Archeological Observations North of the Rio Colorado

Archeological Observations
North of the Rio Colorado

Neil M. Judd

FOREWORD BY
Richard K. Talbot

THE UNIVERSITY OF UTAH PRESS
Salt Lake City

Originally published by the Smithsonian Institution,
Bureau of American Ethnology, Bulletin 82. Washington, DC:
Government Printing Office, 1926.

The Defiance House Man colophon is a registered trademark
of the University of Utah Press. It is based upon a four-foot-tall,
Ancient Puebloan pictograph (late PIII) near Glen Canyon, Utah.

14 13 12 11 10   1 2 3 4 5

Library of Congress Cataloging-in-Publication Data

Judd, Neil Merton, 1887-1976.
Archeological observations north of the Rio Colorado /
Neil M. Judd; foreword by Richard K. Talbot.
p. cm.
Originally published: Washington : Govt. Print. Off., 1926.
Includes bibliographical references and index.
ISBN 978-1-60781-022-3 (pbk. : alk. paper)
1. Utah—Antiquities. 2. Arizona—Antiquities. I. Title.
E78.U55J92 2010
979.2'01—dc22
2010039327

LETTER OF TRANSMITTAL

Smithsonian Institution,
Bureau of American Ethnology,
Washington, D.C., October 28, 1925.

Sir: I have the honor to transmit the accompanying manuscript entitled "Archeological observations north of the Rio Colorado," by Neil M. Judd, and to recommend its publication, subject to your approval, as a bulletin of this bureau.

Very respectfully,

J. Walter Fewkes, *Chief*

Dr. Charles D. Walcott,
Secretary of the Smithsonian Institution.

CONTENTS

ILLUSTRATIONS

FOREWORD

Neil Merton Judd was a pioneer, a man of firsts. In *Observations North of the Rio Colorado* we find the first serious scholarly approach to archaeological survey, excavation, and reporting in western Utah and northwestern Arizona. The result was documentary confirmation of a strong architectural, material, and dietary connection of farming groups in this study area to contemporary Puebloan groups in the greater Southwest. In fact, Judd came at the dawning of archaeological work in the Great Basin and Southwest, and laid the groundwork for others of note: Morss, Steward, Reagan, Gillin, Harrington, and many others. By the time these early archaeologists began their exploratory efforts in the region, Neil Judd had already moved from his Utah field work to Pueblo Bonito in Chaco Canyon, where his legacy would be forever fixed. He was a contemporary and friend of other firsts—Kidder, Cummings, Morris, Nusbaum, Fewkes, Roberts, Douglass, Hodge, and others. He was with his uncle, Byron Cummings, when they "discovered" Rainbow Bridge. He directed the first excavation and restoration efforts at Betatakin in the same year (1917) that he excavated at Paragonah. Later, with A. E. Douglass, he participated in the first efforts to establish tree-ring chronometry in the Southwest.

Born in 1887 in Cedar Rapids, Nebraska,[1] Judd's family moved to Utah in 1901. He was first nurtured under the tutelage of Cummings at the University of Utah, and then E. L. Hewett at the Archaeological Institute of America (AIA) in Washington, DC. Modern American archaeology was then in its infancy and Judd was one of a small cadre of professionals attempting to fill in regional culture histories. Those working in the Southwest were a tight-knit group who freely shared data, and whose opinions usually amplified individual research efforts. Judd was intimately involved in this give and take; with A. V. Kidder in particular he shared "a friendship that lasted fifty years" (Judd 2009:16).[2]

Observations documents Judd's archaeological field work in Utah and northwestern Arizona between 1915 and 1920. It represents a coming out for the young Judd, his first solo field work since earning his BA and MA degrees. In 1915, at age 27, he was sent by the Bureau of American Ethnology (BAE) to investigate reports of Puebloan ruins at Beaver, Utah. Such remains, in an era of growing national excitement and interest in archaeology, suggested a cultural relationship between the more highly publicized ruins of the Southwest and the little known eastern Great Basin. Judd's mission was to confirm that relationship, and to try to determine the distribution of these types of sites.

Upon arriving in Utah, Judd briefly investigated a mound site near Willard reported to the BAE by Don Maguire. Maguire was intimately familiar with many of the sites Judd visited, having dug into them while amassing a private collection, some of which was displayed at the Chicago World's Fair in 1893.[3] Limited testing was sufficient to confirm the presence of a circular subterranean structure that resembled in some ways southwestern pithouses. Moving southward, Judd visited other sites along the eastern rim of the Great Basin, and on the western Colorado Plateau from St. George eastward to Kanab. Some testing was carried out, but only at Beaver were large scale excavations performed. Here Judd established the Puebloan connections he was seeking, as well as a regional distinctiveness, writing that "the culture represented by the major dwellings, whose walls were constructed entirely of adobe, is certainly Puebloan, yet it differs from that of recognized Pueblo areas" (Judd 1926:22). He further noted both similarities and differences in Puebloan pithouses to houses at Beaver and Willard: "Having identified a certain kinship between the prehistoric habitations of western Utah and those of the San Juan drainage, for example, the 1915 expedition suddenly assumed a new function, namely, that of exploration" (Judd 1926:26).

Work conducted in subsequent years would result in important excavations at Paragonah (1916 and 1917) and in Cottonwood Canyon near Kanab (1919). Along the way were reconnoitering, documentation, and artifact collection efforts at sites across that same eastern Great Basin and southwestern Utah/northwestern Arizona region, north of the Grand Canyon. The latter included mostly reconnaissance work on and surrounding the Kaibab, Walhalla and Paria plateaus (1918, 1920).

Judd also relied heavily on local informants to describe the location and nature of important sites he did not have time to visit. Considering the vastness of the study area and the minimal project budget (Judd 1926:2), Judd's diligence on following up with these many contacts was both commendable and necessary. Yet these communications are equally relevant and insightful, as many report on sites that either no longer exist or are now covered by modern development. At the Beaver mounds, for example, he noted the timeliness of his visit, since field plowing had destroyed many mounds and threatened to destroy the few that still remained. Similar observations on pending site destruction were made in subsequent years at Paragonah. The highly complex "Big Mound" at Paragonah in particular would have been a sad loss of critical scientific data had Judd not spent a portion of his very busy 1917 field season excavating the mound.

Observations can appropriately be called the first official scientific examination of the distribution and nature of what later would become known as the Fremont and the Virgin branch of the Ancestral Pueblo (Anasazi) regions.[4] And, as noted, it documents many important sites, most of which current and future archaeologists will never see. But it is more. In this documentary work are the seeds for understanding late Fremont and Virgin area site design and community social structure,[5] and the initial classifications of material culture unique to those two regions. Judd further recognized both passive as well as very active styles in architecture and material remains that suggested the significant regional interplay and influences affecting both areas, themes often ignored even today.

Archaeologists today are specialists. They are frequently inculcated in a particular theoretical paradigm and to a specific analytical specialty, and as such are easily hyperfocused on particular issues. Judd and his contemporaries were primarily generalists who pondered the "big picture." *Observations* is a big picture view of an archaeological landscape that in some respects no longer exists. In it is the culture historical framework upon which Fremont and Virgin area archaeology is built. Indeed, theoretical posturing and modeling often teeter on the edge of realism, and are meaningless without hard data to back them up. Time and again, the current view of things must answer to the archaeological record, the foundations of which were established by men like Neil Judd. We all follow in the footsteps of someone, and we can only hope that the path created was true and good. But Neil Judd was a man of firsts, a trailblazer whose efforts influenced (whether he knew it or not) a century of archaeologists, and whose work will continue to do so for the next century.

Richard K. Talbot

NOTES

1. Judd was born in tiny Cedar Rapids, Boone County, Nebraska, and not the much larger Cedar Rapids, Iowa.
2. To convey the life story and rich contributions of Neil M. Judd to American archaeology would require considerably more space than allowed here. This foreword, then, focuses specifically on Judd's *Obser-*

vations effort and the contributions thereof. Details of Judd's life and insights can be found in his autobiographical *Men Met Along the Trail,* including important insights by Don Fowler in his foreword to the most recent reprinting (2009) of that highly entertaining tale. Also see obituaries and synopses of Judd's life, including bibliographies of Judd's writings, by Brew (1978), Glen (1982), and Wedel (1978).

That richness, however, can be conveyed in a brief synopsis of Judd's exploits. Prior to his field work reported in *Observations,* Judd taught briefly in Utah public schools, served as a volunteer assistant to Cummings (1907–1909) on expeditions to the four corners region, was student assistant to Edgar L. Hewett on an AIA expedition to New Mexico, and, finally, obtained a BA degree from the University of Utah in 1911. In that year he began a lifelong connection with the United States National Museum, Smithsonian Institution, in Washington, DC, serving first as an aide in the Division of Ethnology (1911), assistant curator (1918) and then curator (1919) of American Archaeology in the Department of Anthropology (1918), and, finally, curator of archaeology at the National Museum (1930–1949). He received an MA degree from George Washington University in 1913 and in 1914 was a member of an AIA expedition to Guatemala. Between 1915 and 1920, the period that the *Observations* field work was being carried out, Judd served as treasurer for the American Anthropological Association (1916–1918) and was director of a partial excavation and restoration effort of Betatakin (1917). Toward the end of World War I (1918), Judd also enlisted in the Signal Corps.

Following his *Observations* field work, and besides the Pueblo Bonito work from 1921 to 1927, Judd served as vice president of the Anthropological Society of Washington (1920–1923); member of the board of managers of the Washington Academy of Science, as well as president of the Anthropological Society of Washington (1925–1927); member of the National Research Council (1925–1928; 1931–1932; 1937–1939); president of the Society for American Archaeology as well as vice president and chairman, Section H, of the American Association for the Advancement of Science (1939); and president of the American Anthropological Association (1945). Between all of these duties Judd managed to squeeze in important field work in the American Southwest along with various other responsibilities both before and after his formal retirement in 1949. Judd passed away on December 19, 1976.

3. It appears that much of the impetus for the first expedition came from the 1914 letter (and possibly additional correspondence) from Don Maguire, reprinted on page 5. Judd (2009:62) specifically noted that his initial 1915 field work focused on visiting many of the village sites that Maguire had explored.

4. Don Maguire, Henry Montgomery, Edward Palmer, and others—including various government surveyor groups—had visited and collected from many sites, but none followed the systematic archaeological approach introduced by Judd.

5. The Beaver and Paragonah excavations both encountered the unique structural features today referred to as Central Structures, posited to

have served a Fremont community integrative function (Talbot 2000). Both likewise exhibit courtyard areas for implied communal use (Janetski and Talbot 2000).

REFERENCES

Brew, J. O.
1978 Obituary, Neil Merton Judd, 1887–1976. *American Anthropologist* 80, no. 2 (1978): 352–54.

Glen, James R.
1982 *Register to the Papers of Neil Merton Judd*. Smithsonian Institution.

Janetski, Joel C., and Richard K. Talbot
2000 Fremont Social and Community Organization. In *Clear Creek Canyon Archaeological Project: Results and Synthesis*, by Joel C. Janetski, Richard K. Talbot, Deborah E. Newman, Lane D. Richens, and James D. Wilde, pp. 247–262. Museum of Peoples and Cultures Occasional Papers No. 7, Brigham Young University, Provo.

Judd, Neil M.
1926 Archeological Observations North of the Rio Colorado. Smithsonian Institution Bureau of American Ethnology Bulletin No. 82. Washington, DC.

2009 *Men Met Along the Trail: Adventures in Archaeology*, with Foreword by Don D. Fowler. The University of Utah Press.

Talbot, Richard K.
2000 Fremont Architecture. In *Clear Creek Canyon Archaeological Project: Results and Synthesis*, by Joel C. Janetski, Richard K. Talbot, Deborah E. Newman, Lane D. Richens, and James D. Wilde, pp. 131–84. Museum of Peoples and Cultures Occasional Papers No. 7, Brigham Young University, Provo.

Wedel, Waldo R.
1978 Obituary of Neil Merton Judd, 1887–1976. *American Antiquity* 43, no. 3 (1978):399–404

ARCHEOLOGICAL OBSERVATIONS NORTH OF THE RIO COLORADO

By Neil M. Judd

INTRODUCTION

The present paper records a succession of archeological observations in western Utah and northwestern Arizona, undertaken by the writer for the Bureau of American Ethnology during the years 1915 to 1920, inclusive. Each season's reconnaissance was conducted under the authority of a permit issued by the Secretary of the Interior; each has been briefly reviewed in the annual explorations volume of the Smithsonian Institution. The cultural objects gathered during the six years have all been transferred, as required by law, to the United States National Museum.

Just as laboratory research frequently leads into paths not previously suspected, so the field observations herein considered have assumed larger proportions and have covered a wider range than was originally intended. The initial investigation, that of 1915, had for its prime purpose examination of certain alleged prehistoric Pueblo ruins near Beaver City, in west central Utah. But it was also planned, should these ruins appear in any way related to ancient habitations south and east of the Rio Colorado, to seek information regarding the distribution of their kind throughout western Utah. Such a survey, it was thought, would fully explain the nature and probable significance of that apparent relationship.

A cursory examination only of the mounds at Beaver sufficed to establish a cultural kinship between them and recognized Pueblo ruins elsewhere; in consequence, the writer set forth on a rapid reconnaissance which led southward to St. George, thence east to Kanab and back to Beaver. The outstanding result of this hurried survey was realization of the number and the relative importance of archeological sites in the region traversed. Each exhibited, in greater or less degree, the effect of environment, but each had been occupied unquestionably by individuals we have come to regard as Puebloan.

Following this initial expedition, Mr. Frederick W. Hodge, then ethnologist in charge, determined to continue and expand the reconnaissance, with certain definite limitations. Owing to the meager funds available for the purpose, it was the opinion of Mr. Hodge that as large an area as possible should be examined in preference to attempting detailed investigations at one or more sites. In this way, so it seemed, the bureau could render a greater service to students of prehistoric southwestern cultures. The incompleteness of some of the following observations may perhaps be pardoned, therefore, if the reader will bear in mind that these studies have been pursued under an annual appropriation of $500, or less, of which fully one-half was required for railroad transportation. Except where unforeseen circumstances intervened, the broad plan of procedure originally outlined by Mr. Hodge has been followed from year to year.

The area of reconnaissance extends from the Grand Canyon, in Arizona, to fhe northern shore of Great Salt Lake, in Utah; it reaches eastward to the Green River, and on the west fades into the barren deserts of Nevada. Not all this vast territory has been examined personally by the writer; resident and nonresident observers have largely been depended upon for information regarding the number and character of ancient ruins in those localities not actually visited. The fact that more attention has been devoted to the country surrounding Kanab, Utah, than elsewhere is a result of accident rather than design. Kanab is the gateway through which one enters the plateau regions of northwestern Arizona, and plans for a survey in the spring of 1919 of the uninhabited mesas and valleys west of Kanab Canyon were necessarily abandoned after reaching the field, owing to lack of water and forage for pack animals. This interruption, however, afforded a welcome opportunity for additional observations in Cottonwood Canyon, northwest of Kanab. The survey which had proved impracticable that year was made, but only in part, the following spring (1920).

Were the Bureau of American Ethnology to acknowledge fully its indebtedness to those who have contributed toward the success of these observations it would needs mention nearly every individual with whom the writer has come in contact during the course of his archeological studies in the region above indicated. To each of these good friends the bureau extends its grateful thanks, and trusts that this impersonal word of appreciation will afford evidence that innumerable acts of kindness did not pass unnoticed. Especial acknowledgment is due, however, to Messrs. George Harding and J. L. Edwards, of Willard; to Messrs. Dave Geordge and Jarm Bradshaw, of Beaver; to Mrs. Martha J. Openshaw and Mr. Isaac

Bozarth, of Paragonah, for courteous permission to conduct excavations on their property. Mr. Don Maguire, of Ogden, has furnished helpful notes regarding numerous archeological sites in Utah explored by him between the years 1880 and 1905; Mr. E. M. Mansfield, former manager of the Grand Canyon Cattle Co., graciously tendered the hospitality of his field headquarters and the use of fresh horses during the earlier observations in House Rock Valley, Arizona. Whatever success resulted from the excavations of 1917 at Paragonah is due mainly to former President John A. Widtsoe and Prof. L. E. Young, of the University of Utah, whose invitation to the Smithsonian Institution made possible the joint expedition of that year. An individual word of appreciation is also due Messrs. B. A. Riggs and Delbert Riggs, of Kanab, who not only placed their home in Cottonwood Canyon at the disposal of the bureau's representative, but repeatedly sacrificed their own interests in order to assist the investigations when other aid was not available. Without the whole-hearted cooperation of these and others, the present record of archeological observations north of the Rio Colorado would have been less extensive and far less helpful to those students of prehistoric man who some day will retrace the trails now dimly outlined.

Each season's field work was intended to cover an area not previously examined. For this reason chiefly it seems preferable, in presenting the results which follow, to consider the various localities and ruins pretty much in the order in which they were visited. Such procedure tends naturally toward a certain geographic grouping of the archeological sites, and enables the writer to include with each new group those additional notes which have been gathered concerning prehistoric remains not personally examined by him. The cultural material collected during the course of the reconnaissance is described in a separate section, which seeks to follow the same general sequence as that indicated for the ruins but without special reference to the year of collection. Two appendices contain, respectively, United States National Museum catalogue numbers of the specimens illustrated and such individual room measurements as were made at the various sites explored.

I. FIELD WORK, SEASON OF 1915

Although the objective of this first visit to western Utah was a number of prehistoric ruins, described as of Pueblo origin and located near Beaver, the writer did not proceed at once to his destination. Unforeseen circumstances delayed his journey beyond Salt Lake City, and what promised otherwise to be a week of enforced idleness was devoted to several small mounds near Willard, on the northeastern shore of Great Salt Lake (pl. 1). The existence of these mounds had been known through correspondence, and the unexpected opportunity for examining them, while not fully appreciated at the time, proved very timely indeed, since the counterpart of the rude shelter each covered was subsequently found in direct association with adobe dwellings farther south. Our work on the Willard mounds, therefore, supplies a natural and fitting introduction to that which follows.

Included with this first season's record of archeological observations north of the Rio Colorado are various notes volunteered by chance acquaintances or gleaned from the writings of early travelers through the Great Interior Basin. In most instances these memoranda agree so closely with our own findings that they may be accepted as fairly accurate indexes to the character of prehistoric remains in the localities to which they severally refer.

MOUNDS NEAR WILLARD

Willard is a small farming community, founded in 1853.[1] It occupies a narrow Bonneville terrace that stretches along the eastern shore of Bear River Bay and separates the latter from a wall of brown, desolate hills. In springtime flowering orchards and rows of stately poplars add an atmosphere of quiet and contentment entirely unknown in ancient times, when the trees, if any, bordered a few small rills meandering down from hillside springs.

Less than a mile west of the village, just where the arable bench land dips down to the marshes[2] that fringe Great Salt Lake, a

---

[1] Bancroft, 1890, p. 318.

[2] The writer was informed by several of the older residents that when Willard was settled the lake covered this marshland and washed the foot of the terrace on which the present village and the prehistoric house sites are situated. The fact that arrowheads are frequently found on the "barrens," as these swampy flats are locally known, suggests that formerly, as in recent years, the volume of water in Great Salt Lake has varied, and that the shore line advanced or receded in proportion to that variation.

MAP OF THE AREA UNDER OBSERVATION

CONJECTURAL APPEARANCE OF EARTH LODGES AT WILLARD

number of low mounds mark the site of a primitive settlement that dates from remote antiquity. The fields in which these mounds lie had been cultivated for many years, although they were mostly used for pasture in 1915. Where not wholly demolished by plow and scraper, the mounds offered abundant evidence of promiscuous relic hunting. At least some of these earlier excavations were made by Mr. Don Maguire,[3] of Ogden, who describes his results in a letter of January 15, 1914, as follows:

The farthest north in the State of Utah at which such work (excavations in ancient ruins) was done by me was west about 1 mile from the town of Willard, in Box Elder County, and within about half a mile of the shore of Great Salt Lake. The ruins there consisted of a number of mounds; altogether there were 14 then in evidence. Of these I opened 7, unearthed 15 skeletons, a considerable quantity of broken pottery, also a quantity of stonework, such as lance heads, arrowheads, steatite slickers used in polishing and straightening arrows. Also a number of Indian hand mills of superior make and size, made from granite, and hand stones to the same. On the floors of the rooms opened in the above mounds we found, in a charred condition, considerable quantities of beans, corn, corncobs, and also cloth fiber in a charred condition.

Maguire may have overlooked a number of mounds on the occasion to which he refers, for the present writer identified 25 sites at the beginning of his investigations (fig. 1). Most of these had been completely razed during successive years of soil cultivation, but their former positions were determinable by the earth color and by fragments of burnt roofing clay, potsherds, worked stone, etc., strewn over the adjacent surface. Of the original number less than a dozen house sites existed as recognizable mounds in 1915, and of these only one remained in a relatively undisturbed condition. · It seems safe, nevertheless, to accept this one as typical of all, since superficial examination and trenching of other neighboring elevations disclosed the same characteristic features and artifacts of similar workmanship. This single mound [4] stood near the brow of the old lake terrace already mentioned. Although approximately 40 feet (12.16 m.) in diameter, its summit lay scarcely 3 feet (0.91 m.) above the surface of the surrounding field.

In beginning excavations a test trench 2 feet wide and extending through the black surface soil to the undisturbed clay beneath was cut from the north to the south edges of the mound. From the middle of this a second trench advanced eastwardly. Near the junc-

---

[3] Mr. Maguire, a consulting and mining engineer by profession, became interested in American archeology during the course of vocational travels in Mexico and Central America. Between 1880 and 1905 he gathered a considerable private collection as a result of excavations in prehistoric ruins throughout Utah.

[4] The mound is on land then owned by Mr. J. L. Edwards, whose generous permission to excavate has previously been acknowledged.

tion of the two and at a depth of 2 feet 6 inches (0.76 m.) there was discovered a well-defined earthen floor, the surface of which was hard, smooth, and blackened through continued use. As the work of exposing this pavement progressed quantities of burned roof clay

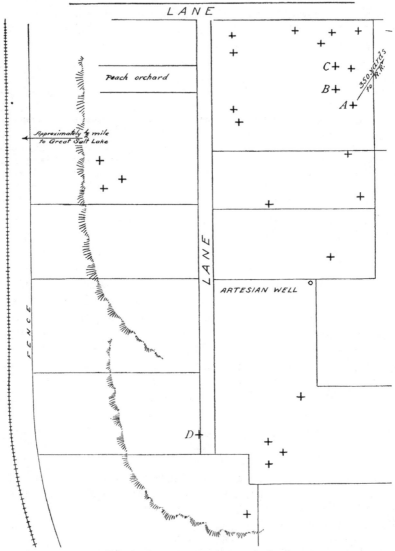

FIG. 1.—Location of mounds at Willard

were encountered, bearing impressions of logs, willows, and grass. Most of these were uncovered at or near the floor level, but others occurred between that and the surface. Above the floor was the rich black soil of the cultivated fields; beneath it the sandy clay and gravel of the Bonneville terrace.

In the middle floor lay a circular fireplace 31 inches (0.78 m.) in diameter and 3½ inches deep (fig. 2). Wood ashes, streaked with striae of fine sand, filled the basin. Beyond its raised rim and about 4 feet (1.2 m.) from each other were four postholes, varying somewhat in depth, but each measuring 7 inches (17.7 cm.) in diameter. Between those holes and the fireplace were various materials that indicated, in part at least, the manner in which the former dwelling had been constructed. Fragments of charred poles, from 1 to 4 inches (2.5–10 cm.) in diameter, lay across the fire pit or sloped from it upward and outward toward the surface. Over one group of such fragments and resting on the north edge of the basin was a charred mass of coarse grass and reeds (*Phragmites communis* Trin. and *Calamagrostis canadensis* Beauv.); above this were portions of burned and smoke-stained roofing clay, the impressed side usually being down. These chunks ranged in thickness from 2 to 6 inches (5–15 cm.); a few bore marks on each side showing that the plastic mud had been forced between the timbers at the time of building.

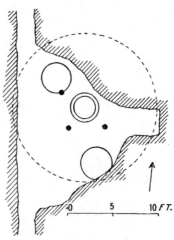

FIG. 2.—Mound D, Willard

Two circular receptacles had been dug into the floor on opposite sides of the fireplace, probably to serve for storage purposes. Their sides were only slightly darker than the undisturbed clay surrounding them and afforded no evidence of having been plastered. The westernmost of these bins measured 3 feet 3 inches (0.99 m.) in diameter, and 12 inches (30.4 cm.) in depth; that edge nearest the fireplace was pierced by one of the postholes previously noted. The second pit was slightly larger than the first; on its northern rim, with worked side down, lay a relatively thin, unshaped granite bowlder showing slight use as a metate or milling stone. No other artifact was found in or near the two bins. That both of these were intentionally dug subsequently to completion of the shelter seemed quite evident from their immediate surroundings and their position in relation to the fireplace and roof supports.

Maguire has stated that he found charred beans and corn in the Willard mounds. Although the present writer was less fortunate, cultivation of the latter food plant in northern Utah in prehistoric times is at least suggested by the frequency with which well-shaped and deeply ground metates occur at this aboriginal village site.

Numbers of them have been unearthed and stacked along the fences. They possess one characteristic feature more fully described on page 145.

Bearing in mind the several objects found about the fireplace and their obvious relationship to each other, it seems possible, tentatively, to restore such a dwelling as that represented in the mound at Willard. The four upright and perhaps notched posts supported crosspieces upon which lay lighter poles and split timbers. Over these were spread, in succession, layers of willows, reeds, or grass, and mud, the latter fitting closely about the two former and retaining their impressions perfectly after fire or natural decay had removed all other traces of the vegetable matter. The relatively small, flat portion of the roof between the uprights probably contained a smoke vent for the fireplace directly beneath.

That the sides of this lodge sloped from the ground to the crosspieces supported by the four central posts seems obvious from close examination of the floor. About the fire pit and within the square formed by the four pillars the earth had been tramped hard and smooth through constant use. Elsewhere the floor was traceable in indirect proportion to the distance from its center, and in no place could it be followed with certainty more than 7 feet (2.1 m.) from the rim of the fireplace. Further, the two pits previously described were so situated as to be well under a sloping roof, and therefore of least inconvenience to the inhabitants of the hut. Although no marks were found which might indicate the former resting place of inclining wall timbers, the mere fact that the floor, so distinct in the middle, became less plain toward its borders, suggests that this ancient structure was circular in ground plan, and in outward appearance not unlike the earth lodges of certain western tribes, or, for example, the familiar winter hogan of the Navaho (pl. 2).

Following the first published references [5] to the crude dwellings exposed by the excavations at Willard, attention was called to the seeming resemblance between them and southwestern pit houses such as those discovered by Dr. Walter Hough [6] near Luna, New Mexico. This apparent similarity becomes less evident, however, upon closer comparison of the outstanding characteristics of the two types. The northern Utah structures were erected over a cleared space which may have been slightly below the general ground level,[7] while the true pit houses were largely subterranean. These latter were not infrequently as much as 5 feet in depth. The

---

[5] Judd, 1916; 1917a.

[6] 1907, p. 63; 1919.

[7] No indications of earthen walls or embankments, or of masonry of any sort, were observed in the mounds trenched at Willard.

former may be pictured as truncated cones, the flat portion of their roofs being directly above a central circular fireplace; the latter as sunken cylinders whose tops, at or slightly above the ground level, were supported by posts placed close to the wall of the excavation. Rimmed fireplaces do not occur in the Luna pit dwellings, but they are present in similar structures recently discovered in Chaco Canyon,[8] northwestern New Mexico. An earth lodge on the Mesa Verde National Park, Colorado,[9] and a semisubterranean structure figured by Kidder and Guernsey [10] in their most valuable and instructive report on explorations in northeastern Arizona, are each represented as having had a conical roof supported by poles which extended at an angle from a low encircling bench to a common meeting place above the middle of the dwelling. In these two instances, as in the case of the Luna pit houses, the supposition is that access was gained by means of steps or a ladder leading through an opening in the roof. In the shelters at Willard no trace of a doorway could be found. The entrance may have been at or near the ground level, or with equal plausibility it may have been through the flat roof section above the fireplace, in which latter case it would have served also as a smoke vent.

Brief examination of three other mounds in the Willard group disclosed sufficient evidence to warrant the statement that they covered the remains of shelters similar to that already described. Each of these three, unfortunately, had been thoroughly gouged out years before, when teams and scrapers were employed in the work of excavation. But the sides of the old cuts showed that from 2 to 4 feet of black earth had gathered upon the original floor level following its abandonment, and that the customary stone chips, potsherds, charcoal, etc., were not lacking in this soil.

Fragments of deer bone and antlers were present at each of the four sites above mentioned, but only in such quantities as to lead one to believe that these larger animals were not readily available as a source of food supply to the ancient inhabitants of this vicinity. The bones of small mammals and a variety of birds, on the other hand, were fairly abundant. No human burials were discovered.

Metates, manos, hammerstones, arrow shaft smoothers, bone awls, arrow points, potsherds, etc., were collected during the course of our observations. The pottery is invariably a gray plain ware, smoothed but undecorated. Several shards of black-on-white ware are said to have come from the earlier excavations, although none was found in 1915.

---

[8] Judd, 1924.   [9] Fewkes, 1920, p. 58.   [10] 1919, p. 44.

A large mound about 1½ miles north of Willard, frequently described as of human origin and but little disturbed, proved upon examination to be of natural formation. It is composed almost wholly of coarse gravel and small cobblestones, loosely cemented together, and is probably an isolated remnant of the old Lake Bonneville terrace on which the modern village stands. No human artifacts of prehistoric origin were observed in the neighborhood of this lone elevation.

Mounds North of Willard

Notice of the occurrence of pottery fragments on mounds north of Great Salt Lake reached the writer during the course of his observations at Willard, but as yet there has been no opportunity to confirm such reports. It is not unreasonable to suppose, however, that house remains similar to those just described exist along the borders of the fertile Cache and Bear River Valleys in Utah, and perhaps as far north as the Snake River in Idaho.[11] Mounds have been reported at the base of the Blue Springs Hills, northwest of Tremonton, Utah, and it is not at all unlikely that camp sites will be discovered near the obsidian outcroppings on Promontory Point, one of the sources of supply for the ancient arrow makers of the Willard bench.

In a cave on the western slope of the ridge, about 12 miles (19.3 kilos) north of the Southern Pacific station on Promontory Point, Professor Cummings [12] observed pieces of rope and moccasins made from buffalo hide, buffalo bones, and a few fragments of pottery resembling those at Willard. On the rear wall of the cave there had been painted in red ocher the figure of a square-shouldered man with triangular head. No other evidence of human handiwork was noticed. Mr. Thomas Whitaker, discoverer of the cavern, had been led to it by recollection of an old Indian tradition which related how the survivors of a separate tribe had been destroyed there by Shoshonean warriors.

Several years ago the writer observed a number of low mounds on the northeast outskirts of Blackfoot, Idaho, in cultivated fields adjoining the city cemetery. From the train the knolls appeared to be artificial, as did others a few miles farther north. The unfortunate limitations placed on governmental research into the prehistory of our country has alone prevented close examination of these ele-

---

[11] So far as the author is aware, the numerous letters and journals left by the early American and British fur trappers—those intrepid explorers who penetrated into the far corners of the Great Basin between 1812 and 1840—contain no reference to ancient ruins or other prehistoric remains.

[12] 1913.

vations. Inquiries addressed to various residents of Blackfoot have failed to elicit any response.

Garrick Mallery reports[13] the occurrence of colored pictographs near Oneida, Idaho, and Isaac I. Stevens[14] refers to similar work on a cliff at Pend d'Oreille Lake, in these words:

> The painted rocks are very high and contain effigies of men and beasts and other characters, made, as the Indians believe, by a race of men who preceded them as inhabitants of the land.

That these pictographs bear any relationship to such prehistoric remains as those at Willard appears highly improbable, and yet the vague possibility that other structures of the Willard type may be found in the northwestern United States should encourage the extension of archeological research in that direction. Students of American history might turn with some degree of confidence, in the writer's opinion, toward the north or west for the ancestral home of the ancient Willard potters.

Mounds West of Great Salt Lake

Definite information concerning prehistoric human remains within or bordering upon the Great Salt Lake Desert is very meager indeed. So far as known fur traders who combed this inhospitable region between 1825 and 1830 in search of new trapping grounds left no record of ancient ruins seen by them. Reports of military and other Federal explorers following closely upon the tracks of the trappers are almost equally destitute of information within the province of this paper. One brief note only commands attention.

While exploring the northwestern shore of Great Salt Lake Capt. Howard Stansbury[15] wrote in his diary for May 14, 1850, that "some broken specimens of Indian pottery were found at this camp, and also some pieces of obsidian. The latter, probably, had been procured elsewhere by the savages for making arrowheads." The exact spot at which these specimens were seen can not be determined from the text itself, but consideration of the work with which the party was then engaged would seem to place the camp mentioned east or northeast of the Hog Mountains. Excepting a very hurried and unsuccessful attempt to locate alleged " Indian mounds covered with pottery " near Kelton, the present writer has not sought to extend his reconnaissance into this section of Utah.

Vague rumors of mounds and " Indian crockery " in northern Nevada prompt the thought that an archeological survey of the

---

[13] 1886, p. 37.

[14] 1885, p. 150. See also Report, Commissioner of Indian Affairs, Washington, 1854, p. 222; and H. J. Rust, "A brief historical and archaeological sketch of Lake Coeur d'Alene, Idaho," The Archaeol. Bul., vol. 3, No. 2, Madison, Ind., 1912.

[15] 1852, p. 182.

upper Humboldt River may disclose some faint trace of that primitive culture left by ancient housebuilders throughout the eastern half of the Great Basin. We have no definite statement concerning this western district, but notices of the mounds and pottery have come through hearsay from cattlemen and sheep herders supposedly familiar with the country.

Garrick Mallery [16] notes the occurrence of pictographs incised upon basalt rocks at the lower extremity of Pyramid Lake, western Nevada. Others, both pecked and scratched, were observed in considerable numbers on the western slope at Lone Butte, in the Carson Desert, and a third large group, including representations of human figures and footprints, circles, and waving lines, appeared on the cliffs bordering Walker River, near Walker Lake. William Epler reports [17] hieroglyphics in Star Canyon, Humboldt County. Still another series, on a block of basalt at Reveille, was regarded by G. K. Gilbert, of the United States Geological Survey, as of " apparent Shinumo or Moki origin." Mallery questions this identification,[18] and with good cause.

Students of ancient southwestern cultures would unhesitatingly identify most, if not all, of the Nevada pictographs as of Shoshonean workmanship. In view of recent discoveries, however, the writer would urge that general decisions be held in abeyance until further, more detailed information is available. Relatives of the western Utah housebuilders erected adobe dwellings along the Rio Virgin, in southeastern Nevada; it is not at all improbable that their characteristic civilization will be found represented also in valleys to the westward. Sites that attracted historic Indians would also have appealed to more ancient peoples, and rock carvings of human footprints, circles, and snaky lines have a distinctly Puebloan flavor.

Unverified reports have been received of mounds near Grantsville, south of Great Salt Lake, and certain caves northwest of Tooele Valley[19] are said to be heavily smoked and to contain other evidence of aboriginal occupancy. Such visible records as exist in those caverns may be, and probably are, of comparatively recent origin, but there is an equal possibility that the same caves were also occupied by Indians in prehistoric times. It is not to be supposed that the ancient inhabitants of Salt Lake Valley, for instance, refrained from venturing out upon the level, if barren, plains south and west of Great Salt Lake.

---

[16] 1886, p. 24.
[17] 1898, p. 121.
[18] 1886, p. 25.
[19] Tooele Valley, named for the tule growing there, was explored by the Mormons in the fall of 1849.—Bancroft, 1890, p. 315. Fur traders had covered the same ground before 1830.

Mounds Near Ogden

That narrow but remarkably fertile strip of farm land which separates the northern extension of the Wasatch Range from the alkali flats bordering Great Salt Lake unquestionably contained at one time the remains of many earth lodges, and perhaps even a few isolated adobe dwellings. Half a century or more of continued cultivation has served so completely to obliterate such ruins, however, that little if any prehistoric evidence is now visible. Among the older local residents are some who recall the occasional finding of metates, manos, and other stone utensils, but no masonry walls. Fragments of burned roof adobe, such as those exposed in the excavations at Willard, are invariably referred to as portions of ancient " kilns " or " smelters "—identifications which will not confuse the student of western archeology. Since the writer has personally examined but a relatively insignificant portion of this district, he has, from necessity, depended largely upon the observations of others.

About 1900 several low mounds were razed at Ogden, Utah, during the grading of a road in the neighborhood of Thirtieth Street and Madison Avenue. Fragments of pottery, bone, charcoal, etc., exposed by the excavations attracted considerable local attention at the time. Mr. Andrew A. Kerr,[20] among others, became much interested in these discoveries and has kindly furnished the information here recorded. No walls were noted and no effort was made to ascertain the probable method of construction employed in the ancient dwellings at this site, the search for curios which followed initial discovery being confined to promiscuous digging by individuals at the side of the new road and in trenching several mounds in adjacent fields.

Although the historical importance of these inconspicuous mounds was entirely overlooked or disregarded at the time they were destroyed, Mr. Kerr fortunately recalls much of the cultural material exposed in them.[21] This material includes the customary chipped arrow and spear heads, stone metates and manos, and a considerable quantity of gray potsherds, most of which were heavily smoke-stained. In addition, a fragment of lead ore, a piece of yellow paint,

---

[20] Mr. Kerr has permitted his boyhood interest in antiquities to develop into a professional enthusiasm, now recognized by his connection with the University of Utah museum. As representative of the University of Utah during the excavations of 1917 at Paragonah, he rendered valuable and efficient assistance—assistance inadequately acknowledged by this brief reference.

[21] It is said that the owner of the property on which certain neighboring mounds were located retained most of the objects found in them, although Mr. Kerr secured and still preserves a few of the smaller ones as part of his private collection. Whole bowls were reported, but Mr. Kerr was never able to verify this rather dubious statement.

and 13 "horn" beads were recovered. Subsequently, Mr. Kerr found an obsidian disk, "about as large as a half dollar and three times as thick." Arrowheads and other artifacts are still occasionally found along the little stream at the foot of the hill on which these mounds formerly stood.

In the general search for relics two or three human skeletons were found, but nothing is now known as to the fate they suffered. It is a matter of profound regret that they were not preserved, since skeletal material must be depended upon, in large measure, to substantiate such deductions as may eventually be made regarding the probable relationship between those ancient people of northern Utah and the builders of pre-Pueblo ruins nearer the Rio Colorado.

The discovery of mounds on the old Bonneville terrace just south of Ogden gives credence to other reports that similar indications of prehistoric habitations have been noted north of the city. The mountain waters of both Ogden and Weber Rivers flow through beautiful valleys much frequented by Indians until the middle of the nineteenth century; the unprotected knolls and benches left by the ancient lake would have proven equally attractive to their less nomadic predecessors.[22] Neither Kerr nor Maguire has observed ancient remains at the actual mouth of Ogden Canyon; both regard as modern Indian graves those several small mounds occurring within the canyon itself.[23]

Mounds in Salt Lake Valley

The railroad connecting Ogden and Salt Lake City runs through a veritable garden of fruitful orchards, well-watered fields, and green pastures. Close on the east rises a wall of bare mountains; westward, beyond the arable land, alkali flats stretch away floorlike to the blue depths of Great Salt Lake. Stately poplars guard each winding roadway; wide-spreading trees shade every farmhouse. Here, finally, is complete realization of that vision of a Promised Land which buoyed the first Mormon pioneers on their arduous pilgrimage to Salt Lake Valley in 1847.

But the present charm and restfulness of this fertile section is entirely a development of the past 50 years. Fur traders and trappers trailing back and forth across its drab hills a quarter century

---

[22] Mr. Felix T. Moore, in a letter of September 26, 1924, reports the finding of bone tubes, a perforated bone awl, a tubular stone pipe, and a human image in clay on the lake bottom bordering Bear River Bay.

[23] It will be recalled that Peter Skene Ogden, the Hudson Bay Co. agent, established headquarters in this region about 1824 for a considerable following of Canadian and Indian trappers. "Ogden's Hole" remained a famous trading center for several years, and it is not unlikely that some of these graves date from that period. Ogden Canyon is said to have been a favorite retreat for the mountain Indians long before the coming of the whites; a small hot spring in the canyon was supposed to possess great medicinal properties.

in advance of the Mormons found little of beauty in it. Roving bands of mountain Indians claimed the region when the trappers arrived, but in a far more distant past, long before our written history began, other and entirely different Indian peoples came to occupy the valley. We know but little of these ancient folk, for the evidence of their former presence has mostly been destroyed. A few thin threads of information only have been held for us by early visitors to Utah, but these threads, happily, are strong enough to bind the prehistoric inhabitants of Salt Lake Valley to those blood brothers farther south regarding whom we know more.

Don Maguire states [24] that he observed several mounds west of Farmington, and still others on the east side of the Jordan River at a point about 5 miles northwest of Salt Lake City. In a short paper on the Great American Desert Mr. Henry S. Poole notes [25] that a farmer uncovered fragments of rude pottery [26] and a "hollowed stone for grinding corn" while plowing the surface of a small offshore island in Great Salt Lake not far from Bountiful. Here, as at Ogden, no trace of walls appears to have been noticed— negative evidence which may or may not indicate house remains similar to those at Willard. Additional mounds, according to this same writer, were opened during construction of the Utah Central Railroad (now the Oregon Short Line) through the valley.

That Salt Lake City occupies the site of one or more prehistoric settlements is apparent from the fact that various artifacts peculiar to sedentary or semisedentary peoples are even now reported from time to time during excavations for buildings, pipe lines, etc. In 1870 Dr. F. V. Hayden, of the United States Geological Survey, collected several fragments of pottery [27] "on Fourth Street, 4 feet below the surface." Similar finds were made in Salt Lake City during the years covered by this report, but local interest was such that they were permitted to pass unnoticed. The fragments themselves seem not to have been preserved.

Preceding Hayden came another observer, Mr. W. F. Rae, who writes:[28]

By accident I learned that this valley (Salt Lake) had a special attraction for the archaeologist. Indian burial mounds of great antiquity are situated in its midst. . . . Taking the road which runs west (from the city), and crossing the Jordan, we then proceeded in a southwesterly direction. . . The labor

---

[24] The information is given in a personal letter to the writer, dated Ogden, Utah, Oct. 11, 1916.

[25] 1874, p. 212.

[26] Earthen vessels are not known to have been manufactured by the Indians of the Great Basin within the historic period.

[27] These are in the national collections at Washington, Cat. No. 9761. They include a rim fragment with a round handle attached, and shards of a plain gray cooking pot, decorated around the neck with three parallel bands of thumb-nail impressions.

[28] 1871, pp. 162–164.

of a few hours proved to us that they (low "sand hills") were in reality the places of sepulture of an ancient Indian tribe. Flint spearheads, flint arrowheads, stone implements, and fragments of rude pottery ware we disinterred from the sand. . . . All of them were found in the larger of the three mounds.

Bancroft [29] quotes an article from the Salt Lake Telegraph, reprinted in the San Francisco Evening Bulletin of October 9, 1868, which contains the following additional information, presumably originating with Rae, regarding the same "sand hills:"

The mounds, as they exist to-day, do not exhibit much uniformity, but this can be accounted for by the disintegrating action of rains and winds, to which they have been so long subject. Immediately north, south, and west of the largest barrow, traces can be seen of others now all but obliterated, and the locality bears unmistakable evidences of once being the site of very extensive earthworks. In one mound or barrow only, the largest, were remains found, and they were exposed on or very near the surface of the sandy soil, in one or two large hollows near the center. The other barrows were destitute, at least on the surface, but what there may be below it is hard to say. Of all the relics, except those of charred bone, which are comparatively plentiful, and some in a state of petrification, that of pottery is the most abundant, and to this day some of it retains a very perfect glaze. Much of it, however, is rough, and from the specimens we saw the art does not appear to have attained to so high a degree of perfection as among the ancient nations that inhabited the Mississippi and Ohio Valleys. The largest piece of pottery seen was not above three inches square, and it appeared, as did all the others pieces, to have formed a portion of some rounded vessel, probably a cinerary urn or something of that kind. Other articles were seen, such as a fragment of pearly shell, several other shells, a white cylindrical bead, a small ring, probably a bead also, and a stone knife.

Arrowheads of various materials and granite mills are also mentioned as having been found.

Although the locality is not described with such exactness that it can readily be revisited by one pressed for time, we are, nevertheless, fortunate in having these references from an obviously accurate observer. More might have been added, but due allowance should be made for the time represented. Salt Lake Valley is 15 miles (24.13 kilos) wide. Salt Lake City numbered less than 12,000 souls in 1868. Rae was a chance traveler, not a student of antiquities. He crossed the Jordan River and drove in a southwesterly direction, which within a very few miles would have brought him to a flat, unwatered, barren portion of the valley not likely to have attracted ancient house builders. After riding for some distance it became apparent that his driver did not know the exact location of the mounds he sought; they were discovered only after additional inquiries had been made. The wandering search of this stranger may well have brought him back to the border of the placid river, where semisedentary Indians would have found far more agreeable surroundings.[30]

The newspaper correspondent quoted by Bancroft [31] also mentioned an "extensive fortification or entrenched camp," with walls from 4 to 8 feet high and doorways plainly marked, at the head of Coon's Canyon, some 20 miles southwest of Salt Lake City. There is a distinct flavor of exaggeration in this particular reference, especially so to one at all familiar with the general appearance of the Oquirrh Mountains. Their treeless slopes are not likely to have tempted prehistoric man from more favored locations in the broad Salt Lake Valley.

Half a dozen sizable streams flow down from the Wasatch Range, on the east, to meet the sluggish Jordan. These mountain creeks, with an abundance of clear, cool water, with shaded glens and a vast acreage of fertile soil near by, would have proven as irresistible to primitive farmers as they have to recent graduates of the State agricultural college. The latter, indeed, are said to have encountered several ancient village sites during cultivation of their fields southeast of Salt Lake City. One of the most extensive of these is reported on the old Bonneville terrace between Mill Creek and Big Cottonwood Canyon, but the writer was unsuccessful in his hurried search for it. Manos, or smoothing stones, arrowheads, and the rejectage from blade manufacture were found, however, as far north as Red Butte Creek. None of these possessed the distinctive earmarks of pre-Shoshonean peoples.

It is naturally a matter of profound regret that during these archeological observations north of the Rio Colorado a more comprehensive examination of Salt Lake Valley proved impossible. Meager though our information be, it is sufficient to warrant the belief that house remains of a sedentary or near-sedentary people formerly existed there in considerable numbers. Some of these prehistoric dwellings were probably of the Willard type; others more closely resembled those in Utah Valley, if one may judge chiefly from circumstantial evidence. Ancient adobe walls have long been known near Payson; walls of like construction, in valleys farther south, received much attention during the bureau's reconnaissance. Fragments of earthenware vessels found in direct association with such walls agree, in each instance, with shards recovered sparingly in Salt Lake Valley; hence the presumption that at least some of the prehistoric habitations in the latter district resembled those known to have occurred in the former.

---

[30] The collections in the Deseret Museum, Salt Lake City, contain several earthenware vessels said to have been found on the banks of the Jordan River.

[31] 1875, p. 715.

Mounds in Utah Valley

The Jordan River, repeatedly mentioned in the preceding paragraphs, conveys the fresh waters of Utah Lake [32] northward to the saline expanse of Great Salt Lake. In its slow way the river passes through a narrow gorge, locally known as " The Narrows "— the only interruption in a ridge of low, treeless hills that effectually separates Salt Lake Valley from Utah Valley. The latter borders Utah Lake on the east, and is well watered by Provo River (Timpanagos) and lesser mountain streams flowing down from the Wasatch Mountains.

Provo lies in the heart of Utah Valley. On the margins of near-by streams and on the lower Bonneville terrace through which they flow are the reported remnants of several prehistoric mounds. The present studies were not extended into this particular section, but the observations of earlier writers furnish a clue to the nature of the ancient remains and establish a relationship between them and the more southern ruins, next to be considered.

In 1872, during the course of a Government topographic survey of the Great Basin, " excavations were made near Provo, Beaver, and Paragonah, Utah. At the former a number of stone mills, pestles, arrowheads, pottery, bones of animals, several domestic implements, and an almost perfect skeleton were discovered." [33] The excavations near Beaver appear to have centered in a Paiute burial ground on a hillside east of the village; those near Paragonah and Provo were in low mounds whose origin was unknown both to the white settlers and the Indians they had so lately supplanted. An imperfect picture of the latter group, that near Provo, is to be found in the report of Mr. Mark S. Severance [34] and Dr. H. C. Yarrow:

West of the town, on its outskirts, and within 3 or 4 miles of the lake, are many mounds of various construction and in different states of preservation. Mormon farmers have leveled some of them, plowed into others on the edges, and removed from others the rich soil for use elsewhere; in no case has there been a special attempt at exploring them. Those examined were on low ground, almost on a level with the lake and with the Provo River, a mile distant on the north. Overflows from both the river and the lake sufficient to inundate the area of country occupied by the mounds are not at all unlikely to have occurred during the long lapse of time since the building of the mounds, though at the present time the climatic character of the region is such that overflows are of rare occurrence; not infrequent to a mild degree, however, after the melting of the snows in the lofty Wasatch Range, from which the Provo River issues.

---

[32] The " Laguna de Nuestra Señora de la Merced de Timpanogotzis " of Escalante, the northernmost point reached in his memorable journey of 1776.—Bancroft, 1890, p. 11. William H. Ashley built a fort here in 1825, and two years later mounted a 6-inch cannon on its walls.—Ibid., p. 21.
[33] Wheeler, 1889, p. 57.
[34] 1879, p. 393.

On the next page of the same report we read further:

Mounds 1 and 2 are higher and less disturbed than Nos. 3, 4, 5, and 6, which are almost entirely demolished. The excavation made in mound No. 1 was continued for about 12 feet from the outer limit, with a breadth of about 8 feet. The mound was 45 feet in width, 60 feet in length, and 10 feet high in the middle. A few pieces of pottery and broken bones were also found.

Since the Wheeler surveys the plow of modern civilization has turned its annual furrow and the mounds once noted near Provo have slowly merged into the surrounding fields. In fact, several lifelong residents of Utah Valley, when questioned, expressed surprise that evidence of prehistoric occupancy had ever been observed in this vicinity. We are thus led to suspect that such elevations as attracted the attention of Yarrow and Severance have since largely, if not wholly, disappeared. Although no mention is made of walls encountered by these early investigators, it may safely be assumed, and chiefly because masonry is not specifically reported, that the Provo mounds concealed adobe dwellings similar to those near Payson.

PAYSON, about 15 miles south of Provo, also occupies the middle of an extensive and prosperous agricultural district. If any trace of prehistoric habitations is now present in this vicinity it has seemingly escaped the notice of local residents. But in 1876 Payson received a brief notoriety as a result of excavations in several near-by mounds, and more especially through circulation of certain utterly absurd stories regarding objects alleged to have been found in them. Popular interest at the time centered about "an air-tight stone box, encased in mortar or potter's clay, and containing another stone box of about two quarts capacity," in which grain "similar to Chilean club wheat" [35] was securely stored away. Although this entire question arose from what may or may not have been intentional exaggeration on the part of the original discoverer, it is quite possible to gain from the printed statements, and especially that following a personal investigation by Dr. Edward Palmer,[36] sufficient information to enable us to judge of the character of the ancient house remains in this particular locality.

It appears that in 1876 there were at least six mounds in the Payson group, and that each of these contained the shattered walls of adobe dwellings. Palmer refers to the component parts of these walls as "sun-dried mud bricks," but he says, describing them fur-

---

[35] Wirt, 1880, p. 28. The entire story will be found in the Proceedings of the Davenport Academy of Natural Sciences, vol. 2, pp. 28–29, 82, 167–172. Conant, 1879, pp. 67–69, quotes a letter from Amasa Potter, leading figure in the Payson fraud, to the Eureka (Nev.) Sentinel; the same letter reappears in Popular Science Monthly, vol. 12, 1877, pp. 123–124. Such facts as may be separated from the fiction are summarized by Palmer, 1880, pp. 167–172.

[36] 1880, pp. 167–172.

ther, "a close examination shows that while the clay was soft it was taken up by the hand and laid in the wall, and another similar lot laid over this, and the upper surface and sides smoothed with the hand." From this description it is obvious that the walls of the prehistoric houses at Payson were constructed of successive masses of adobe mud, shaped in place to conform with those already laid, rather than of individual blocks or bricks dried separately and later added one above the other, as in modern building operations. Such methods are exactly those noted during the excavations at Paragonah in 1916 and 1917 (p. 70), where traces of roof construction agree also with those observed by Doctor Palmer at Payson 40 years earlier. This pioneer explorer of the western Utah mounds also marked the frequent superposition, in whole or in part, of these earth dwellings, a condition more fully considered in our chapters on the remains near Paragonah.

SANTAQUIN, a few miles southeast of Payson, is said to be the site of several mounds apparently identical with those just considered. Others in the same vicinity have been razed in recent years through enlargement of the cultivated fields.

In Summit Canyon, southeast of Santaquin, there is an extensive series of rude carvings representing men, animals, and various geometrical patterns of unknown import.[37] These have been pecked into the south face of innumerable bowlders lying along the north side of the canyon. They appear more nearly related to a similar series west of Parowan (p. 38) than to characteristic pictographs of unquestioned Pueblo origin. A well-known Ute trail, no longer traveled, connects Utah Valley and Thistle Valley by way of Summit Canyon.

A. A. Kerr knows of at least two mounds covering fragmentary adobe walls about 2 miles northwest of Nephi. Less trustworthy informants place the number as high as 20. Additional mounds, presumably of the same character, have been reported in San Pete Valley, between Manti [38] and Mount Pleasant.

Incomplete and unsatisfying though these casual references be, they nevertheless serve one definite purpose—they extend the area known to have been occupied by the prehistoric house builders of western Utah, and in consequence bridge a considerable gap otherwise left by this reconnaissance. As will appear from the following pages, a cultural relationship exists between the ancient inhabitants of the adobe houses in Millard, Beaver, and Iron Counties on

---

[37] J. D. Putnam, 1876, p. 143.

[38] A series of pictographs near this village is figured by Lieut. J. W. Gunnison in his book, The Mormons, 1853, p. 63 and reproduced in Schoolcraft's History of the Indian Tribes of the United States, vol. 3, pl. 42, and in Bancroft's Native Races of the Pacific States, 1875, p. 717. The highly amusing "translation" quoted by Gunnison is briefly commented upon by Garrick Mallery, 1886, p. 251.

the one hand, and those of the Willard lodges on the other. The foregoing notes enable us to project the culture of the localities next to be considered into those districts with which we are less familiar.

That adobe as a building material was so consistently employed by the prehistoric people of western Utah is a result chiefly of environment. Generally speaking, stone suitable for wall construction was not available to those primitive folk dwelling north of the drainage of the Rio Colorado.

MOUNDS NEAR BEAVER

Coming finally to Beaver, the original objective of the 1915 survey, we may gather from its ancient house remains some idea of what might have been disclosed had the mounds of Utah Valley received more careful examination at the time of their discovery.

Beaver is a charmingly quiet and peaceful farming community situated only a few miles below the mouth of Beaver River Canyon. Fifteen minutes' walk eastward from the village square brings one to a number of low mounds, the only visible evidence of an ancient settlement of considerable size. Standing in fertile fields as obstacles to the even cultivation of the soil, it was not to be expected that these mounds could long endure as monuments to a prehistoric past. In fact, most of the original group had been razed prior to 1915, and those few remaining [39] were threatened with early and complete destruction. The present observations, therefore, were indeed timely.

The Geordge-Bradshaw mounds occupied a slightly elevated area in the broad alluvial flat built up in geological times by the once wandering Beaver River, a clear mountain stream whose shaded waters now hug the north base of an old Bonneville terrace [40] that reaches far out from the west slopes of the Tushar Mountains. A mile to the northeast a similar low, bare bench separates the course of Beaver from that of North Creek.

Prior to the advent of Mormon settlers in 1856 Beaver River and the streams that closely parallel it on the north had proved favorite retreats for nomadic tribes of the mountain country, and long before their time more sedentary peoples had likewise sought the quiet

---

[39] Two of the number stood in the fields of Mr. Dave Geordge, and the remaining six on the adjoining property of Mr. Jarm Bradshaw. One of the eight had been chosen as the site of a new barn; another had been bisected by the foundation walls of the Bradshaw house, in process of construction at the time of the writer's visit. Of the remaining six, three had been utilized as available sources for loose earth, and all bore the scars of random amateur digging. The willingness with which Messrs. Geordge and Bradshaw granted permission to excavate has previously been acknowledged.

[40] The Paiute burial ground examined by members of the Wheeler survey (see p. 18) is situated on this terrace.

and contentment that still reigns here. It is a matter of frequent observance that the location or the environment which appealed strongly to primitive man also attracted his European successor, and therefore modern communities have oftentimes established themselves, innocently enough, on the very site of a prehistoric village.

The house remains exposed near Beaver are of interest to students of southwestern archeology for two reasons, chiefly: (1) The culture represented by the major dwellings, whose walls were constructed entirely of adobe, is certainly Puebloan, yet it differs from that of recognized Pueblo areas; and, (2) directly associated with these major dwellings are lesser structures essentially identical with the rude shelters observed near Willard. The presence of these latter structures in the Beaver mounds and in those south of Beaver forms one of the strongest cultural ties between the ancient house builders of southwestern Utah and the primitive folk who erected earth-covered lodges on the northeastern shore of Great Salt Lake. The occurrence of adobe houses in western Utah mounds had been previously noted [41] and the individualistic nature of their ceramic remains had been partially illustrated,[42] but no detailed study had ever been attempted of the primitive culture both represent.

THE GEORDGE MOUND.—A few moments before the writer first visited the Geordge-Bradshaw mound group, brickmakers, gathering clay for their mixer, had disturbed several masses of burned adobe. Each of these bore the impress of grass, willows, or split timbers— roof material that immediately suggested dwellings of the Willard type. It was a simple task with borrowed shovel to clear the floor that lay just beneath these adobe fragments.[43]

Once exposed, the ruins of this primitive habitation confirmed our initial impressions. There lay a well-marked but unsurfaced area slightly more than 17 feet (5.2 m.) in diameter; in the middle of this a rimless fireplace 39 inches (0.99 m.) in diameter and 3 inches deep. At an average distance of 4 feet 6 inches (1.37 m.) from the pit and about 8 feet 5 inches (2.56 m.) from each other were four postholes whose charred and decayed contents indicated the former presence of substantial roof supports. Between the two southern posts were the fragments of a black-on-white bowl and two plain-ware cooking pots, shattered by a large, unworked stone which fell with the burning timbers. In the southwest quarter of the lodge, and among its charred roofing poles, were the burned

---

[41] Palmer, 1880.

[42] Holmes, 1886.

[43] Mr. Ambrose E. McGarry, then a student at the University of Utah, not only rendered most helpful and efficient assistance during the 1915 excavations at Beaver, but also accompanied the writer on that hurried survey which extended southward to St. George and back again to Beaver. For this trip a team and light buckboard were employed; our observations, therefore, did not extend far from passable roads and trails.

bits of six bone awls; to the east of these were four manos (hand stones for use on the metates or grinding mills) and part of a metate. Other artifacts and several unworked cobblestones lay strewn over the floor; also a number of split animal bones.

The following day excavations were commenced in the larger of the two mounds on the Dave Geordge property. According to the owner, this mound had formerly extended more than 50 feet farther west (fig. 3), but a portion had been sacrificed about 1910 when the adjacent field was leveled. Mr. Geordge recalls that adobe walls were encountered in the section destroyed, and that earthen floors in some of the rooms rested upon layers of cobblestones.

Elsewhere, but chiefly along the northern and southern borders of the elevation, quantities of earth had been removed by individual

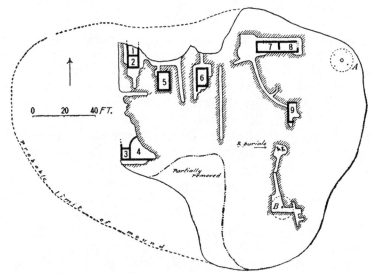

FIG. 3.—Sketch of the Geordge Mound, showing trenches cut and walls exposed in 1915

citizens. Since it was quite obvious that the opportunity for preparing a complete ground plan of this prehistoric community had been irretrievably lost, excavation of the entire mound was not undertaken. Those walls already in evidence were exposed and limited search was made for still other undisturbed remains. The observations made during the course of this brief investigation may be considered as a unit.

The nine rooms in the Geordge mound wholly or partially excavated were never more than one story in height. Their walls had been constructed entirely of adobe mud laid in relatively large masses which appear as courses of from 16 to 20 inches (40.62–50.7 cm.) in thickness. Contrary to popular belief, these courses or layers do not prove that the aborigines employed movable frames in constructing their rectangular earth dwellings. On the contrary, close examination shows that each wall course was composed of innumerable masses of plastic adobe mud, each as large as an individual could handle conveniently, forced into position and there smoothed by hand.[44] These masses followed the line of the wall and others were thrown on top, care only being exercised that the weight of the added material did not press out of alignment the mud already in position. The very nature of the material utilized, therefore, explains the occurrence of longitudinal courses in prehistoric adobe walls, for each successive layer was permitted to dry, in part at least, before another similar layer was placed upon it. In many instances the lines of demarcation were obliterated at the time of construction as the builders molded and pressed the clay into position, or as they subsequently erased visible irregularities with a surfacing of liquid mud.

Evidence of former doorways was not observed, and it must be inferred, therefore, that the individual rooms were entered through hatchways or roof openings. Several stone disks that may well have served as covers for such openings—disks from 18 to 30 inches (45.68–76.2 cm.) in diameter and 2 inches thick—were found at or near the surface of the mound. Shattered wall material—that is, broken chunks of dried adobe—formed a considerable proportion of the débris in each chamber.[45] With this was the age-long accumulation of dust carried and deposited by the wind.

Fireplaces were not present in any of the rooms opened, nor were there any charred timbers or smoked walls to suggest burning of the ceiling members. In nearly every instance the floor was spread over a foundation layer of cobblestones; always it was hard and slightly darkened through use. On the floors, but more frequently in the débris above them, potsherds, bone awls, and occasional stone artifacts were exposed in satisfactory numbers.

An initial example of the superposition of dwellings, repeatedly found during subsequent excavations, especially those at Paragonah (p. 69), was furnished by room 2, which had been erected upon 14 inches of wall material and loose earth covering the floor of an earlier house. Beneath the latter, at a depth of 6 inches, were the remains of a third dwelling. The area of these lower floors was not ascertained.

It is apparent that the earth walls of the two earlier structures had been thrown down in succession, the rubbish leveled, and the third or last dwelling constructed above the whole. The larger masses from the razed walls were doubtless carried away, but the finer

---

[44] Identical methods of wall construction in a prehistoric adobe ruin near Moab, Grand County, Utah, are described by Cummings, 1910, p. 19.

[45] Dimensions of the individual rooms examined will be found in Appendix II.

refuse was left where it fell. The work of destruction ceased when this refuse and the razed walls reached a common level.

A few special features may be noted. In room 1, adjoining room 2 on the north, there had been a 2½-inch post standing near the west wall. It probably served as an auxiliary beam support. A curved, though badly broken, wall stood against the outer northeast corner of room 3. While its original function was not determined, it was obvious that the curve was of secondary construction, and that it joined a rectangular room whose south wall continued for several feet toward the east. Nothing was discovered to suggest a similarity of purpose between this room and the problematical kiva exposed in the Bradshaw mound (p. 32).

Rooms 7 and 8, in the northeastern portion of the Geordge mound, were separated by a partition built subsequently to the main walls. A doorway, 16 inches (40.62 cm.) wide, through this partition furnished a means of ready communication between the two chambers. In the north wall of room 7, and 3 feet 8 inches (1.1 m.) from its northwest corner, was what at first appeared to be a doorway. It was 14 inches (35.5 cm.) wide and its slightly rounded sill (the convex upper surface of a wall section) lay 17 inches (43.2 cm.) above the floor. But the sides of this doubtful door were noticeably irregular, a fact which led to the conclusion that the opening had been cut by a badger, whose tunnels were repeatedly cross sectioned elsewhere.

The floored areas, each with rimless circular fireplace, suggesting additional structures of the Willard type, were disclosed in the southeastern portion of the mound. In these two instances, however, the postholes characteristic of the Willard type lodge were not discovered. The southernmost of these pavements possessed little of interest other than numerous fragments of burned roofing clay, found in or immediately surrounding the fireplace. In tracing the second floor, however, an adult skeleton was encountered, its head and shoulders resting upon four large unworked stones lying within the fireplace. The body had been buried at full length with its head to the northeast and its arms folded across the chest. A second skeleton, that of a child, lay with its head to the northwest and its lower leg bones crossing and touching those of the adult. Miscellaneous shards were found about the thighs of each skeleton; both burials had been encased in a single mass of adobe mud.[46]

After four days' exploratory work in the larger Geordge mound our excavations were temporarily discontinued. From the evidence

[46] Mr. Geordge recalled that an adult skeleton had been exposed near the original southewestern limit of the mound, but he remembered no details in connection with the burial.

obtained it seemed quite obvious that a cultural relationship, however puzzling, existed between the prehistoric inhabitants of Beaver
and those of various explored areas south and east of the Rio
Colorado. With this realization the one fundamental purpose of
the 1915 expedition had been met. The Beaver houses, to be sure,
were constructed entirely of adobe; they stood mostly as individual
structures, yet grouped to form a fairly compact settlement. Among
the minor antiquities the pottery, especially, was unquestionably
Puebloan, although it possessed characteristics which differentiated
it from all other known wares of similar origin.

Having identified a certain kinship between the prehistoric habitations of western Utah and those of the San Juan drainage, for
example, the 1915 expedition suddenly assumed a new function,
namely, that of exploration. Because of Dr. Edward Palmer's excavations near St. George in 1876 (p. 40) such a relationship as
that mentioned had been more or less anticipated. The writer now
set forth on a too-hurried reconnaissance of southwestern Utah with
the object of determining the probable distribution of such structures as those exposed at Beaver.

Altogether 15 days were devoted to this survey, during which
approximately 340 miles were traveled by team and ten localities
of more than passing archeological interest were superficially examined. The fifteenth day found us again at Beaver, prepared for
a week's investigation of the mounds on Mr. Bradshaw's property.
It seems well to consider these latter in this place, inasmuch as no
subsequent observations have been made in the vicinity.

THE BRADSHAW MOUND.—As previously stated, six mounds were
visible in the Bradshaw field in the spring of 1915. Of these, one had
largely been replaced by the cellar walls of a dwelling then in course
of construction; a second was occupied by a workshop; and a third,
at once the largest and least disturbed of all, was shortly to have been
leveled as the site for a new barn. The latter mound was selected
for excavation.

The results of this work were summarized in a short paper [47]
presented some years ago, but further more detailed consideration
is deemed advisable in the present report. Attention should be
directed especially to the remains of several shelters of the Willard type and their obvious association with adobe structures which
comprise the principal habitations of this prehistoric village. Although such relationship is fully illustrated in the ground plan (fig.
4) of the house group, the nature and probable significance of that
relationship are discussed in the paragraphs which follow.

---

[47] Judd, 1917a.

The more permanent buildings in the Bradshaw mound, of which
four only are contiguous, were constructed of successive courses of
adobe mud after the manner already described (p. 23). They had

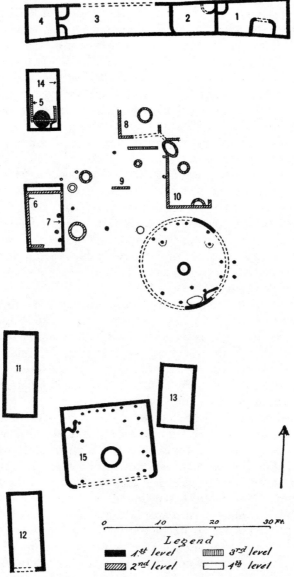

Fig. 4.—Arrangement of house remains in the Bradshaw Mound

flat roofs of clay supported by large and small timbers, willows,
and grass; they seem to have been entered through openings in the
ceiling, since no indications of lateral doorways were observed.

In these adobe dwellings fireplaces rarely occur (the only exceptions are rooms 8, 10, and 15) and there is always a marked absence of ashes, potsherds, and similar kitchen refuse. In general, these major structures convey the impression that they were utilized exclusively as sleeping quarters, perhaps, and for the storage of foodstuffs.

The domestic activities of the community, on the other hand, appear to have been pursued in lesser structures near the main dwellings. There, at least, is found the usual accumulation of débris that gradually collects about primitive habitations and leaves its meager evidence of human industry. Such records, in the Bradshaw mound, are largely restricted to that portion of the village immediately east of rooms 7 and 14. Kitchen refuse near the four southernmost dwellings, while present, was so insignificant in quantity as to be almost negligible.

That household tasks were concentrated in one relatively limited area is obvious from the fact that east of room 7 no less than four distinct levels of occupancy were exposed. These levels were easily recognized surfaces or pavements, each with house or lodge remains, separating the successive layers of camp refuse and floor sweepings. Each layer included masses of burned adobe bearing impressions of grass and willows—roofing material from temporary shelters that once stood in this section of the village.

Examination of the remains of these temporary structures shows them in each case to have been of the type exposed at Willard; that is, they were shelters whose individual roofs were supported by four posts surrounding a central fireplace, usually with raised rim.[48] If any difference existed between these structures as erected at Willard and at Beaver, it is to be found at the latter site in a seeming tendency to slight or even omit the inclosing walls.

At Willard the floored area became less definite with increased distance from the fireplace, thus suggesting a slanting wall. At Beaver the same was sometimes, but not always, true. Some of the Willard type shelters at Beaver certainly were roofed with inclined earth-covered poles; others just as surely lacked the inclosing walls, for their clay floors extended without interruption far beyond the normal limits of such habitations. Instances of the latter sort suggest that the Willard type lodges underwent certain modifications at Beaver, or at least served a new function, while their builders depended mostly upon the more stable adobe dwellings. As modified, the central fireplace remained, together with the flat roof directly above it, but the side walls of the lodge were occasionally omitted, leaving the fireplace accessible from all sides. In other

---

[48] The only unrimmed fireplace noted in the Bradshaw Mound lay on the fourth level, near the projected northwest wall of the supposed kiva.

words, when associated with rectangular adobe buildings the Willard type lodge was apparently reduced in importance to an arbor or court shelter in which the cooking and other household tasks were performed. The meager remains in the Bradshaw mound warrant this view of lesser importance for structures of the Willard type; still further modifications are evident as we journey southward.

Circular fireplaces, a characteristic feature of these bowers or " kitchens," are not present in the more permanent rectangular dwellings. Only three exceptions to this statement were observed in the Beaver mounds, namely, rooms 8, 10, and 15 of the Bradshaw group. The last mentioned differs from all the other rooms and appears to have been designed for some definite though unknown purpose. Rooms 8 and 10, on the other hand, are identified by fragmentary walls on the second level of occupancy; it is not certain that either of these two buildings was ever completed.

The adobe walls of room 8 could not be traced beyond the points indicated on the ground plan. Within these fragmentary walls was a fireplace 26 inches (0.66 m.) in diameter and 4 inches deep; half of this depth was represented by an encircling rim of adobe 3 inches (7.6 cm.) wide at the base. No postholes were noted near this ash-filled basin.

Room 10 is likewise marked by incomplete adobe walls, barely traceable in places. Built on the floor against the southern wall is a semicircular fireplace 7 inches (17.7 cm.) deep and with an 11-inch (27.9 cm.) radius. A second fireplace, 22 inches (55.4 cm.) in diameter and about 4 inches deep, lies 4 feet 6 inches (1.37 m.) north of the one last mentioned. Although our notes connect this second fireplace with the second level of occupancy, we may be guilty of an error in observation, for the floor at this point was somewhat irregular and two postholes through the third level stand just outside the west wall of the room. Other post positions were not determined, but the two mentioned are correctly placed for association with the doubtful fire pit.

An elliptical third-level fireplace, 32 inches (0.81 m.) long by 20 inches (50.7 cm.) wide and 10 inches (25.4 cm.) deep, had been built above the northwest corner of room 10. Just west of this pit and on the same floor with it was a wall fragment 4 feet 6 inches (1.37 m.) long and 8 inches (20.3 cm.) high. It stood upon a soft fill and lacked the usual base or foundation of cobblestones. Fourteen inches of ashy earth separated the second and third levels at this point.

Other second, third, and fourth level fireplaces were exposed west of room 10. Each of these was surrounded by a well-packed floor and the postholes so characteristic of Willard type shelters, although no effort was made accurately to locate all such holes or indicate their relative positions on the ground plan.

Room 15, the third dwelling in which a fireplace was observed, deserves special consideration. It was at once the largest and most unusual house in the whole village. Its adobe walls averaged 8 inches in thickness and illustrated more clearly than usual the course or layer method of construction. These layers varied in height from 18 to 23 inches (45.6–58.1 cm.), and each was divided by numerous vertical cracks, a few only of which could be identified as intentional joints. Similar cracks, less regular, to be sure, were caused by roots of sage and other surface plants, which had followed the wall faces to their very foundations. The cleavage powers of growing roots may, in part at least, explain the rather widely disseminated belief that primitive adobe structures such as those at Beaver were always constructed of large blocks of mud, molded and placed upon the walls.

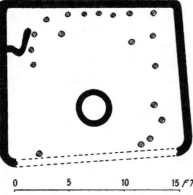

0   5   10   15 *FT.*

FIG. 5.—Room 15, Bradshaw Mound

Near the middle of this room was a circular fireplace, 36 inches (0.91 m.) in diameter and 6 inches (12.6 cm.) deep as measured from the top of its low surrounding rim (fig. 5). Between this fireplace and the southeastern corner of the room were two large corrugated ollas, each standing upon a rest or stool of clay 6 or 7 inches in height and approximating the diameter of the vessel. While still plastic the upper surface of these mud rests had been molded into shallow basins to fit the rounded bottoms of the jars. Each pot was covered with a flat stone and, excepting for a little dry earth which had sifted in and a single arrow point found in one of them, was empty.

In the northwest corner of the room a low, irregular adobe wall formed a binlike structure the original purpose of which is not clear. This partition did not completely inclose the angle of the room, and its lack of uniformity does not admit of satisfactory explanation. It seems evident, however, that the inclosure was designed for storage purposes—perhaps the storage of material having a ceremonial significance and employed in connection with this particular building. At any rate the reader will readily recall the occasional mention of small bins or closets possessing unusual form which have been noted in kivas and associated rooms in other sections of the Southwest. This particular bin was quite barren of cultural objects.

Chiefly along the north and east sides of room 15 were a number of postholes, averaging 5 inches in diameter but varying in depth from 8 to 24 inches (20.3–60.9 cm.). The distance one from the other differed also, and leads to the belief that these holes mark merely the former positions of roof supports which had been added, following the completion of the dwelling, as a means of sustaining the weight of a roof otherwise too heavy for the thin earthen walls. That such additional support might have been necessary, especially after the upper walls had been softened by rain, is the more easily understood if the reader will recall the manner in which these prehistoric adobe dwellings were roofed. First two or more sizable beams were placed upon the walls across the shorter dimension of the room; upon the beams, but at right angles to them, were smaller poles or split timbers, and above these in turn was a layer of brush or grass. A surface layer of adobe mud varying in thickness from 2 to 5 inches (5.1–12.7 cm.) covered the grass; the whole formed an enormous weight for earth walls only 8 and 10 inches (20.3 and 25 cm.) thick.

Rooms 1, 2, 3, and 14 also are first-level rooms containing small corner bins whose functions as storage receptacles will scarcely be doubted. In each instance the relatively thinner walls of the bin had been constructed after completion of the house itself. As a rule the bin walls were drawn in at the top, forming orifices smaller than their corresponding floor areas; in only one instance (the larger bin in room 1) were the walls more than 12 inches in height. A pothole or subfloor receptacle, 36 inches (0.914 m.) in diameter and 26 inches (0.65 m.) deep, was observed in the southwest corner of room 14. Its opening was surrounded by an adobe rim 3 inches high and 5 inches thick at the base; the inner surface of the cist remained unplastered.

After room 14 had served its period of usefulness its adobe walls were razed to within 20 inches (50.7 cm.) of its floor, a layer of cobblestones was spread upon the wreckage, and room 5 erected above it. This bowlder foundation reached eastward 3 feet farther than necessary and northward to the outer wall of room 4. Although No. 5 has been designated as a third-level dwelling (the only one in the whole group), there is here some likelihood of error, for its northern half and the adjacent court level on the east had previously been destroyed. As nearly as could be judged the floor of this structure lay 23 inches (58.1 cm.) above that of room 4 and between 3 and 4 inches above the second level, upon which rooms 8 and 10 stood. Few objects of interest were found within the walls of room 5, but among them a single squash seed is most noteworthy.

Of all the first-level structures in the Bradshaw mound none is more interesting or more important, perhaps, than that represented by two sections of a curved wall immediately south of room 10 (fig. 6). The room was plainly circular in outline, and for this reason, chiefly, it has previously and provisionally been referred to [49] as a kiva. If this designation be correct then the room under consideration is indeed important, for its geographical location marks it as the most western known prototype of the true kiva, or ceremonial chamber, in prehistoric Pueblo communities of the upper San Juan and elsewhere.

As exposed during the course of excavation, the two sections, built of adobe and in the same manner as in secular structures, are enough to give an original diameter of approximately 16 feet (4.87 m.) to the room. The western half of the circular wall had fallen inward and lay in broken masses upon the floor; its former position was plainly indicated by the successive layers of refuse that had accumulated against its outer face.

In common with similar structures throughout the ancient Pueblo area, the middle floor of the Bradshaw kiva was occupied by a circular fireplace, in this instance 24 inches (0.61 m.) in diameter and 7 inches (17.7 cm.) deep, as measured from the crown of its clay rim. Surrounding the pit at an average distance of 5 feet 6 inches (1.7 m.) from its center were four postholes, each marking the former position of a substantial roof support. These pillars were erected prior to completion of the floor, and conical masses of adobe mud had been pressed about the two northern posts as a sort of base. Similar masses, if formerly existent at the other pillars, were no longer traceable.

Excepting its west quarter, the inner circumference of this room was closely paralleled by nine additional postholes, but slightly smaller than those surrounding the fireplace. Although the original function of the posts that once occupied these holes could not be ascertained definitely, it seems entirely plausible that, as in the case of room 15, ceiling braces were found necessary after the kiva had been finished and perhaps utilized for a time. It should be remembered that the relatively thin walls of this structure, like those in other rooms, were built from masses of clay mud pounded into position and allowed to dry in the wind and sun. Further, unless sufficiently shielded by protruding eaves, these adobe walls would yield readily when damaged by rain or snow, virtually melting under the enormous weight of the roof. Exposed beam ends even would act as conveyers of moisture, and unless speedily repaired after each rain the early collapse of such nonreinforced walls would prove inevitable. It was solely to counteract such

---

[49] Judd, 1917a; 1917b. M. R. Harrington (1925, p. 75) has recently reported a small kiva near St. Thomas, Nevada.

destructive effects of moisture, in the writer's opinion, that the builders of the Beaver ruins resorted to secondary roof supports in their larger structures.

East of the fireplace and just within the kiva curve were two post-holes that seemed to pair with two others on the outside of the wall. Although purely conjectural, it seems not improbable that a thin, perhaps wattled, wall, all traces of which have since disappeared, once connected the posts that filled these two pairs of holes, thus forming a subwall passageway comparable in function to the so-called ventilators so characteristic of circular kivas throughout the San Juan drainage.

South of this problematical passage and adjoining the eastern end of the wall segment was a triangular bin whose adobe walls were unequal in thickness and plainly erected after completion of the kiva. The inner walls of this chamber measured 28 inches (0.71 m.) on the west and 4 feet (1.22 m.) on the north; their height was about 15 inches (38 cm.). One of the four central ceiling supports stood against the outer northwest corner of this alcove.

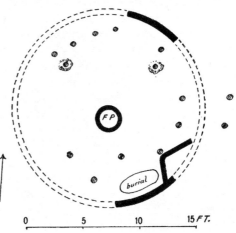

FIG 6.—Problematical kiva, Bradshaw mound

West of the bin, in the angle formed by its shorter side and the adjoining kiva wall, lay the skeleton of an adult male. The body had been deposited in a shallow, basinlike depression excavated for the purpose and was covered with a 2-inch layer of adobe mud that reached 5 or 6 inches above the otherwise regular surface of the kiva floor. The exceptionally compact and worn condition of this covering suggests that the presence of the burial was not allowed to interfere with continuation of those practices which normally occurred within the room. As exposed, the skeleton lay on its back with head to the east. Owing to the burrowing of rodents, certain of the lesser bones were out of position, and some few were entirely missing. No artifacts were found with the burial, and no evidence existed to show that the individual had met other than a natural death.

GENERAL REMARKS ON THE BRADSHAW MOUND.—A brief review of our observations among the prehistoric habitations in the Bradshaw mound seems desirable, chiefly by way of emphasis, before passing on to other, equally ancient structures in neighboring valleys. Here, for the first time, Willard type lodges were found directly associated with rectangular adobe dwellings. In consequence it is desired that the reader have in mind a fairly complete picture of these two types of aboriginal buildings as we proceed southward to similar groups, and finally into the red-rock country with its natural caves and the cliff dwellings they shelter.

The first-level structures exposed in the Bradshaw mound are entirely similar, despite a certain variation in size and interior furnishings and notwithstanding the fact that the floors were slightly higher in some than in others. In each major dwelling the walls had been constructed of superposed masses of plastic clay, forced into place and shaped by hand. Owing both to the nature of the building material and the methods employed, the union of these masses usually resulted in courses or layers frequently separable into blocks of unequal length. It would appear that all walls of adobe had been erected in the same manner, and that most of them had been smoothed or surfaced inside with an additional thin coating of mud before the wall itself had quite hardened.

Fragments of roofing clay, charred beams, etc., indicate that these boxlike habitations were each roofed after the manner most common to the ancient Pueblo area; that is, logs crossing the shorter dimension of the rooms supported, in succession, layers of poles, willows, grass, or reeds, and adobe. House floors as a rule were of clay spread over a foundation of cobblestones that usually, but not always, extended under the four walls. These dwellings had no windows and no doors other than roof openings, which were closed when desired with heavy stone disks averaging 30 inches (0.76 m.) in diameter.

Near and closely associated with these more substantial buildings were the remains of secondary structures that appear to have housed the numerous domestic activities of the several families. Such structures are of the Willard type, identified by an earthen floor and a central fireplace surrounded by four roof supports. Some of these shelters were inclosed by slanting walls; others were open on all sides. Camp refuse naturally accumulated about these workrooms, and as it became an obstacle it was smoothed out and new lodges erected upon the surface thus formed. In the earthy rubbish between these successive floor levels fragments of plain and corrugated pottery, split animal bones, and like objects were found—objects that afford evidence both of the nature of the food supply at this prehistoric village and the degree of cultural advancement to which its inhabitants had attained. Fragments of charred corncobs were found both in the room débris and in the refuse separating the several court levels; a handful of pine nuts was collected just outside the eastern wall of room 13, and, as previously related, a single squash seed came from room 5. No other evidence of vegetable foods was revealed.

Consideration of all the data available points to the conclusion that the Willard type shelters and the rectangular adobe dwellings in the Bradshaw mound were erected by one and the same people; that they were occupied contemporaneously; and that no great period of time elapsed during accumulation of the four distinct levels of occupancy noted in the vicinity of the shelters.

ADDITIONAL OBSERVATIONS NEAR BEAVER

Several small elevations, presumably marking the sites of one and two room houses, were noted on upper Indian Creek. Each mound was identified by a blanket of sagebrush and scattered fragments of pottery and chipped flint. In no instance were walls visible.

Mr. Ambrose McGarry, who conducted the writer to the above groups, reports similar mounds near "the old sheep corral," about 3 miles (4.8 kilos) northeastward from Minersville. Other mounds are said to exist along the course of Devils Creek, and still others on Pine Creek or Cove Fork, about 20 miles north of Beaver. No excavations were made in those few visited, and therefore no information was gathered which might supplement that from the Bradshaw and Geordge mounds. An interesting fact in connection with these small elevations, however, is that they were not grouped into compact settlements, as were those near Beaver.

On the "Milford flats," west and northwest of Minersville, many small mounds are said to have been razed during recent years. Mr. McGarry reports seven undisturbed mounds on his farm 5 miles southeast of Milford as quite comparable, at least superficially, with those excavated at Beaver in 1915 when he was present as an assistant.

Although pictographs are not wholly lacking in this section of Utah, it is, of course, quite impossible to say that they bear any relationship to the builders of the adobe dwellings. A large and important series of such glyphic records, if one may judge from verbal reports, covers a high bluff on the north side of Clear Creek, about 4 miles westward from its junction with Sevier River. Most of these, it is said, are from 15 to 30 feet (4.6–9.14 m.) above the present base of the cliff. Additional glyphs, on the opposite side of the creek and one-half mile farther downstream, are described as fully 100 feet (30.4 m.) above the talus and about 20 feet (6.1 m.) from the top of the cliff. A third group, that at "The Gap," westward from Parowan, is considered on a following page. So far as known, prehistoric habitations are not found in the immediate neighborhood of these rock carvings.

MOUNDS IN PAROWAN VALLEY

Taking up the work of the reconnaissance, the writer and his driver set forth from Beaver in a light buckboard with the knowledge that not more than two weeks could be devoted to the survey in prospect. This limitation necessarily restricted operations to those localities easily accessible by team on a triangular route which included St. George and Kanab, yet avoided the lofty, rugged heights of Colob Plateau.

PARAGONAH, the first objective, is about 30 miles (48.3 kilos) south of Beaver, on the east side and about midway of Parowan Valley. The village was founded during the winter of 1855 [50] as a colony from the neighboring settlement of Parowan. Two streams, Little Creek and Red Creek (known also as Paragonah Creek), flow down from the mountains and make their way in a northwesterly direction toward Little Salt Lake.[51] Paragonah took its position on the banks of the latter stream, occupying the very site of an extensive prehistoric settlement.[52] Most of the mounds that formerly marked this ancient village have disappeared with development of the modern community. Between 40 and 50 of them, however, were still visible in 1915, yet the sage-covered fields in which they stood were even then being prepared for cultivation, during which process the mounds were doomed to complete destruction. Here and there the newly plowed fields showed brown scars—the barren clay beneath ancient dwellings but lately razed. Masses of wall material and fragments of burned adobe roofing were visible about these leveled house sites; potsherds were numerous, and stone implements, including many manos and metates, lay scattered about.

One and one-half days were spent at Paragonah in 1915. In this time four small mounds were explored. Three of these, standing about a mile north of town, had previously been mutilated, and two of the three revealed no certain indications of aboriginal habitations. The two elevations containing house remains may be considered briefly.

---

[50] On Red Creek, about 20 miles north of Cedar City, a small settlement was formed in the autumn of 1852, named Paragoonah, the Pi-Ede name for Little Salt Lake.— Bancroft, 1890, p. 318. According to local residents, Indian attacks forced abandonment of the earlier venture. Recent maps change the spelling to Paragonah.

[51] Little Salt Lake, that appeared in the days of Fremont as quite a sheet of water, has since entirely evaporated, leaving alone alkaline flats.—Wheeler, 1889, p. 48. The volume of water probably varies from year to year, depending upon the amount of rainfall.

[52] Carvalho remarks (1858, p. 207) that the first Mormon settlers to reach Paragonah observed "the remains of a town built of adobe."

Mound No. 1 was practically undisturbed, although its covering of sagebrush had been cut shortly before, and some soil had already been scraped from its borders. Excavations disclosed a single room 20 feet 3 inches (6.2 m.) long and averaging 6 feet 4 inches (1.9 m.) in width; one section of wall stood 3 feet (0.91 m.) high and 12 inches (0.36 m.) thick. All four walls had been so carefully plastered, both inside and out, at the time of construction as to remove all traces of their component adobe masses, yet no doubt remains but that each had been erected after the manner already described (p. 23). The long axis of the room lay slightly east of north. Against the outer southeast corner was a short section of wall representing either a buttress or an incipient addition to the dwelling.

In clearing the room only a few bone awls, three chipped arrow points, and a mere handful of miscellaneous shards were recovered. Against the south wall and occupying the entire width of the dwelling was a benchlike affair, 19 inches (48 cm.) wide, built up of adobe mud after completion of the building itself. The original purpose of this platform was not disclosed; it stood 5 inches high at one end and 19 inches at the other. The north wall, while fairly plumb inside, was so thick at the base that the outside surface sloped perceptibly. The floor was packed and smoothed through use; the cobblestone foundation characteristic of adobe dwellings at Beaver was lacking.

Mound No. 2 spread out like a huge oyster. Trenches revealed a single room 7 feet (2.1 m.) wide and more than 14 feet (4.26 m.) long. The south wall had disappeared completely. The adobe walls were composed of courses averaging 14 inches (3.5 cm.) in height, but without any trace of vertical joints. The long axis of this room was almost exactly north and south. A large metate lay near the surface on the west side of the mound, and a stone disk 18 inches (45.6 cm.) in diameter was found 8 inches (20.3 cm.) below the surface and directly above the northeast corner of the room. Potsherds were scattered upon and through the earthy accumulations.

In both mounds thin layers of compact clay and gravel were encountered between 30 and 36 inches above the room floors. These layers were unquestionably deposited by water long subsequent to abandonment of the ancient habitations, and the most logical source of that water would have been floods from Paragonah (Red) Creek, the former course of which runs some 40 yards east of mound 2. The entire flow of this mountain stream is now impounded for irrigation purposes, but in olden times spring and summer freshets spread at will through the fields until absorbed by the sandy soil. In passing the modern village Red Creek carved a considerable channel, but this has more recently been partially refilled, chiefly with earth from near-by mounds. Mr. Timothy Robinson recalls that when he reached Paragonah, about 1880, this now abandoned course was fully 10 feet deep. In the vicinity of the two mounds under consideration a slightly lower elevation obtains, however, and here the stream did not leave such a pronounced pathway as that noted above.

A third mound had been gouged out years previously by team-drawn scrapers. No floor or wall surfaces were observed on the sides of this central cut, although two squash seeds, several bone awls, and a collection of miscellaneous shards were recovered during a few moments' work with shovels.

A mile or more from Paragonah, "within the walls of Red Creek Canyon and 30 feet above the ground, is a series of pictographs which represent," according to Carvalho,[53] "the human hand and foot, horses, dogs, rabbits, birds, and also a sort of zodiac." If these carvings are as old as we are expected to believe them, it is obvious that a fertile imagination has aided in their interpretation.

PAROWAN, the parent village of Paragonah, is located 5 miles southwest of the latter. Don Maguire intimates[54] that he observed several mounds near Parowan about 1892, although earlier travelers through Parowan Valley seem to have found no such evidence of prehistoric habitations. Residents of the village to-day deny all recollection of ancient mounds destroyed during cultivation of their fields, and yet Dr. W. H. Holmes credits to this locality a remarkably fine example of a corrugated olla.[55]

HIEROGLYPH CANYON,[56] or "The Gap," as it is more frequently called locally, breaks through the low hills southwest of Little Salt Lake to join Parowan and Rush Lake Valleys. Near the western end of this rocky defile an extensive series of pictographs (pl. 4), pecked into the smooth faces of innumerable basaltic bowlders, lines the roadway. Some few of these carvings are undoubtedly of great antiquity, for they can only be discerned under favorable lighting; the larger proportion, however, are obviously of Sho-shonean origin. Interspersed among these are still others that appear to be attempts, perhaps by itinerant sheep herders, to imitate the ancient records.

Sunset and a veritable cloud of mosquitoes were at hand as we emerged from The Gap and approached Rush Lake. No mounds were observed from the road which skirts the eastern margin of the valley, but it is quite within reason that more careful search here will disclose evidence of prehistoric human activity. Unfail-

---

[53] 1858, p. 206. Carvalho is quoted at some length by Bancroft, 1875, pp. 715–717.

[54] The present notation from Mr. Maguire and those which follow are taken from a personal letter to the writer, dated Ogden, Utah, Jan. 15, 1914.

[55] 1886, p. 291, fig. 245.

[56] So designated by O. E. Meinzer in Water-Supply Paper 277, U. S. Geological Survey, Washington, 1911.

a, Room 1, from the northeast

b, Room 11, from the southeast

ROOMS IN THE BRADSHAW MOUND

a

b

PICTOGRAPHS IN HIEROGLYPH CANYON

ing springs issue from the rocks at Ward's ranch; waterfowl abound in the broad marshes, and surely before the advent of white men deer and antelope frequented this one favored portion of Escalante Desert. Like the mountain Indians of a much later period, the ancient inhabitants of Parowan Valley would have turned eagerly toward Rush Lake in search of game; and it is only natural to suppose that, sooner or later, they would have erected their characteristic adobe dwellings on the open alluvial slopes near by.

SUMMIT stands at the southern end of Parowan Valley. Maguire includes the village in the list of archeological sites visited by him, and although not on the route of our reconnaissance, it was learned that a few now almost indistinguishable mounds are still recognized as of prehistoric origin. One of these, larger than the others, lies about a mile north of town. Sporadic digging in it has disclosed adobe walls.

ARCHÆOLOGICAL SITES IN CEDAR VALLEY

The notes of the 1915 reconnaissance include references to several lesser mound groups south of Paragonah. These will be considered briefly in passing, together with such additional data as have been gathered subsequently.

ENOCH, like its Biblical predecessor, was built on the edge of the desert. Five miles to the northeast is Summit; close on the west, Cedar Valley opens out upon the alkaline nakedness of Escalante Desert.

About 1912 Mr. J. L. Lee razed several small mounds on his farm 3 miles east from the village, but he recalls having seen nothing in or about them except potsherds and fragments of bone. He is aware of no other mounds in this section of Iron County.

Westward from Enoch are the Iron Mountains, and at their northern termination, Antelope Springs. During the excavations at Paragonah Mr. Timothy Robinson remarked that "sand knolls covered with pottery" lie on either side of the road connecting Antelope Springs with Modena, and continue southward as far as the Modena-Hamblin road. In the vicinity of these mounds, according to our informant, a ditch "cemented with clay" extends for miles across the desert. This ditch is widely known as "the canal"; it is always partially filled with blown sand and has never been traced to its limits. The writer doubts that this "canal" represents prehistoric human handiwork.

CEDAR CITY is situated at the mouth of Coal Creek, on the eastern margin of Cedar Valley. Remy and Brenchley, from "the quantity of fragments of colored pottery which has been discovered in the vicinity," concluded [57] that Cedar City occupies the site of an extensive prehistoric village. In this deduction the gentlemen were quite correct, but they repeated a fallacy which has persisted since the time of the Spanish conquest by ascribing such ceramic remains to the Aztecs. When they add that " furnaces for pottery are still traceable " we may suspect they saw the burned roof covering of adobe or Willard type houses.

Personal inquiry elicited diversified opinions as to the number and physical appearance of the mounds seen near Cedar City in pioneer days. It was agreed, however, that such elevations as did exist have mostly been destroyed during development of the town and its surrounding fields. The only positive information came from Mr. Harry Hunter, who reported several mounds on his farm 3 miles to the north. As described they probably cover one-room adobe dwellings similar to those exposed at Paragonah.

Just prior to our visit Mrs. A. W. Webster had discovered several obsidian blades while making improvements on her town lot. She had subsequently loaned them to the Deseret Museum in Salt Lake City, but from oral description the blades were judged to be mostly broad and leaf-shaped. A few in the series were long and thin; others were notched at one end.

KANARRA or KANARRAVILLE, toward the southern end of Cedar Valley, is given by Maguire as the location of several mounds visited during his travels. No trace of these was seen in 1915, and inquiries made while passing through the town brought no helpful reply. It is quite probable that here as elsewhere annual cultivation of the surrounding fields has destroyed all evidence of a small cluster of prehistoric dwellings whose inhabitants tilled the very same soil.

ARCHEOLOGICAL SITES NEAR ST. GEORGE

The St. George neighborhood, in Washington County, is affectionately known throughout Utah as " Dixie." Situated 50 miles from a railroad station, it enjoys delightful seclusion yet suffers materially in consequence. Its fertile fields and fruitful orchards have made it a " land of milk and honey "; it is the home of the fig and the grape.

It was in this favored section, or rather at Santa Clara, 4 miles northwest of St. George, that Dr. Edward Palmer made his notable archeological discoveries in the seventh decade of the last century. Some of his collections are now in the United States National Museum at Washington; some are in the Peabody Museum of Harvard University. Palmer's work here represents the very first attempt

---

[57] 1861, p. 364.

at scientific investigation of Puebloan ruins in the Southwest, and his results have been characterized by Professor Holmes as "the first collection of importance known to have been made by exhumation." [58] The one regrettable thing in connection with these early explorations is that Palmer's notes have been widely scattered, if not, indeed, utterly lost to science.[59]

Upon inquiry at St. George it was learned that all the mounds in Santa Clara Canyon have long since been effaced, and that nothing would be gained by a personal visit to the locality. Partial compensation for this disappointment was found, however, in a chance meeting with Mr. R. A. Morris, one of the three men who assisted Doctor Palmer in 1875. Mr. Morris's memory is quite clear on certain phases of these early excavations, and in consequence of this fortunate fact it is now possible slightly to increase our meager knowledge of the ancient house remains as gleaned from published references to Palmer's investigations. These are few indeed, but Holmes in describing the St. George collections [60] notes that Palmer's Santa Clara mound was roughly circular, less than 10 feet in height, and covered about half an acre.

On page 198, Eleventh Annual Report of the Peabody Museum, we read: " The notes and descriptions furnished by Doctor Palmer show that most of these mounds in Utah are in reality the remains of adobe or mud houses, and that in some instances new houses have been successively erected on the remains of the old. In other instances the mounds are formed by the decay of a collection of houses built in such a way as to form a nearly continuous wall about an area thus inclosed. . . ." This quotation obviously conveys Doctor Palmer's conclusion after several years' explorations throughout western Utah, and more especially at Payson. With further reference to the Santa Clara mound, Mr. Morris recalls that in addition to adobe houses others were exposed which seemed to be semisubterranean and whose low earth walls were plastered with about 1 inch of clay. In one such house there were " four posts, arranged as a square, standing 6 feet or more above the floor. On this floor were many masses of clay, some bearing impressions of the human hand." In another instance the walls consisted of willows plastered with mud, and a fireplace stood in the middle of the floor.

The height (6 feet) given for the four posts is probably an erroneous recollection, for Mr. Morris remembers these same mounds as

---

[58] 1886, p. 307.

[59] Doctor Palmer's explorations were biological and botanical as well as anthropological. The present writer has sought to bring together such of the Palmer memoranda as relate specifically to prehistory; should the results of this search warrant, it is hoped later to publish the findings in connection with a review of his archeological collections.

[60] 1886, p. 288.

having been low and relatively insignificant elevations, composed largely of sandy soil. The original height of the posts, while an interesting question, is not of prime importance. It should be borne in mind, however, that here in Santa Clara Canyon prehistoric habitations were found whose walls in some instances were of adobe, in others of wattle construction, and in yet others of clay plastered on the face of an excavation which inclosed four posts or roof supports arranged to form a square. Each of these wall types was disclosed during the excavations of 1917 at Paragonah,[61] thus establishing an architectural relationship between the ancient inhabitants of the two localities. According to Morris, one or two mounds which Doctor Palmer opened in the immediate vicinity of St. George possessed the same characteristic features of construction observed in Santa Clara Canyon.

Mr. Don Maguire writes [62] of a large sandstone block covered with pictographs in the fields southwest of St. George, and of a mound on the bank of the Virgin River [63] east or southeast of the village. The latter may be the low elevation from which gravel was being hauled in 1915, since we learned of no other existent mounds in the vicinity and did not take the time for an actual search of the wide valley.

At the time of our visit local attention was centered on this latter mound, because only a few days previously burials accompanied by several fine earthenware vessels [64] had been uncovered by teamsters at work on the gravel bank. The elevation in question, while of considerable circumference, was quite inconspicuous and exhibited no indications of having been occupied by prehistoric habitations. Very few potsherds lay upon the surface, and Mr. Cottum, who made the discovery, was not aware that he was disturbing an ancient burial ground, although skeletons had been exposed there on other occasions. The bodies had been interred in holes of from 2 to 3 feet in depth, dug into the hard and partially cemented calcareous gravel of which the knoll is formed. In one or two instances, according to reports, stone slabs had been noticed underneath the burials.

Although no evidence of human habitations remained on this particular elevation, there were, a few yards to the north and on the bluff overlooking the river, several smoothed areas that appeared to be the floors of ancient dwellings. All traces of walls had been

---

[61] Judd, 1919a.

[62] In a personal letter dated Ogden, Utah, Aug. 9, 1915.

[63] In 1826 Jedediah Strong Smith named this Adams River, in compliment to the President; it was renamed the Virgin a year or two later, probably for Thomas Virgin (or Virgen), a member of Smith's 1827 expedition. (Dale, 1918, p. 188.) The spelling Virgen appears on the older United States maps.

[64] The specimens, all in possession of a young Mr. Cottum, included an undecorated jar, a plain-ware cooking pot, one corrugated pot, several black-on-white bowls, and a black-on-red bird-shaped vessel with unusually long neck.

washed and blown away from the bare, hard surface of the river terrace; relatively few shards and flint chips were visible.

Archeological Sites East of St. George

East and south from St. George is a region widely diversified in its physiographic features. Generally speaking, that portion lying north of the Arizona border consists of high wooded plateaus with bold red cliffs; south of the State line the country is relatively more open and with less of color as it continues, in a series of broad, barren valleys and rugged escarpments, to the Rio Colorado. Archeologically this entire section is unknown. A few small cliff houses occupy shallow caves in Mukuntuweap Canyon, now Zion National Park; others have been reported " in the upper Aubrey of the gorge cut into the western edge of the Uinkaret Plateau at the Hurricane fault. This is just south of the village of Hurricane Bench, Utah." [65]

Short Creek, a little more than midway between St. George and Kanab, in Kane County, was chosen by prehistoric man as a temporary place of abode, and encourages the belief that ancient habitations will be found also toward the east, west, and south. Report has it that cave dwellings exist in the red cliffs from which Short Creek flows, and that open pueblos stand on the low mesas about 12 miles to the west. This northern extension of Antelope Valley was being homesteaded, fenced, and plowed in 1915, and in consequence travel by team met with numerous obstructions. Reported ruins in these new fields were not sought out, but from descriptions they are believed to approximate those on the Jack Galligher ranch, 6 or 8 miles southeast of Short Creek Canyon.

Among the latter were several disconnected house sites within a stone's throw of the Galligher well and but recently razed. From superficial examination the scattered remains appeared to represent primitive adobe dwellings of the type exposed at Beaver and Paragonah, but it was noted also that numerous stone spalls lay in association with the fragments of wall material. Whether these stones had been utilized as wall and floor foundations or whether they originally formed a part of the wall construction was not determined. Masses of impressed roofing clay suggested the presence also of characteristic court shelters or lodges. Visible stone implements and potsherds were identical with those noted elsewhere.

Small mounds " like those at Galligher's ranch " are to be found throughout Antelope Valley, according to cowboys. The same informants, however, insist that cliff dwellings and mesa pueblos seen by them are alike built of stone and mud. This is entirely to be

---

[65] H. W. and F. H. Shimer, 1910, p. 247.

expected, since that portion of Utah and northern Arizona draining
into the Grand Canyon of the Colorado is largely capped with sandstone formations, which provided prehistoric man with a building
material almost as available as, and certainly more durable than,
the adobe so widely utilized throughout the eastern half of the Great
Basin. It would appear that here, in the sandstone or " red rock "
country, adobe walls were generally superseded by those of masonry;
that is, stone blocks laid in adobe mortar. This statement is made,
be it understood, not as a result of exhaustive study but rather as a
presumption grown out of our reconnaissance north of the Rio
Colorado.

PIPE SPRING [66] flows from the base of the Vermilion Cliffs, that
form the north wall of Antelope Valley, to furnish the only dependable water supply on the 62-mile road connecting Hurricane, Utah,
and Fredonia, Ariz. It offered a prize well worth striving for in
ancient as in modern times. About 1863 cattlemen from Mormon
settlements on the Virgin won control of the spring at the cost of
several lives; the present buildings, known as "Windsor Castle"
(pl. 5, b), date from the reestablishment of Kanab in 1870. Port-
holes in every room and the broken hinges of heavy gates that once
swung between the adjacent dwellings evidence the bitter struggle
for possession waged with the Indians half a century ago. Between
1870 and 1890 Navaho tribesmen forded the Colorado at the old
" Crossing of the Fathers " to direct periodic raids against the Pipe
Spring outpost. Cattle and horses that had ranged too far from
protection of the ranch buildings brought wealth and independence
to the nomadic Navaho.

Just below the spring potsherds and flint chips mark the approximate location of prehistoric homes now entirely obliterated. On the
red ledges back of the corrals and along the base of the cliffs north
of "the castle" are many small masonry ruins, mostly one and two
room structures. Although these sites are so numerous as to suggest
the presence of a considerable resident population, no large pueblos
were observed in the vicinity. Scattered potsherds offer no marked
variation from types noted elsewhere.

Report has it that a large series of mounds exists near Moccasin,
some 3 miles north of Pipe Spring; a small cliff house, probably a
cache, is described as standing under a low ledge about 4 miles to
the east. The traveler approaching from the west will observe
several ancient house sites, all within a stone's throw from the road
and within 5 miles from the old ranch. Cobblestones and blocks of
laminate sandstone are present at most of these ruins; in a few

[66] By presidential proclamation, Pipe Spring was designated a national monument May
31, 1923, " as a memorial to western pioneer life."

a, Road from Pipe Spring to Fredonia

b, "Windsor Castle," at Pipe Spring

a, Room 4, Paragonah, 1916

b, Rooms 16–19, Paragonah, 1917

instances surface indications suggest dwellings constructed solely of adobe.

Following the road from Pipe Spring to Fredonia, no prehistoric ruins were observed until within sight of the latter settlement. Here several inconspicuous mounds and one larger elevation stand on the borders of the arroyo southwest of town. That these and other near-by sites have not escaped local attention is apparent from the number of earthenware vessels decorating Fredonia homes.

Archeological Sites Near Kanab

Kanab, seat of Kane County, is situated where Kanab Creek emerges from the Vermilion Cliffs, 3 miles north of the Arizona border. Unknowingly the village has spread out over several groups of prehistoric habitations. Some few of these now lie concealed by alluvial deposits; more have been effaced through cultivation of the soil. Their former presence, nevertheless, is established by the pottery and stone utensils unearthed from time to time by the industrious village folk. Unfortunately no helpful observations were made on the occasion of such discoveries, but it would appear that only in rare instances did surface indications give warning of the close proximity of aboriginal remains. Relatively few of the specimens so found were available for inspection in 1915.

At the time of our visit Miss Delna Farnsworth possessed a number of interesting antiquities found in or near Kanab. Three of these may be mentioned: A small corrugated cooking pot with handle; a jar, $4\frac{1}{4}$ inches (10.7 cm.) high, with black-on-white decoration on the neck and shoulders and vertically perforated lugs at each side; a second cooking pot, 8 inches (20.3 cm.) in diameter, decorated about the shoulder with an incised design. Incised pottery is apparently unusual in ruins of southwestern Utah.

In 1913 or 1914 Kanab Creek floods enlarged their channel and did considerable damage to the property on the west side of town. They also exposed an old house site on the rear lot of Mrs. Vinnie Jepson. With the caving bank several pieces of ancient pottery were dislodged. From among those obtained at the time Mrs. Jepson kindly presented one to the national collections. It is illustrated in Plate 40, c.

The only one of these oft-mentioned casual finds which the writer had the privilege of examining was made on the property of Mr. Russel Cutler, in the very heart of Kanab, during excavations for a new house.[67] At a depth of about 4 feet (1.2 m.) several fine

---

[67] This particular discovery occurred while the writer was out on his 1920 reconnaissance; building operations were already under way when the site was examined.

earthenware vessels were exposed; no surface indications of a pre-historic dwelling had been noticed. Of the specimens found Mrs. Cutler had three small corrugated jars and two black-on-white vessels, a bowl and a jar. The young man employed for the digging had retained as his share a black-on-red heart-shaped jar, half filled with red paint, and two coiled pots. These he had taken with him when leaving Kanab. Among the broken specimens obtained at the time and later restored are those illustrated in Plates 39, *b, d;* 43, *b.* Absence of masonry walls leads one to believe the ancient dwellings were constructed of adobe.

A half mile west of Kanab, across the arroyo and close to the thin cedar fringe that borders the valley, are several mounds which probably cover house remains such as those observed at Beaver and Paragonah. No walls were traceable, but burned roofing adobe bearing impressions of the willows and grass on which it formerly rested, flint chips and potsherds lay scattered about. A majority of these shards were from plain ware and corrugated vessels, but black-on-white and black-on-red fragments were also present, the latter in greater proportion than was noticed at individual sites farther north.

The largest of these elevations had been partially covered with blown sand, and it was thus impossible to gauge the extent and depth of the accompanying refuse heap. The contour of the mound, however, suggests contiguous dwellings so arranged as to form three sides of a square, open to the east.

"A few miles south of Kanab," writes Professor Holmes,[68] " stands a little hill—an island in the creek bottom—which is literally covered with the ruins of an ancient village, and the great abundance of pottery fragments indicates that it was for a long period the home of cliff-dwelling peoples."

In the broad valley extending from Kanab to Johnson Run and on its low dividing ridge, known locally as the " Cedar Flats," many ruins are reported. Those farthest from available sources of building stone may prove to have been constructed of adobe. Three ruins on the north side of the valley were built of masonry; the sandstone blocks incorporated in their walls were mostly from near-by outcroppings and entirely unshaped. Two of these three ruins consisted of single rooms only; the third included several adjacent single rooms arranged to form two and part of the third side of a square. The open side of the group faced the southeast. No suggestion of a circular room was observed. At each of these three sites potsherds were present. They included the familiar plain,

---

[68] 1886, p. 281.

corrugated, and black-on-white varieties, with a few shards only of black-on-red.

JOHNSON CANYON, 8 miles east of Kanab, has long been known to have harbored prehistoric peoples. It was here, buried in the sandy floor of a cave, that Dr. Edward Palmer discovered several interesting Cliff-dweller artifacts in March, 1877.[69]

Under the belief that open ruins, or valley pueblos, would be found in proximity to such caves, the present writer proceeded to the mouth of Johnson Canyon in 1915 for such observations as could be crowded into a single day. The morning hours of that day were devoted to examination on foot of the newly plowed fields and the sage-covered slopes on the farm of Mr. Jacob H. Crosby; in the afternoon a neighboring branch of the canyon was partially explored on horseback.

Several small ruins, chiefly situated on low sandy knolls, were visited on the Crosby place. No excavations were attempted, but in three or four instances the wind had blown away the sand to reveal portions of ancient walls. At one particularly wind-swept site a cluster of binlike rooms with walls of upright slabs had been thus exposed. Some among these were roughly circular and from 4 to 6 feet (1.2–1.8 m.) in diameter; their floors consisted of sandstone slabs overlain with 3 inches of adobe mortar. Lesser bins, varying in size according to the width of the component slabs, may once have served for storage purposes. The interior walls of two such bins showed unmistakable evidence of fires. Most of the slabs as exposed ranged in height from 14 to 20 inches (35.5–50 cm.); rarely were they 30 inches high. About 20 of these structures, each independent from the others, were visible at one site. Stone implements, flint chips, and potsherds typical of southwestern Utah were plentiful. With these artifacts were many fragments and chips of sandstone. Since the slabs themselves exhibited no evidence of shaping processes, it is inferred that the sandstone bits were utilized in some sort of superstructure designed to increase the height of the upright slabs.

A small ruin, with masonry walls, stands on a projection of the low mesa just behind Mr. Crosby's stable. It is not improbable that careful search of this rim rock would disclose many similar remains which have thus far attracted but little, if any, attention.

The afternoon ride up an unnamed branch of Johnson Canyon failed to discover an alleged cliff dwelling, the exact location of which was uncertain even to our informant. We did observe, however, a number of mounds comparable in size and superficial appear-

[69] 1878, pp. 269–272.

ance with those on the Crosby property. Others of the same type are reported in neighboring canyons.

Returning from this quest our trail crossed a short arroyo from one bank of which the bones of a human skeleton protruded. Although most of the bones had disappeared with caving of the bank, is was noticed that burial had been made in a hole dug 3½ feet into compact white sand. The grave had been refilled with sand of a reddish-brown color, and subsequently a 6-inch layer of clay had washed down from the hillside, effectively concealing the interment.

A mile or more above the Crosby place and on the west side of Johnson Creek is the Greenhough farm, where several mounds had been leveled during the years immediately preceding our 1915 visit. The house walls razed with these mounds are thought to have been of masonry. Mr. David Greenhough, son of the owner, retained such artifacts as were exposed at the time; from among these a flint knife and three earthenware vessels (pls. 40, a, d; 41, a) were generously presented to the national collections.

KANAB CREEK, originating in the rugged southwestern borders of Paunsaugunt Plateau, flows for 30 miles through successive mesa walls before it passes the Vermilion Cliffs and on through Kanab Canyon into the Rio Colorado. Our reconnaissance did not penetrate this lower gorge, but the testimony of cattlemen credits it with a variety of ancient human habitations. From verbal descriptions these are thought to be comparable with the cave ruins actually visited in the more accessible upper portions of Kanab Creek and with those exposed pueblos seen in 1920 in the lower reaches of Toroweap Valley (p. 127).

In the 10 miles of canyon immediately north of Kanab it would appear that every habitable cave had been occupied by prehistoric peoples. Traces of such occupancy, although often meager, are visible at most of the sites. A number of implements and utensils taken from these caves are now owned in the village; a still larger number, prized for a time, have been lost or destroyed. Two mummies, said to have been found in this section, have likewise disappeared. In addition to the cave ruins, small pueblos of masonry stand on exposed knolls at frequent intervals throughout the canyon. They are undoubtedly contemporaneous with those cliff dwellings in which stonework predominates.

One such ruin, 2 miles north of Kanab, was razed in 1911 when the town reservoir was rebuilt. The ancient settlement occupied a low sandy ridge on the west side of and overlooking the stream channel. No trace of house walls was observed, according to Mr. Delbert Riggs and other informants, but several slab cists, remembered as fireplaces, were noted. Near these structures the team-drawn scrapers uncovered 23 skeletons, each interred on its back with limbs flexed. All had been buried within a space 30 feet square. Several pieces of pottery and a number of long chipped blades were recovered at the time. A handful of arrow points accompained one burial; with another were half a dozen fragments of copper-stained rock.[70] All this material, skeletons and cultural objects alike, has since been lost or widely scattered.

About a mile above the dam the wagon road cuts through a narrow pile of earth and rock washed down from the adjacent cliffs. Some prehistoric family had chosen this elevation as a desirable site for its home, but only a few fragments of the old masonry have survived the picks of the road-building crew. Similar small ruins are perhaps more numerous throughout the north half of Kanab Creek than one would suspect from a chance ride up the canyon.

Besides building houses in the open valley, the prehistoric Indians appear to have utilized every suitable cave, erecting habitations in many of them. Two such caves are found in Riggs (Chokecherry) Canyon, on the east side of Kanab Creek and just below Crocodile Spring.[71] Each of them shelters the remains of ancient buildings; each has been more or less ravaged by relic hunters.

The best preserved of the structures in these two caves is illustrated

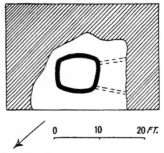

FIG. 7.—Cave ruin, Riggs Canyon

by Figure 7. It lies well within a relatively narrow cavern toward the east end of the canyon; its broken walls stand between 5 and 6 feet (1.5–1.8 m.) high. Rude masonry comprises the bulk of the building material, but this is topped by masses of adobe mud reinforced with rabbit brush. Sandstone slabs on edge form a base for the inner walls. The room was plastered inside and out. There is no door. Absence of smoke stains would seem to indicate that the room had been intended for storage purposes.

Toward the front of this same cave there may be seen the dim outlines of two small circular structures. Scattered through the loose rubbish were bones of two human skeletons, an adult and an adolescent. It is said that the accompanying skulls, together with several cultural objects, were removed about 1916.

---

[70] One gentleman identified these as pieces of turquoise.

[71] Slight delays in beginning the explorations of 1920 permitted two days' additional observations north of Kanab. Such notes as were then made have been incorporated here with the 1915 records. In January, 1926, the writer was informed that these two Riggs Canyon caves were despoiled the previous summer by boys from Kanab who retained several wooden implements and other articles that appear, from verbal description, to be of Basket Maker origin.

The second cave, near by, is much larger than the first. It has collected a vast quantity of blown sand, but through this, at the east end, there appear the partially razed walls of a round-cornered, D-shaped room, 7 feet 10 inches (2.3 m.) wide by 9 feet (2.7 m.) long. Its exposed portions were built of adobe mud surrounding bunches of grass and twigs. At least the inside surface was plastered, and the lower part of this had been washed with a thin reddish clay, the color of which stands out in marked contrast to the drab adobe above.

Additional structures of the same general type unquestionably await detection here. At the rear of the cave are a number of exposed rocks on which stone axes have been sharpened. The leg bones of an adult skeleton and part of a sandal lay upon the surface of the sandy accumulations. Against the cliff wall some playful aborigine had left the red impress of his paint-stained hands.

Perhaps 2 miles above Riggs Canyon there is a large cave in which Mr. Thomas Robinson stores the hay from his Kanab Creek farm. While scraping out the sand in 1911, by way of preparing the cave for his own purposes, Mr. Robinson exposed several skeletons. The body bones seem to have attracted little or no attention at the time, but three of the skulls, each lacking its lower jaw, were promptly reburied. A fourth skull, complete, was presented to the local grade school, there to serve as an object lesson in primitive anatomy. With Mr. Robinson's help the first three were recovered in 1920, and the fourth specimen, minus all its teeth and lower jaw, but painstakingly decorated with black ink, was subsequently exhumed from a pile of discarded books in the engine room of the school. Unfortunately the remaining portions of the skeletons have been irretrievably lost, but these four salvaged craniums are now permanently preserved in the United States National Museum.[72] Each of them lacks the occipital flattening so characteristic of the Cliff-dwellers. This fact, together with the reported absence of house walls, leads to the belief that the Robinson cave was originally occupied by Basket Makers. Cedar bark was noticed during the clearing operations, but there is no recollection of slab cists, baskets, or other artifacts.

A number of other caverns lie within easy distance of that last considered. Two of these, and several others farther up canyon, were hurriedly examined from horseback. Most of them exhibited some trace either of Basket Maker or Cliff-dweller peoples. Cattle and sheep annually seeking shelter in the caves since the advent of white settlers have destroyed nearly every vestige of ancient walls; smoke stains on the cave roofs usually mark herders' temporary camps.

---

[72] Catalogue numbers 315643, young adolescent, probably female; 315644, adult female; 315645, adult male; 315646, adult female.

Despite the obvious destruction caused by these herdsmen and their stock, the larger proportion of the caves merit examination and promise at least helpful data for the archeologist who seeks to contribute to the prehistory of our Southwest.

THREE LAKES CANYON, emptying into Kanab Creek about 5 miles above Kanab, contains half a dozen caves that also invite attention. With one exception they are relatively shallow, but they afford such shelter as would naturally have appealed to prehistoric peoples. Small, exposed dwellings, built of coarse masonry, may be seen standing singly or in groups at intervals along the margins of the canyon. Each such site is identified by a low mound. Rectangular adobe structures of the type unearthed at Beaver and Paragonah have not been certainly discovered, so far as we are aware, in this or other sections of the Kanab Creek drainage.

In Cave Lakes Canyon, the south fork of Three Lakes Canyon, are at least a dozen spacious caves in which primitive man could have found ample shelter. Fully half of these stand at the upper end of the valley, where numerous perennial springs water a grassy meadow that shows delightfully green against the red sandstone cliffs. Sand blown across the rim rock has lodged among the willows and oak to form effective barriers that impound seepage waters and create pools within several of these canyons. But unmistakable smoke stains on their ceilings show that at least some of them were occupied in ancient times. Since the advent of Mormon colonists, early in the fourth quarter of the last century, one or more families have dwelt here during the major portion of each year.

All the larger, drier caves now furnish refuge for farm animals pastured on the meadow. One such cavern, just above the ranch house of Mr. Wilfred Robinson, contains visible sections of ancient masonry walls. Quite similar walls have been erected near by within recent years to serve as granaries. Shelters smaller than those noted in the canyon proper are certain to be found on the higher ledges, although no special search in such places has been made by the present writer.[73]

Small pueblos observed among the cedars on the sandy mesa at the head of Cave Lakes Canyon show that the ancient sedentary peoples did not restrict their dwelling sites to the rock-walled valleys.

COTTONWOOD CANYON

During our sojourn in Kanab we had heard much of certain cliff dwellings near the upper end of Cottonwood Canyon, about 11 miles from the village, and altered our intended course to inspect them.

---

[73] In the fall of 1920, Mr. Jesse L. Nusbaum, of the Museum of the American Indian, Heye Foundation, explored a Basket Maker cave of vast archeological importance near the Robinson ranch. See Nusbaum, 1922.

Toward its head Cottonwood is well watered, and its low inclosing cliffs afford easy access to fair grazing on the surrounding hills, factors which early prompted establishment of a small cattle ranch now owned by Mr. B. A. Riggs. As the writer and his companion drove up to the door Mr. Riggs, one of Kanab's few surviving founders, appeared to voice the cordial welcome so typical of the western frontier; half an hour later he was guiding us to the ruins we sought.

This particular group included a kiva and four disconnected dwellings (pls. 15, 16). They were situated at one end of a shallow cave in an eastern branch of the canyon and were entirely hidden by a dense growth of oak. Several drawings of men, painted with red and yellow ocher and plain clay, showed on the rear wall of the cave; geometrical figures in white were present also. At the opposite end a tiny spring trickled from a bed of columbine, to lose itself presently in the loose talus.

The kiva was more than half filled with fallen masonry, blown sand, and blocks of sandstone dropped from the cave roof. Two of the four dwellings were fairly intact, their ceilings of poles, cedar bark, and earth being still in place; the others had suffered from time and the rubbing of cattle. Each of the five structures was built of laminate sandstone laid in adobe mortar. The stone itself, although tabular, showed no marked evidence of attempts at shaping; the mortar had been freely used and tended in places to cover the masonry. Sandstone spalls and occasionally potsherds were utilized as chinking to protect the adobe from weathering.

While breakfast was in preparation the next morning just prior to our departure from Cottonwood, hurried examination was made of a second cave about 200 yards from the ranch house. Here were visible remains of three slab bins or cists and two circular rooms with standing walls. These latter structures were built of adobe reinforced by rabbit brush and the slender shoots of black sage; at the base of their inner walls sandstone slabs set on edge formed a sort of wainscoting. On the cliff behind, a number of excellent pictographs, done in red, white, yellow, brown, and plain clay, immediately suggested a Basket Maker origin. Similar drawings had been observed the previous afternoon in caves of Farm Canyon.[74]

Leaving the agreeable hospitality of the Riggs ranch, we made our way through deep sand to Mount Carmel, Orderville, and Glendale, in Long Valley on the upper Virgin; thence over the divide to Hatch

---

[74] Such scanty notes as were taken during this too brief visit to Cottonwood Canyon in 1915 were largely augmented four years later when unforeseen circumstances again turned our attention to the same quiet valley. The reader will find more detailed descriptions, with photographs and text figures, in those paragraphs covering the field season of 1919.

and Panquitch, on Sevier River, and back to Beaver by way of Fremont Pass. On this ride no prehistoric ruins were observed and no information was gained which would indicate that mounds or other prehistoric remains had been seen by local residents. In Long Valley, and again in the vicinity of Panquitch, conditions are favorable for an ancient occupancy, and it is not improbable that more painstaking search than was permitted us will yet disclose in these two localities traces of primitive adobe dwellings or the wattled walls that frequently go with them.[75] In addition, the pink cliffs that border Colob and Markagunt Plateaus on the west, and Paunsaugunt Plateau on the east, should provide caves in which primitive man sought shelter as he did in Cottonwood Canyon. These are areas that still await investigation.

Following the return to Beaver, one week was devoted to excavation of the large mound on the Jarm Bradshaw property, as previously reported, and the 1915 reconnaissance of western Utah was brought to a close.

---

[75] Mr. T. C. Hoyt, connected with the Ogden office of the United States Forest Service in 1915, has described a cave high in the cliff at the mouth of Sanford Canyon, about 8 miles north of Panquitch, which is thought to have been occupied in ancient times. Owing to its inaccessible location, the cave had not been entered up to that time.

II. FIELD WORK, SEASON OF 1916

Among all the archeological sites visited during the reconnaissance of 1915 none was so extensive as that at Paragonah. Here were many mounds covering the disintegrating walls of prehistoric adobe dwellings—fast-disappearing representatives of a primitive culture widespread throughout western Utah in ancient times. These crude habitations promised little in the way of spectacular discoveries, but they offered an opportunity for investigative work the equal of which was not observed elsewhere. Then, too, the Paragonah mounds were threatened with early and complete destruction; they stood as a last thin line of survivors awaiting the irresistible advance of modern agriculture.

Captain Wheeler quotes from the report of Dr. H. C. Yarrow that between 400 and 500 mounds were seen near Paragonah in 1872.[1] Within 20 years this number had been reduced to about 100, according to Prof. Henry Montgomery [2] and Mr. Don Maguire, both of whom engaged in excavations here in January, 1893. Less than 50 mounds remained in 1915, and of these most were doomed soon to disappear with contemplated enlargement of adjacent cultivated fields. It seemed imperative, therefore, that additional investigations be made at this site without delay, a realization which prompted a return to Paragonah for inauguration of the 1916 reconnaissance.

OBSERVATIONS AT PARAGONAH

On the farm of Mr. Isaac Bozarth, situated at the north margin of the village, were several massive mounds whose size alone prevented their demolition the previous year when surrounding fields were plowed for the first time. One of these was selected for excavation. It concealed a group of individual rooms, the relationship of which is illustrated by Figure 8. Evidence of earlier digging, identified by the workmen as that of Maguire, was plainly visible at the southeast end. An unfinished cut about 20 feet (6.09 m.) wide ran longitudinally through the elevation. Despite this mutilation, the site promised something of information in the time at our disposal. House remains were not always found where expected. Among dwellings examined only those exhibiting special

---

[1] Wheeler, 1889, p. 57.   [2] 1894, p. 303.

54

features will be described. The others were quite the counterpart of those excavated at Beaver in 1915.

Room 1 was long and narrow.[3] It had been cleared previously and its walls leveled to a uniform height of 15 inches. The earth with which the chamber was subsequently refilled had been deposited by wind and water and so compacted that it did not separate readily either from the walls or the floor. Against the outer west end was what appeared to be a buttress, 3 feet 6 inches (1.06 m.) long by 6 inches (15.2 cm.) thick; any former connection between this and the north side of the room had completely disappeared. No artifacts were found within the house.

Room 2 was divided subsequent to construction by a partition 6 inches thick, in contrast to its 10-inch (25.4 cm.) inclosing walls.

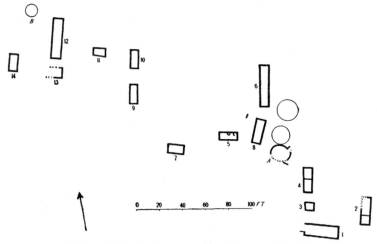

FIG. 8.—Adobe dwellings exposed at Paragonah in 1916

Although it still stood to a height of 12 inches, the division exhibited no trace of a former doorway. Like the main walls, it was built of individual masses of adobe mud forced successively into position and carefully smoothed on both faces. Horizontal lines of cleavage, so frequently noted in walls of this character, had been carefully obliterated. Bone awls, potsherds, and fragments of stone implements were found in the room. The floor of this dwelling lay approximately 18 inches above that in room 1.

Between rooms 2 and 3 was a large ash heap, the bottom of which was fully 3 feet below the floor of room 2. In this débris were many bone awls, fragments of split mammal bones, potsherds, and stone implements, in addition to blocks of discarded building material.

---

[3] The dimensions of each excavated room will be found in Appendix II.

Room 4, with carefully surfaced walls 10 inches thick, proved to be one of the neatest and best-constructed houses in the entire group. After it had been occupied for some time the room was divided by a relatively thin partition composed of willows bound horizontally to several 2-inch posts and the whole plastered with mud. A doorway, with sill 10 inches above the floor, opened through this partition at its junction with the west wall of the room. Numerous artifacts were exposed in the smaller section of the dwelling; none in the larger.

The east wall had collapsed at a point 2 feet (0.61 m.) above the floor, and at this level there appeared a 1-inch layer of gravel extending over the entire area of the room and irregularly to the northeastern limit of the mound. Thinner lenses of coarse sand were visible both above and below this gravel layer, a condition noted in nearly every one of the Paragonah mounds examined. As postulated in a previous paragraph (p. 37), these sandy layers were deposited by flood waters from Red Creek, whose former course lies less than 100 yards north of the house group under consideration.

Room 5 contained in its northeast corner the remains of a small bin, but far greater interest attaches to the superposed levels, with their evidence of long-continued domestic activity. The north wall of the room had been razed to within 8 inches (20.3 cm.) of its base, at which point a new floor was spread. This pavement joined the inner east and south walls of the abandoned house, extending over and beyond its partially razed north wall. On this secondary floor, but just within the former north limit, was a rimless fireplace 4 inches (10.2 cm.) deep. There was no evidence that the fireplace had ever been roofed, although it seemed quite obvious that the fragmentary south and east walls of room 5 were utilized as a partial protection for those household industries centering about the fire.

When camp litter, and more especially wind-blown sand and clay, became a nuisance in this sheltered corner the hearth was abandoned in favor of another constructed on top of the accumulation a short distance away. Four additional fireplaces were observed immediately north of that above room 5. Each consisted merely of a clay-lined basin about 30 inches (0.76 m.) in diameter and 4 inches (10.2 cm.) deep, surrounded by a well-trod pavement whose outer edge merged with the loose earthy content of the refuse pile. That the latter grew with some degree of rapidity is at least suggested by the apparent effort made to keep kitchen fires on a level with the increasing refuse. Each of the five fireplaces in this section of the mound occupied a separate, rather restricted plane; one of them, that just outside the east corner of room 5, is no less than 38 inches (0.96 m.) above the floor of the latter.

Room 14 contained two floors, the second 21 inches (53.2 cm.) above the first, and like it curving slightly upward to join the walls of the dwelling. The fill between these two floors consisted of clean, sandy clay. Potsherds and other artifacts were not present; neither were there fragments of adobe to indicate that house repairs had preceded construction of the second pavement. Absence of broken wall material between floors is so unusual as immediately to attract attention.

Circular room A was a curious structure. The southern portion of its curved wall had been entirely demolished, but the remaining sections showed a maximum diameter of 15 feet (4.6 m.), with a circular rimmed fireplace occupying the middle floor. Masses of roof adobe, some of which were burned to the point of vitrification, lay strewn about, and beneath them numerous charred fragments of ceiling poles.

Two features of this room deserve special notice. First, it had been excavated from a pile of loose, ashy débris and adobe mud was spread directly upon the bank to form its walls. That this rubbish was not compact enough to withstand the weight of the roof is apparent from the fact that the plastered sides had settled outward to a considerable degree. The original north wall, for instance, although reduced to within 20 inches (50 cm.) of its base, inclined 22 inches (55.9 cm.) from the perpendicular. Efforts to correct this defect had been made with four successive layers of mud plaster, each markedly thicker at the top than at the bottom. This settling tendency of the wall may well account for the ultimate abandonment of the room. Two posts, not indicated on the ground plan, had been erected as auxiliary roof supports, but the inherent weakness of the structure could not be overcome. Finally, the upper walls were thrown down and their wreckage roughly leveled to form an open court. In this at least one fireplace was subsequently built, resting, curiously enough, upon the sloping north wall of the ruined chamber.

The second feature to be mentioned is the problematical eastern entrance or ventilator. Only one side of this passage, and that incomplete, remained at the time of excavation; for this reason it was quite impossible to gain any adequate idea as to its original dimensions or function. A separate wall fragment just outside the southeast quarter likewise remains unexplained. But, considered as a whole, this round room seems to have been designed for some special purpose; for the present, at least, the writer prefers to regard it, like the circular structure in the Bradshaw mound at Beaver, as a prototype of the true Pueblo kiva.[4]

---

[4] Judd, 1917b.

Circular room B, at the northwestern limit of the house group, when first exposed was also thought to have been constructed with special requirements in mind. But it is perhaps more closely related to the secondary Willard type shelters found at Beaver. Its southwestern quarter had been dug from a low clay bank; further, at some time during its occupancy, a triangular bench had been built against the inner north wall of the room. This platform, only 4 inches high, was made of clay mud, its edges being rounded to meet the floor. In the middle of the latter stood a rimmed fireplace, and about it three postholes. Traces of a corresponding fourth post at the north were not discovered.

As in circular room A, the floor of this chamber was covered by quantities of burned roof adobe and charred timbers. Fragments of a coiled basket lay beside the fireplace; several earthenware vessels, each shattered by the fallen roof, were recovered from the débris. Charred corncobs and husks were observed among the litter; likewise numerous bone and stone artifacts.

Secondary shelters, or kitchens, of the Willard type seem largely to have lost their individuality in this particular group of ancient dwellings. There were no fireplaces in the rectangular adobe houses. All cooking and all those diversified industries with which primitive people busy themselves were done in the open. That the same convenient spots were utilized year after year in the performance of necessary household tasks is indicated both by the accumulations of camp refuse and the frequency with which fireplaces were observed throughout this débris. It is also obvious that these centers of domestic activity were shifted from time to time in an effort to keep them always on top of the constantly increasing rubbish and wind-blown earth. Surrounding each fireplace was a small trampled area. Well-defined floors with postholes or other evidence of a roof—features characteristic of secondary court shelters at Beaver—were generally lacking at Paragonah.

One of the best local examples of this lesser type of habitation stood just north of and almost adjoining circular room A. Here was an unmistakable floor about 15 feet (4.56 m.) in diameter, its western periphery cut 3 inches into native red clay. The customary fireplace was present; almost the entire floor was strewn with charred poles and roof adobe, showing the effect of the intense heat generated when the room was destroyed. Another similar floor, 18 feet (5.5 m.) in diameter, lay immediately north of that last described. These latter were the only recognizable secondary shelters observed during the 1916 excavations. In numerical contrast to these two, more than a dozen unprotected fireplaces were exposed in the refuse piles adjacent to the house group.

During the course of the Paragonah investigations four human skeletons and fragments of an infant's skull were exposed in the near-by field of Mr. T. A. Topham, where several small mounds were then being razed. Each of these elevations covered a single adobe room, whose walls were quite comparable with those already considered. No two of the rooms were closely associated, and none of them possessed an adjacent débris heap of noticeable size.

As to the skeletons themselves, one was buried within the walls of a dwelling and under a layer of sandstone slabs which formed a second floor about 8 inches (20.3 cm.) above the original. It is uncertain whether these slabs had been surfaced with adobe mud. A second body had been exhumed just outside the north wall of the same house; as with the first, no definite information was obtainable as to the method of interment. A third skeleton,[5] buried in the open field with head to the west and knees elevated, had been slightly damaged during leveling operations. Below the raised knees were two fragments of the frontal bone of an infant. The fourth skeleton, also buried in the open field, was so thoroughly broken by the plow which exposed it that no effort toward preservation was made.

EXPLORATIONS IN MILLARD COUNTY

Garrick Mallery figures[6] a few drawings made by I. C. Russell of crude pictographs seen at Black Rock Spring, on Beaver River, some 20 miles (32.2 kilos) north of Milford, Utah. They are incised or pecked on the vertical faces of basalt bowlders, as were those in The Gap west of Parowan (p. 38). In the opinion of Mallery, Shoshonean Indians produced the Black Rock carvings which are "generally of an 'unintelligible' nature, though the human figure is drawn in complex forms. Footprints, circles, etc., also abound."[7]

According to this same author, Mr. Gilbert Thompson, of the United States Geological Survey, visited a second series of similar drawings in Fool Creek Canyon (probably that draining the middle west slope of the Canyon Range, at the northeast margin of Sevier Desert). Some of the Fool Creek characters are thought strongly to resemble those in Arizona commonly credited to the ancient Pueblo; they differ further from the Black Rock series in that many of them were drawn in red, and apparently at three different periods. Neighboring pictographs were pecked on the canyon walls, while yet others were both pecked and painted.[8]

[5] U. S. N. M. Cat. No. 292012; adult male, slight occipital compression.

[6] 1886, p. 230.

[7] Ibid., p. 27.

[8] Ibid., p. 229.

Mallery notes the further occurrence of pecked and incised char-
acters at various locations in Nevada, specifically at the lower end of
Pyramid Lake; on the western slope of Lone Butte in the Carson
Desert; on Walker River near Walker Lake, and at Reveille.[9] These
figures are said to be numerous and of wide variety; they appear, in
most instances, at least, on the smooth faces of basaltic bowlders.
Although most of the carvings are thought to be the work of
Shoshonean tribes, the series at Reveille is reported as of " apparent
Shinumo or Moki origin."

Whether this last-quoted opinion has any real basis in fact is
unknown to the present writer. As a rule the prehistoric housebuilders of western Utah north of the Colorado drainage erected
their adobe dwellings on slight elevations in broad, open valleys,
where few, if any, rock surfaces were present to tempt the pictorially
inclined. It seems too early, therefore, to suggest any possible connection between these ancient folk and the carvers of pictographs on
basaltic bowlders at various localities throughout the Great Basin.

That the primitive peoples of western Utah wandered over into the
desert valleys of Nevada, there to build their characteristic adobe
dwellings, is entirely to be expected. Already, in fact, evidence of
such dwellings has been noted in the vicinity of Las Vegas by Dr.
A. V. Kidder and Mr. N. C. Nelson. Both gentlemen have observed
fragments of corrugated and black-on-white pottery—usually an
infallible sign of the close proximity of prehistoric Pueblos. Mr. M.
S. Duffield [10] reports the occurrence of potsherds, stone implements,
etc., in the Spring Mountains southwest of Las Vegas. Early reports
of adobe ruins and pictographs in the lower drainage of the Rio
Virgin were abundantly verified when M. R. Harrington, late in
1924, exposed dwellings of the Paragonah type near St. Thomas.[11]
Nevada, therefore, may yet be expected to make a substantial contribution toward solution of the archeological problems raised by
the prehistoric housebuilders of the Great Basin.

SNAKE VALLEY.—Paralleling the western border of the county is
Snake Valley, a semiarid trough that heads in Nevada, crosses the
Utah line and continues northward a distance of 80 miles or more
until it gradually merges into the Great Salt Lake Desert. From
the archeological point of view Snake Valley is still unexplored,
although assurances of a prehistoric occupancy have been received.[12]

---

[9] 1886, pp. 24–25.

[10] 1904, p. 148.

[11] Harrington, 1925, p. 74. While this report was still in press much new information
has resulted from researches of the Museum of the American Indian, Heye Foundation,
near St. Thomas, Clark County, and elsewhere in Nevada. See Harrington, 1925, a–c,
1926; and Kidder, 1925.

[12] The writer's sole source of information is Mr. George Bishop, of Smithville and
Garrison, from whom several letters were received between 1916 and 1920.

Our informant mentions a ruin some 30 by 40 feet (9.1 by 12.1 m.) in area from which four low wall sections of excellent masonry protrude (subsequent efforts to relocate this ruin appear to have been unsuccessful), and expresses the belief that ancient houses will be discovered beneath the numerous mounds in the valley. Whether this surmise has any foundation in fact may not be said, but it is well to bear in mind that many of the Snake Valley mounds are of natural origin, grown up about flowing springs.[13] On the other hand, although no potsherds were observed near the so-called masonry ruins above mentioned, they have been frequently observed elsewhere in the valley.

On the George Bishop ranch at Smithville is a large cave, difficult of access, the dimensions of which are given as 80 feet by 80 feet, with a rear width of only one-tenth that at the mouth. A small spring flows from the back wall. The floor of this cave is covered with fine red earth; in the middle is a pile of charcoal at least 3 feet high. About the old hearth were a number of mountain sheep horns, two or three pairs of which were later sent by Mr. Bishop to a Salt Lake City museum. He adds that nine pairs remained in the cave. Other similar caverns are reported in this vicinity, yet we have no information as to their size or probable contents. Especially to the west, among the mountain ranges just across the Nevada border, topographical features would seem to suggest the possible occurrence of ancient dwelling sites.

An earthen vessel, filled with corn and sealed, was found by children at play in a cave at the upper end of Snake Valley, some 35 or 40 miles (64.4 kilos) southwest of Garrison, according to our informant. Later the specimen was accidentally broken and then discarded.

The alleged dams and reservoirs mentioned frequently in the correspondence from which the above notes were taken are, perhaps, adequately explained by Meinzer in these words:[14]

Conspicuous shore features were constructed by the waves (during the highest stage of Lake Bonneville) in Snake Valley Bay. Especially characteristic are large terraces bordered on the outside by heavy embankments resembling railroad grades and forming natural reservoirs. So perfect and regular are these embankments that they are believed by some of the inhabitants of the region to represent the labors of an ancient people.

SEVIER DESERT.—Several mounds covering prehistoric habitations were razed during preparation of the irrigated fields that now surround Oasis, Deseret, and Hinckley, in the very heart of the

[13] Oscar E. Meinzer, Water-Supply Paper 277, U. S. Geol. Survey, Washington, 1911, pp. 130–131.
[14] Ibid., pp. 127–128.

Sevier Desert. Reports as to the probable original number of these mounds vary widely, but it seems safe to assume that the total was not inconsiderable. Indeed, it is not at all unlikely that prehistoric agriculturists built their adobe houses in every favorable location along the borders of Sevier River between Sevier Canyon and the Cricket Range.

In the one day at his disposal the writer made personal inquiries at the three towns above mentioned, drove from Hinckley to Abraham, thence westward into the sterile desert, and back to Oasis.[15] Local residents had observed low elevations and had found various objects of antiquity while cultivating their fields. In no instance, however, were these mounds of such size as to require special reductive measures.

Between Abraham and Hinckley a half dozen prehistoric dwelling sites were examined. Each of these was identified by scattered potsherds, flint chips, and broken stone implements; in each case every vestige of former house walls had disintegrated and had been washed or blown from the clay hardpan. That these ancient habitations were constructed of adobe seems indisputable, for suitable building stone is entirely wanting throughout this portion of the desert.

On the northern outskirts of Hinckley a farmer had razed three or four low mounds during the summer of 1915 to provide space for additional haystacks. Each knoll is recalled as having concealed a single room with adobe walls; two or three small earthen vessels, bone awls, stone balls, etc., were found during the work of demolition. When this site was visited during the course of the 1916 reconnaissance fragments of burned roof adobe lay strewn over the surface, and in the loose earth scraped from the mounds were numerous shards of prehistoric pottery. These represent both plain and corrugated jars and bowls decorated on the inside only. As at Beaver and Paragonah, the bowl fragments were a dull, slaty gray, ornamented with black geometric designs.

PAVANT VALLEY.—The lofty Pavant Range forms the southeastern boundary of Millard County. Clear, cool streams flow down its western slopes and into the irrigation ditches of half a dozen agricultural communities. Any surplus or sudden increase in stream volume runs past the villages and out into the monotonous expanse of Pavant Valley.

In ancient times primitive farmers cultivated the fertile soil along the margins of these same streams, hunted antelope among the lava beds that form the western wall of the valley and deer that sought

---

[15] Mr. C. O. W. Pierson, of Oasis, possessed a small collection of local archeological specimens in 1916. Among them was a fine plain-ware cooking pot obtained southeast of the village.

shelter on the pine-covered mountain ridge. These prehistoric farmer-hunters, with an apparent preference for the gentle slopes at the western base of the Pavant Range, built adobe dwellings within hailing distance of each other, or perhaps grouped them into miniature settlements. The ruins of such dwellings, now marked by low earth mounds, are still to be seen at intervals throughout the valley; many similar remains have long since been sacrificed to the plow and scraper.

Fillmore, the county seat of Millard County, is situated on an old Bonneville terrace close beside Chalk Creek, the second largest stream entering Pavant Valley. In this particular locality, and it is perhaps equally true elsewhere, prehistoric peoples seem to have favored the borders of the stream as dwelling sites, since existing mounds, and many no longer visible,[16] follow the course of Chalk Creek from the canyon mouth to the barren flats northwest of town. After passing the Lake Bonneville bench Chalk Creek formerly changed its course with each season, leaving the neighboring bottom lands more or less covered with thin layers of gravelly deposits. Some of the older settlers recall this shifting tendency of the stream, and at least one old Indian from the Pavant village near Kanosh believes that the prehistoric inhabitants here were driven out by Chalk Creek floods.

During the single day of reconnoitering northwest of Fillmore approximately 25 mounds were observed. None of these appeared to conceal the remains of more than one room; all were low and relatively inconspicuous. Potsherds, flint, and obsidian chips, etc., were present in each instance. At some sites plain ware formed a majority of the visible shards; at others, black-on-white apparently predominated. In no case was there the slightest evidence that stone had been utilized in wall construction.

On the north rim of the " Devil's Kitchen," some 10 or more miles southwest of Fillmore, is a small series of pictographs pecked into the vertical faces of basaltic bowlders. Most of these carvings are

---

[16] Mr. John J. Starley, chief informant during our observations near Fillmore, pointed out the former locations of numerous mounds. Mr. Starley recalls vividly a brief visit made by Dr. Edward Palmer and an escort of soldiers from Fort Douglas about 1874, when two or three small mounds were opened. In one of these an earthen jar was found ; the vessel was half filled with sunflower seeds, and these in turn were covered by a layer of corn or broken corncobs. Both corn and seeds were charred. Despite these excavations, Starley remembers Doctor Palmer as " a collector of bugs and grass," who " nailed every lizard he saw and grabbed every insect, and usually had his pockets bulging with such stuff." Palmer made other visits to this locality between 1869 and 1877, for Fillmore was one of the principal stations on the stage route from Salt Lake City to St. George. About June 1, 1870, according to manuscript notes in possession of W. E. Safford, of the U. S. Department of Agriculture, Palmer " spent two days at Fillmore and made a nice collection." The nature of this collection is not stated ; likewise none of the scattered notes with which the writer is familiar conveys any information as to the extent or results of Palmer's archeological observations in Pavant Valley. The coiled jar illustrated in Plate 41, c, was obtained near Fillmore in 1888 by Dr. H. C. Yarrow.

scarcely traceable and appear very old. It is not at all improbable that other groups of like character will be found among the lava fields on the western border of the valley. Here was the source of the obsidian so commonly used by the prehistoric arrow makers in this section of the State, and here also the more recent Pavant Indians secreted their dead until white pillagers brought cessation to an old tribal custom.

Meadow, a small settlement 7 miles southwest of Fillmore, was included in the 1916 reconnaissance when word was broadcast of the recent discovery there of several prehistoric earthenware vessels. These had been exposed quite accidentally by Mr. Joseph S. Dame while trenching for a pipe line on his town property.[17] Two small jars (pl. 40, *b*, *g*) found at the same time have been presented to the national collections by Mrs. Edith Bennett. No human bones were observed with this pottery, but elsewhere near the village skeletons have been exhumed during leveling operations.

It is quite obvious that Meadow occupies the very site of an ancient settlement. Many mounds have been razed there during expansion of the modern community. One of the largest of these elevations is thought to have stood directly in front of the Dame lot; if this conjecture be correct, the mound was completely obliterated when the street was graded. In 1916 the only mounds known locally were situated about three-quarters of a mile east of town. Among the number was one large and half a dozen low elevations; the latter, no doubt, covered but single rooms.

Superficially the mounds examined near Meadow, Fillmore, and Deseret add nothing to the information previously gained at Beaver and Paragonah. The ancient dwellings observed in Millard County had been constructed of adobe; their roofs were doubtless flat and provided with a hatchway, which could be closed as desired with a stone disk. No noticeable variation in pottery technique is apparent. As a result of our 1916 reconnaissance only one outstanding difference appears between the mounds observed in Millard County and those in Beaver and Iron Counties, for example, and this is that the former are generally lower and smaller in ground area. This does not mean, however, that larger mounds were absent when the present conquest of the country began or that they do not now exist in areas beyond the narrow limits of our survey.

ADDITIONAL ARCHEOLOGICAL SITES

Mounds similar to those at Fillmore and Meadow are reported near Hatton and Kanosh, at the southern end of Pavant Valley.

---

[17] The specimens discovered by Mr. Dame were subsequently purchased for the Bureau of American Ethnology ; three of them are figured in Plates 39, *a* ; 40, *e* ; 41, *b*.

Others are known on Cove Creek, in the extreme southeastern corner of Millard County.

Twenty miles to the east, on the opposite side of the mountains, is Clear Creek and an extensive series of pictographs. Conflicting notices of mounds below the mouth of this stream, especially in the vicinity of Monroe and Richfield, have been obtained from chance acquaintances. Perhaps a fair indication of what might formerly have been expected in this section of the State is conveyed by the following quotation from F. S. Dellenbaugh: [18]

> The ruins in the valley of the Sevier River have generally been found so far, I believe, to consist of adobe. In digging water ditches in the town of Monroe several mounds were cut through and a number of skeletons unearthed, besides some fine specimens of pottery. No one, as far as I could ascertain, knows where the skeletons are now, or the pottery either.

One informant writes that cliff dwellings are to be seen on Otter Creek, a southward-flowing branch of Sevier River in eastern Piute County.

In 1875 G. K. Gilbert, of the United States Geological Survey, observed a number of incised and painted pictographs on Temple Creek, a southern tributary of the Dirty Devil River. Such notes as he made at that time are quoted by Mallery.[19] They include, among others, representations of human beings, animals, bird tracks, human hands and feet, circles, waving lines, etc. There is a possibility that the colored figures especially are products of the Basket Makers, for definite records of these precursors of the Cliff-dwellers have been observed within the gorge of the Rio Colorado a short distance to the east.

Near Escalante, some 45 miles southwest from the mouth of Temple Creek, a number of interesting prehistoric remains are described by Mr. Ambrose E. McGarry [20] as follows:

> Near the top of the mesas there were a number of small caves, and these were all walled up in front with adobe, each containing one or two rooms and one entrance. I found one wall made of wattlework, the small sticks being set in the bottom of the cave and then carefully covered with clay. On top of the mesa I found a large room about 20 feet in diameter, circular, and used perhaps as a lookout, as it commanded a view of Escalante Canyon, Wide Canyon, and the desert to the south. I found a horn scraper about 8 inches long, well formed and rounded at the end. It had two small holes near the top in which I found a thong that had been used to fasten the scraper to the hand.

Additional information on this region was kindly furnished by Mr. D. C. Shurtz, jr., of Escalante, who writes [21] that many cliff dwellings are known between the village and the mouth of Escalante

[18] 1877, p. 178.
[19] 1886, pp. 26–27.
[20] In a personal letter dated Aug. 21, 1916.
[21] A personal letter to the writer dated March 8, 1920.

River. Most of these appear to have been caches or storehouses, but others were habitations, since smoke stains show on their walls and ceilings and artifacts of various sorts have been found in the rubbish they contain. Among these articles are agricultural implements of oak, bone tools, pottery, and fragments of squash rind. Paintings on the rocks in several places are said to be in good state of preservation.

Mr. Shurtz informs us also that a number of ruins, some with masonry walls 3 feet (0.91 m.) high, stand on Kaiparowits Plateau (locally known as " Fifty-mile Mountain "). Laminate sandstone is readily available in this section of Utah, and it is only natural, therefore, that the ancient housebuilders should have utilized it for construction purposes. Cave dwellings with walls of adobe or wattlework such as McGarry mentions are, on the other hand, much less well known.

In the Circle Cliffs country, north of Escalante River and west of the Henry Mountains, prehistoric ruins, if present at all, are doubtless few in number and of little consequence. Mr. Shurtz knew of none; Dr. Herbert E. Gregory observed nothing of moment during his field work for the United States Geological Survey. Yet somewhere south of the Dirty Devil, in this region of sandstone and shifting sand—6,000 square miles awaiting archeological exploration—unmistakable evidence of the passing of prehistoric peoples will yet be found. We may be sure of this, for ancient ruins have been noted by every explorer who has braved the rapids of the Rio Colorado.

On the afternoon of July 28, 1869, Maj. J. W. Powell and his party camped at the mouth of the Dirty Devil River. The next day they passed through a low, red-walled canyon, and the major made the following entry in his diary:[22]

A short distance below its head we discover the ruins of an old building on the left wall. There is a narrow plain between the river and the wall just here, and on the brink of a rock 200 feet high stands this old house. Its walls are of stone laid in mortar with much regularity. It was probably built three stories high; the lower story is yet almost intact; the second is much broken down, and scarcely anything is left of the third. Great quantities of flint chips are found on the rocks near by, and many arrowheads, some perfect, others broken; and fragments of pottery are strewn about in great profusion. On the face of the cliff, under the building and along down the river for two or three hundred yards, there are many etchings. Two hours are given to the examination of these interesting ruins, then we run down 15 miles farther and discover another group. The principal building was situated on the summit of the hill. A part of the walls are standing to the height of 8 or 10 feet, and the mortar yet remains in some places. The house was in the shape of an L, with five rooms on the ground floor, one in the angle, and two in each extension. In the space in the angle there is a deep

---

[22] 1875, pp. 68–70.

excavation. From what we know of the people in the Province of Tusayan, who are doubtless of the same race as the former inhabitants of these ruins, we conclude that this was a " kiva," or underground chamber, in which their religious ceremonies were performed.

We leave these ruins and run down 2 or 3 miles, and go into camp about mid afternoon. And now I climb the wall and go out into the back country for a walk.

*　　　*　　　*　　　*　　　*　　　*　　　*

Just before sundown I attempt to climb a rounded eminence, from which I hope to obtain a good outlook on the surrounding country. It is formed of smooth mounds, piled one above another. Up these I climb, winding here and there to find a practicable way, until near the summit they become too steep for me to proceed. I search about a few minutes for a more easy way, when I am surprised at finding a stairway, evidently cut in the rock by hands. At one place, where there is a vertical wall of 10 or 12 feet, I find an old, rickety ladder. It may be that this was a watchtower of that ancient people whose homes we have found in ruins. On many of the tributaries of the Colorado I have heretofore examined their deserted dwellings. Those that show evidences of being built during the latter part of their occupation of the country are usually placed on the most inaccessible cliffs. Sometimes the mouths of caves have been walled across, and there are many other evidences to show their anxiety to secure defensible positions. Probably the nomadic tribes were sweeping down upon them, and they resorted to these cliffs and canyons for safety. It is not unreasonable to suppose that this orange mound was used as a watchtower. Here I stand where these now lost people stood centuries ago and look over this strange country. I gaze off to great mountains in the northwest, which are slowly covered by the night until they are lost, and then I return to camp. It is no easy task to find my way down the wall in the darkness, and I clamber about until it is nearly midnight before I arrive.

Dellenbaugh, a member of Powell's second expedition, elaborates somewhat upon the major's description of the first ruin group. He adds: [23]

The canyon walls at this point are low, and beaten trails that lead down on both sides indicate that it was an old and well-known crossing. . . . The situation was admirably adapted for defense, and commanded an extensive view in every direction. The lookout house, standing almost upon the brink of the precipice, was red sandstone, rectangular, and some 18 feet long. It had been two stories high. Three walls, 12 or 13 feet in height, still remain standing, and the accurate lines of the angles were remarkable. The fourth wall had fallen in and covered the floor of the building with a compact mass of rocks. Not a stick of timber could be found; but the sockets of the crossbeams were still distinct. Of the mortar, which was most likely the kind ordinarily used, clay and fine sand, not a trace was left. . . . But it was just beneath the uppermost stratum of the cliff that the main portion of the fortification was discovered. Nature had assisted the Shinumos in forming a cozy retreat. A level shelf, varying from about 6 to 10 feet in width, ran along for 150 feet or more. In most places the rocks above protruded as far as the edge of the lower rocks, sometimes further, thus leaving a sort of gallery, generally 7 or 8 feet high. Walls that extended to the roof had been built

[23] 1877, pp. 172–174. The article figures four painted drawings of unquestioned Basket Maker handiwork.

along the outer edge of the natural floor, and the inclosed space being sub-divided by stone partitions to suit the convenience of the builders, the whole formed a series of rather comfortable rooms or houses. At some points, where the upper rocks did not project quite far enough for a roof, an open balcony was left. The back walls of the houses—the natural rock—had on them many groups of hieroglyphics; and further along, where there was no roof rock at all, the vertical faces had been inscribed with seeming great care. Some of the sheltered groups were painted in various dull colors, but most of them were chiseled.

Forty years after Powell and Dellenbaugh rode through the canyons of the Rio Colorado their observations as to the frequent occurrence of aboriginal remains in gorges that might logically be regarded as impassable barriers to aboriginal migrations were confirmed by Ellsworth and Emery Kolb. On their voyage through Glen Canyon the brothers found [24] "many evidences of ancient Indians, who had reached the river through side canyons. We found several ruined cliff dwellings, with broken pottery and arrowheads scattered about. There were strange pictographs of masked figures and of deer and mountain sheep on the walls." Still a decade later, members of the United States Geological Survey added to the pictorial and descriptive record of these prehistoric ruins.

Escalante crossed the Rio Colorado in 1776 over an old Ute trail since known as the " Crossing of the Fathers." When Powell passed this well-marked ford he noted the bleached bones of cattle and the dead coals of many camp fires—relics of Navaho depredations against Mormon settlements at Kanab, Pipe Spring, etc. To check these periodic raids the ledge trail up the west cliff was dynamited about 1890. The Navaho followed the Utes; the Utes followed still older footprints. Long before white men brought horses and cattle to tempt the Indians of the plateau country human beings on foot had marked pathways through the red rock country. Dandy Crossing, Halls Crossing, and the Crossing of the Fathers are trails across the Rio Colorado that found their origin in prehistoric times. For this reason alone ancient ruins southwest of the Henry Mountains are certain to be more numerous than our few brief references would imply.

---

[24] 1914, p. 162.

III. FIELD WORK, SEASON OF 1917

In 1917 archeological observations north of the Rio Colorado were confined to the largest mound in the Paragonah group, excavation of which was undertaken jointly by the Smithsonian Institution and the University of Utah. The essential results of these investigations have already been published [1] and need not be considered again with equal detail. But it does seem desirable to review the salient features of this, the principal adobe village at Paragonah—best-known representative of that prehistoric culture most widely distributed throughout west-central Utah—and, less briefly, to note the occurrence of somewhat similar remains elsewhere before crossing on toward the Rio Colorado and the masonry ruins which lie within its drainage.

It will be remembered that Paragonah was the site of a very considerable settlement dating from unknown antiquity; that most of the 400 mounds seen by Doctor Yarrow in 1872 had long since been razed; that those remaining were threatened with early and complete demolition. In 1917 only the largest mounds had survived, and they chiefly by reason of the labor required in their reduction.

REVIEW OF ARCHEOLOGICAL OBSERVATIONS AT PARAGONAH

Excavation of the " Big Mound " disclosed the remains of 43 quadrangular dwellings, 3 circular rooms, and numerous court shelters. These various habitations, however, did not represent the full size of the ancient village, for additional structures had been destroyed when the south portion of the mound was removed. As the season's excavations progressed successive levels of occupancy were observed (there were seven such levels above shelter L); fireplace had succeeded fireplace with the rapid accumulation of camp rubbish and blown sand; adobe houses had been erected upon the partially razed walls of others, and in at least one instance (kiva I) a circular room was reduced in size for no apparent reason except that its clay-plastered walls were not strong enough to support the weight of its flat roof. This entire group of primitive dwellings was concealed by a single widespreading mound, the largest seen throughout all of western Utah, approximately 225 feet (68.6 m.) in diameter by 10 feet (3.05 m.) high.

---

[1] Judd, 1919a.

69

The Paragonah excavations of 1915 and 1916, being more or less exploratory, had been restricted to lesser elevations. These covered from one to a half dozen or more buildings. The least prominent mounds at Paragonah disclosed nothing not found in the largest; they were contemporaneous with the latter and represented an identical culture. The former developed over isolated houses; the latter covered groups of habitations that might properly be regarded as villages. The only outstanding difference observed between house remains in the larger and smaller mounds had to do with the relatively greater period of time during which the former obviously were occupied.

In every instance noted during the three successive periods of observation at Paragonah (about 60 rooms were examined) the prehistoric adobe walls had been constructed of individual masses of plastic clay, each rounded for convenient handling. Careful examination of the fallen walls showed conclusively that such clay masses were thrown with some degree of force upon those already in place; that resulting irregularities were then smoothed by hand and the walls usually surfaced with thin mud plaster. In contrast to a fairly common practice at Beaver, Deseret, and Fillmore, only one of the Paragonah houses (room 31) was provided with a floor foundation of waterworn cobblestones.

Of necessity the plastic adobe mud from which these walls were built had to dry in the wind and sun before any degree of height could be attained. And it was this very natural requirement that resulted in the much-discussed courses or layers still visible in every wall except where completely obliterated by the secondary surfacing. Molding frames or forms were not utilized. Indeed, they were not required, for a 16-inch course of heavy mud will readily hold its shape if permitted to harden before a second layer is placed upon it.

When the desired height had been reached a flat roof of poles, brush, grass, and mud, in succession, closed in the room. Each ceiling was provided with a hatchway, the sole means of entrance,[2] to be covered, if need be, by a movable stone disk. Although no trace of them has survived, ladders or steps surely led to the roof tops. Being flat, these roofs would not readily shed the torrential summer showers; the water would tend to soften the sun-dried adobe about the beams, thus causing the roof to settle or the walls to collapse. With this probability in mind it will readily be understood why primitive man, lacking serviceable tools for the removal of minutiae, abandoned and replaced any structure that could not conveniently be repaired.

---

[2] The single lateral doorway observed in the outer walls of adobe ruins in western Utah occurred in room 8, Paragonah excavations of 1917.

Measured by our observations, the prehistoric adobe dwellings at Paragonah, as elsewhere throughout western Utah, lacked interior fireplaces. All cooking was done in the open near the houses, or in secondary shelters that rarely appear to have been wholly inclosed. These fireplaces, with their welcome warmth or the tempting aroma of cooking food, would very naturally form centers about which the domestic life of each family revolved. Refuse from the kitchen was tossed to one side; floor sweepings were likewise disposed of, but the rubbish pile thus started was even more rapidly augmented by sand and dust carried on tireless winds and deposited in the lee of every obstacle.

In Paragonah mounds a majority of these fireplaces seem to have been entirely unprotected. They consisted merely of shallow clay-lined basins, discarded in favor of others at the whim of their individual owners. Still other fireplaces, however, followed the prevailing custom noted at Beaver; that is, each occupied the middle of a well-defined floor and was covered by a flat roof supported by four posts. These few details tend to establish a relationship between such secondary shelters at Beaver or Paragonah and the sole type of habitation disclosed by the excavations at Willard (p. 8). Indeed, it was at the latter place that these details were first recognized. Only when the same characteristic features of construction were observed in more southerly ruin groups did the familiar structure come to be thought of as the " Willard type."

In addition to these two distinct kinds of dwellings—those of adobe and the secondary or Willard type shelters—the 1917 excavations disclosed a third method of house construction, namely, that with wattled walls. This latter method (apparent in rooms 20, 39, 40, 41, etc.) appeared a purposeful attempt to combine the more desirable features of the other two. It seemed a desire to surround the living quarters, represented by the court shelters, with a wall affording some measure of the protection found in adobe structures. These wattled-wall houses were quadrilateral instead of circular; their middle floor was occupied by a rimmed fireplace surrounded by four pillars as central roof supports. Their inclosing walls were vertical and consisted of a row of posts plastered with adobe mud. For the most part horizontal willows had been bound to the stakes before plaster was applied; in other instances, and sometimes even in the same dwelling, thick mud was forced between the uprights, and without additional support smoothed off to form the wall faces. The flat roof, extending outward from above the central fireplace, rested upon the wattled walls, and very insecurely it would seem, since the latter never appear to have been more than 5 inches (12.7 cm.) thick. These three distinct kinds of habitations, then—the Willard type lodge, the adobe house, and the wattled-wall dwelling—represent the known architectural achievements of the prehistoric peoples who dwelt on the site of modern Paragonah. That like structures are to be found rather generally throughout western Utah from Provo southward to St. George seems fairly well established by the bureau's reconnaissance.

Aboriginal peoples who build houses make use of the most suitable material at hand. This in the region under consideration was adobe. Building stone was utterly lacking. But the exclusive use of adobe mud in construction work was not peculiar to the ancient peoples of western Utah. In other sections of the Southwest similar architectural handicaps had been encountered.

USE OF ADOBE ELSEWHERE

Along the Rio Gila, in southern Arizona, adobe was the only building material available; its use at Casa Grande and numerous lesser ruins has been described by Fewkes,[3] Hough,[4] Mindeleff,[5] and others. Bandelier[6] observed the remains of adobe ruins repeatedly during his memorable explorations in the southwestern United States; Nelson[7] has noted the occurrence of adobe and masonry walled rooms indiscriminately in Pueblo ruins of the Galisteo Basin, New Mexico.

In 1914 Mr. Earl H. Morris excavated a ruin on the Animas River, northwestern New Mexico, and found adobe walls apparently identical in construction with those at Beaver and Paragonah. Describing this ruin, Morris writes:[8] "As nearly as could be determined, irregular balls or chunks of clay were pressed together to form the core of the wall, after which mud was smeared into the irregularities till the surfaces were smooth and the wall was of a satisfactory thickness." In certain instances foundations of cobblestones were noted. But this ancient village, unlike those in western Utah, was formed by a cluster of adjoining rooms; in addition, the pottery recovered illustrates superiority both in manufacture and decoration. Consideration of their architectural as well as their ceramic remains indicates, therefore, that the prehistoric peoples of the Animas and those of Parowan Valley were separated not only by distance but also by a considerable period of time.

As Morris continued and expanded his observations he came upon certain pre-Pueblo pit dwellings,[9] circular in form and excavated to a depth of from 3 to 6 feet (0.91–1.8 m.). These rep-

---

[3] 1912, p. 25.
[4] 1907, p. 28.
[5] 1896, p. 289; 1897, p. 315.
[6] 1892, pp. 109, 414, 433, etc.

[7] 1914, pp. 51–57, 83–105.
[8] 1915, p. 668.
[9] Morris, 1919, pp. 186–187.

resent an aboriginal culture different from that found in western Utah, but it is interesting to note that the earth walls of the pits had been plastered, as were those in the round rooms at Beaver and Paragonah. Some few of these pit houses possessed floor receptacles quite the counterpart of the two bins exposed in the lodge at Willard (p. 7). Other ruins in this same region (between the San Juan River and .the Continental Divide, 70 miles east of the La Plata) were walled by posts bound together with willows and plastered over with mud; others, outlined by stone slabs on edge, showed corner posts as former roof supports.[10] A further point of interest is that 11 of the 33 skulls Morris collected from the mesa ruins, like some of those exhumed at Paragonah, do not exhibit the occipital flattening so characteristic of Cliff-dweller crania.[11] In spite of these several similarities, outstanding differences obtain between the crude habitations Morris so clearly describes and those equally primitive structures found in west central Utah. They represent different cultures; perhaps different periods.

During the early explorations of the Hayden survey W. H. Jackson observed [12] what he supposed to be adobe ruins northeast of the Mesa Verde, southwestern Colorado. Upon the summit of the mesa Fewkes has more recently discovered a circular semisubterranean " earth lodge," the inner walls of which consist merely of the clay-plastered sides of the excavation.[13] It may be predicted with some degree of confidence, therefore, that future explorations on the Mesa Verde will disclose additional structures of this primitive type, and perhaps even adobe pueblos such as those examined by Morris on the Animas and between the Mancos and La Plata Rivers.

The writings of Doctor Fewkes frequently mention the use of adobe mud in Mesa Verde cliff dwellings. To be sure it occurs most often as an integral part of primitive masonry, but " bricks made of clay are set in the walls of the speaker-chief's house and were found in the fallen débris at its base. These bricks were made cubical in form before laying, but there is nothing to prove that they were molded in forms or frames, nor do they have a core of straw, as in the case of the adobes used in the construction of Inscription House in the Navaho National Monument, Arizona." [14] Reinforced mud " bricks " of the latter type find their Utah counterpart in the round rooms of Cottonwood Canyon (p. 93).

South of the Mesa Verde, in Gobernador Canyon, are several " hogan-like structures " in direct association with masonry ruins.

---

[10] Morris, 1919, p. 190.
[11] Ibid., p. 204.
[12] 1876, p. 369.
[13] Fewkes, 1920, p. 58.
[14] Fewkes, 1911 a, p. 30.

But Kidder [15] regards them as of post-Spanish origin and indicative of Navaho influence. Certainly they have but little resemblance to the flat-roofed shelters at Willard, Beaver, and Paragonah.

The surveys of 1915 and 1916 emphasized the fact that a rather large proportion of the western Utah ruins consists of isolated one-room habitations. Even when grouped into villages, as at Beaver and Paragonah, surprisingly few of these houses join one another. Occupants of the adobe dwellings were individualists; each family stood on its own, and yet, within limits, they preferred to neighbor with their fellows. Separation of dwellings was a characteristic custom among those prehistoric peoples who once dwelt in valleys bordering the Great Interior Basin.

But isolated habitations are not peculiar to the region of our reconnaissance. They are well known throughout the ancient Pueblo area; more especially throughout the San Juan drainage. Prudden [16] has directed attention to the occurrence of one and two room buildings, and to the irregular grouping of such structures about the heads of side canyons tributary to the Rio San Juan. Here also, both in the valleys and back upon the cedar-crowned ridges, are true pueblos—ruins composed of many adjoining rooms. These villages and isolated dwellings are alike constructed of masonry. They differ still further from the adobe houses of western Utah in that each room was provided with a lateral doorway instead of a roof opening.

Dean Cummings [17] describes a ruin near Moab, in Grand County, east central Utah, which is much more closely related to the particular field of our investigation. Like those at Paragonah, the Moab ruin was built of individual adobe masses; these, when positioned, spread slightly, causing artificial cracks that show plainly in an accompanying illustration. There is no question as to the similarity of constructional methods, although the walls at Moab appear not to have been resurfaced, as usually happened at Paragonah. It is interesting to note, also, that the Moab ruin rested on the uppermost of five levels of occupancy—a fact strongly suggestive of conditions observed in Beaver and Parowan Valleys. Still another point of interest is that Dr. A. V. Kidder subsequently photographed near Moab a metate whose grinding surface possessed the secondary depression so characteristic of milling stones found at Willard, and less commonly at Beaver and Paragonah. The present writer recalls no other instance in which metates of this type have been observed in eastern Utah. These several cultural resemblances do not necessarily mean that Grand and Iron Counties were in-

---

[15] 1920, p. 327.   [16] 1903; 1918.   [17] 1910, pp. 18–19.

habited in prehistoric times by identical peoples. Much depends upon the pottery from the adobe ruin at Moab.

Wattled walls, like those of adobe, occur in widely separated sections of the Southwest. They are found in cave dwellings and exposed pueblos; in ruins of stone and mud and in those of adobe only. But wattled work was by no means peculiar to regions lacking suitable building stone, even though extensively employed there. Cummings[18] figures granaries of mud-covered osiers in White Canyon, southeastern Utah, and dwellings with plastered willow walls in cave ruins of Navaho National Monument, northeastern Arizona.[19] Close students of prehistoric cultures in the Gila Valley have made frequent reference to traces of wattled walls, usually associated with large adobe buildings. Fewkes[20] repeatedly noted evidence of such constructional methods, and Hough[21] adds that these plastered walls often stood above others built of bowlders and clay. Superposition of floor levels in ancient ruins at the Spur ranch, near Luna, New Mexico, is also mentioned by Hough.[22] These are only a few of the authorities that might be quoted in connection with the use of wattled walls by our prehistoric predecessors of the Southwest.

The foregoing references should afford sufficient evidence that environments similar to that of western Utah prompted similar methods of house construction. And yet the builders themselves need not necessarily have been blood relatives. As disclosed by our observations, the dominant type of ancient dwelling throughout the southeastern portion of the Great Basin was a detached one-story adobe structure. Rarely were these rooms joined together. Secondary habitations or roofed fireplaces, and less frequently wattled-wall dwellings, appear in conjunction with the adobe houses. These three methods of construction were employed in the same village and very likely by the same family. Such major antiquities, and more especially the artifacts recovered from them, measure the cultural advancement of those prehistoric peoples that dwelt on the site of modern Paragonah. The lesser more than the major antiquities unite in setting the ancient housebuilders of western Utah somewhat apart from their contemporaries of the Southwest. In the chapters which now follow attention will be directed to prehistoric ruins within the drainage of the Rio Colorado. These will be seen to exhibit certain environmental modifications not apparent in the ancient villages of Parowan and other more northerly valleys.

---

[18] 1920, p. 23.
[19] Ibid., pp. 24, 27. See also Fewkes, 1911.
[20] 1909.

[21] 1907, pp. 15, 32.
[22] Ibid., p. 68.

IV. FIELD WORK, SEASON OF 1918

Our chief objective in the spring of 1918 was an alleged circular ruin or watchtower said to resemble those of southwestern Colorado. The location of this structure was given as " the rim of Walhalla Plateau, overlooking House Rock Valley and the Grand Canyon." Only one familiar with the topographical features of this particular section can appreciate the indefiniteness of our directions. It was anticipated that a considerable search might prove necessary, and yet, could existence of the tower be established, the discovery would have far-reaching consequences. With the time at our disposal again limited by the funds available, and with the primary purpose of the expedition already indicated, it was not expected that the season would contribute much in addition to these archeological observations north of the Rio Colorado.

Outfitting at Kanab, the writer and his guide proceeded by team to South Canyon ranger station, close under the western wall of House Rock Valley; thence by pack train to Cape Royal, southernmost extension of Kaibab Plateau, and later back again to the ranger station. During this entire journey a veritable cinema of shifting scenery presented itself. The barren expanse of Johnson Run, east of Fredonia; the forested summit of the Kaibab and the broad yet colorful valley beyond; the wondrous panoramas disclosed from the north rim of the Grand Canyon, 8,000 feet above sea level—all these in turn tempted forgetfulness of the archeological purpose of our mission. Nature was never so lavish as when she created the fairyland below Walhalla Plateau.

The " tower " we wished so much to find was finally located—a circular exposure of weathered limestone. But the trip was not wholly in vain. Prehistoric ruins were seen throughout much of the region traversed. Their walls were rough, unworked blocks of limestone, sandstone, or chert, depending upon the material most accessible to the site occupied. Most of them had so completely collapsed as scarcely to be recognized as one-time human homes. No two of them were exactly alike. Each was distinct within itself, and yet each possessed certain characteristics common to the others.

OBSERVATIONS IN HOUSE ROCK VALLEY

Such ruins as were visited in House Rock Valley lay within sight or easy riding distance of the trails followed. Their locations in

76

a

b

RUINS AT TWO-MILE SPRING, HOUSE ROCK VALLEY

a, Ruin 1 mile north of New House Rock corrals

b, Remains of circular structures at Two-Mile Spring

many instances had previously been indicated by riders for the Grand Canyon Cattle Co.

One interesting ruin group stands on a sloping sand ridge just behind the stone house at Two-Mile Spring, upper House Rock Valley. The ancient dwellings are mostly circular, varying from 4 to 10 feet (1.2–3.0 m.) in diameter; such of their walls as remain consist of red sandstone slabs set on edge and close together. Perhaps a dozen of these structures, all more or less broken, are still visible (pls. 7; 8, *b*).

The upright slabs obviously mark the lower inside diameters of the old houses. Slabs so placed were noted in a cave near Riggs ranch, upper Cottonwood Canyon, in 1915; above them were reinforced adobe walls. Some similar construction must necessarily have completed the dwellings at Two-Mile Spring. Strewn about them are many sandstone spalls, quite numerous, and yet not sufficiently so as to warrant the belief they were used in true masonry.

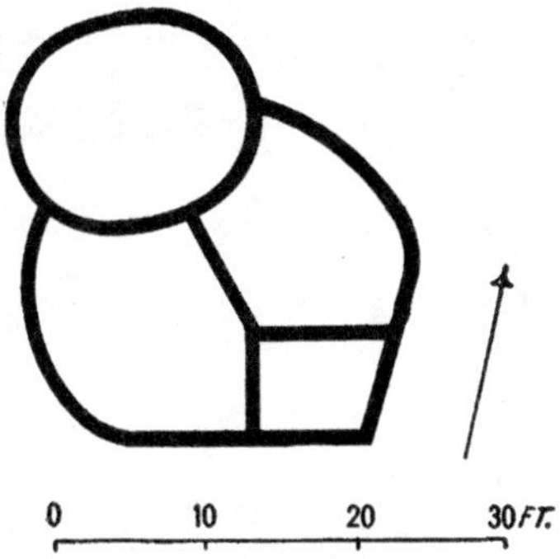

No excavations were attempted here, but the writer was informed that earthenware vessels and several skeletons had previously been exposed by wind action. What disposition was made of these is unknown. Our informant insisted that no trace of an ancient village was evident in 1890; that during the past 20 years, especially, tireless winds have uncovered the old foundations. Pottery fragments are plentiful; metates, arrowheads, flint chips, etc., are also present. Two mealing stones were observed whose grinding surfaces had been cupped, indicating secondary use as mortars.

0   10   20   30 *FT.*

Fig. 9.—Ruin north of New House Rock corrals

Farther up trail, just beyond the mesa rim, two similar sites may be identified by fallen slabs and scattered shards.

West of the road connecting New and Old House Rock corrals are a number of inconspicuous ruins, groups of single and adjoining rooms. For the most part they appear as low, rambling piles of irregular limestone blocks, often bronzed by lichens. Invariably they stand on slight elevations bordering shallow courses that drain the wide valley. The angular blocks, gathered from near-by ledges, rarely exhibit any attempt at shaping. They were used as found, large and small alike. Obviously such misshapen stones required enormous quantities of adobe mortar for proper placement. This mud, as it gradually disintegrated following abandonment of the houses, permitted the walls to crumble into the low mounds now

visible. Except for the student of archeology, there is but little
of interest in these ruined dwellings. The outlines of their individual rooms are not always immediately apparent. Each site, however, is accompanied by scattered potsherds and flint chips; occasionally stone implements are observed.

Perhaps a mile north of New House Rock is a ruin of four rooms,
the walls of which are mostly curved (pl. 8, a; fig. 9). The exceptional form of this particular house cluster is at once evident; no
other ruin of like arrangement was noted during the reconnaissance.
At first glance the circular room might appear to bear some relationship to those at Paragonah, but closer inspection failed to disclose
any evidence that it had occupied either a subterranean or semisubterranean position. Like its neighbors, it seems to have been
built upon the hard, stony floor of the valley. And the latter has
changed but little since prehistoric times.

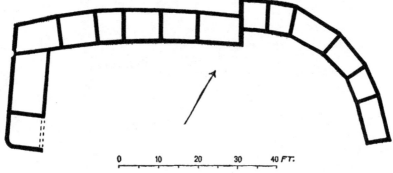

FIG. 10.—Ruin 7 miles south of New House Rock corrals

Fragments of earthenware vessels gathered near by included both
plain and corrugated ware, pieces of black-on-red and the more
prevalent black-on-white. The plain ware—fragments of cooking
pots and smaller jars—predominated here, as at other sites in the
vicinity.

Just how many of these ruins are to be found in House Rock
Valley remains uncertain. At least a dozen were seen north of
New House Rock; others were reported beyond Two-Mile Spring,
and still others south and east from the new corrals. Although a
few ruins exist near springs that issue from the Vermilion Cliffs
on the north side of the valley, a far greater number follow the
main watercourse, dry throughout much of the year, perhaps to its
junction with the Rio Colorado.

About 7 miles south of New House Rock a low red ridge extends
far out from the western plateau. Grouped about the extremity of
this ridge are several bare knolls, and on at least two of them prehistoric ruins may be seen. The ancient walls, built of irregular

limestone blocks, have entirely fallen; rarely does one stone rest upon another.

One of these ruins (fig. 10) occupies a flat-topped hill that parallels the ridge about 100 yards (91.7 m.) west of the wagon road. The main portion of the ruin conforms to the brow of the knoll, but two westerly rooms extend backward at right angles to the others. That this building was occupied for a period is indicated by the quantities of potsherds present, and yet the relatively small amount of visible building stone could not have formed a wall more than 3 feet (0.91 m.) high.

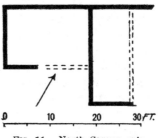

FIG. 11.—North Canyon ruin

Several ruins lie within a quarter mile of Cane Spring,[1] but all their larger stones have gone into construction of the ranch buildings and corrals. The old walls have been still further reduced by

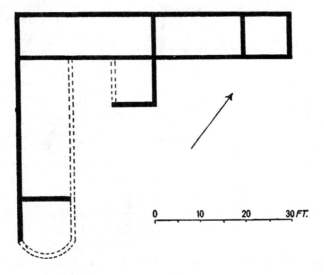

FIG. 12.—Ruin near North Canyon crossing

trailing cattle, yet fragments of pottery furnish mute evidence of domestic activities pursued here long before horses and cows were dreamed of in House Rock Valley.

[1] Headquarters of the Grand Canyon Cattle Co. were located at Cane Spring in 1918. Mr. E. M. Mansfield, local manager, not only welcomed the writer with gracious hospitality, but also loaned fresh pack mules for the toilsome climb to the summit of Walhalla Plateau—courtesies still warmly appreciated.

Ruins similar to those near Cane Spring are reported in Tater Canyon, a few miles south of the ranch. Others stand on the south border of North Canyon, about half a mile southwest of the crossing.[2] Three of this latter group were hastily examined. Two of them (figs. 11 and 12) may be seen from the road, although they appear only as piles of broken limestone. Potsherds lie about these and neighboring sites, but what first attracts attention is the paucity of building stone. The ancient dwellings certainly have never been disturbed since collapse of their walls; no stone has been hauled away. Signs of former occupancy are present, and the thought persists, in consequence, that the builders of these primitive structures raised their masonry to a certain height and then completed it with wattlework or adobe. As elsewhere, limestone was readily accessible. In the northeast corner of the second ruin (fig. 12) several sandstone wall slabs with shaped edges stand in open view.

From a cursory examination it appeared that fragments of black-on-white pottery predominated here, yet the proportion of plain ware and of corrugated ware was fairly high. Even a few black-on-red shards were noted.

A large block of limestone with a concretionary pit in its upper surface stands before the ruin last

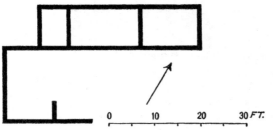

FIG. 13.—Ruin near North Canyon crossing

indicated. This stone might easily be mistaken for a mortar—and it may well have seen limited use as such—but the resemblance is purely accidental, as will be evident upon close inspection.

Between North and South Canyons and some 2 miles west of the wagon road is a serrated ridge known to the cowboys as "The Cocks' Combs." The eastern face of this ridge rises as a gentle slope, sparsely covered with buckbrush and juniper; its opposite side is a sheer cliff, overlooking the north fork of South Canyon. Open ruins, screened by tangled vegetation, are quite to be expected on the rocky west terraces of this fork, but the writer's attention was directed exclusively to caves in the eastern or cliff side of the canyon. Not all these caverns appear to have been inhabited.

The largest cave visited lies under the fourth comb above the ranger station. Two rounded openings had weathered from a thin curtain of rock which otherwise completely closed the chamber. Just inside, the ceiling drooped to within arm's reach; at the rear

---

[2] An abandoned post corral formed a prominent landmark at this point in 1918.

it rose a full 20 feet (6.1 m.). The rocky floor sloped less abruptly than the ceiling, but it invited, nevertheless, construction of several prehistoric dwellings.

Two retaining walls reached outward from the northeast side (fig. 14). Vegetable matter, rubbish, and sand had been packed behind these walls to serve as foundations for houses. Four adjoining rooms could still be traced above the innermost terrace; those below were less readily distinguished. Several narrow ledges at the rear appear not to have been utilized.

On the left a walled recess became a storehouse; opposite this stood a large dwelling, whose ceiling of poles, willows, cedar bark, and sandy clay was still intact. The masonry of this room, like its

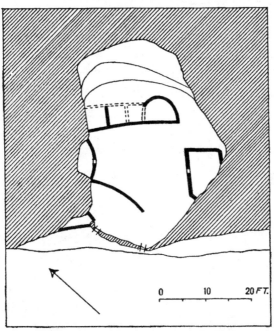

FIG. 14.—Cave dwelling, north fork of South Canyon

neighbors, was loose and crude—unshaped stones, for the most part, laid in mud containing pebbles and much sand.

No excavation was made in this interesting ruin. Fragments of a basket and a wooden vessel were picked up from among the cave litter. Excepting a dozen coiled shards, no pottery was observed within the cavern, but on the talus below its dual entrance fragments of black-on-white bowls appeared. These were of early type—black designs on a white slip that lacked the careful finish and perfection of later periods.

An exposed ruin (fig. 15), constructed mostly of unworked sandstone blocks, lies partly hidden among tall yellow pines about 75 yards (68.6 m.) west of the old ranger station at the mouth of the north fork. Only a few courses of masonry still stand, and the proportion which has fallen seems so insignificant as again to warrant the belief that mud or some equally perishable material originally topped the stonework.

Outcroppings of sandstone furnished this building material. Some of them resemble razed masonry walls, and in at least one instance stones in situ had been utilized by the ancients as a foundation for part of their communal dwelling.

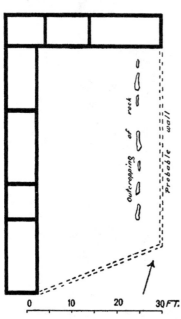

A second ruin, about 100 feet (30.5 m.) south of that last described, consists of a single room measuring 10 by 12 feet (3.0 by 3.7 m.).

Three small storage cists, occupying natural recesses in the yellow cliffs, are visible from these two ruins. Each of the three was built of rough, irregular masonry; each was provided with a diminutive door, capable of being closed by a stone slab. The largest of them could have held no more than 2 bushels of carefully piled corn, yet all three were doubtless built and utilized by the inhabitants of the two dwellings above mentioned.

Fig. 15.—Ruin near ranger station, north fork of South Canyon

Ruins Near Saddle Mountain

Several additional ruins were observed on the ragged south and east slopes of Saddle Mountain. Not all of them were as regular in outline as those represented by Figures 16 and 17. All of them, however, had been constructed of unworked blocks, chiefly limestone, gathered from the nearest outcropping. Those exposed ledges were even utilized as foundations. In most cases the ruins seen in this section are to be distinguished from the natural rock only by close inspection. Many of them are overgrown and partially concealed by buckbrush and sage.

As between the prehistoric dwellings on Saddle Mountain and those in House Rock Valley, stonework was more generally employed in the former—an unimportant difference, to be sure, and one easily explained by the greater accessibility of stone on the mountain. Down in the valley building stone could be quarried, but not without some difficulty, apparently, for it was repeatedly noticed that the amount of rock at any given site was rarely sufficient to have completed a wall of average height. For this reason it is thought that adobe or wattled work surmounted a half wall of masonry. In the Saddle Mountain ruins, on the other hand, stonework played a more important part, but even here one may question whether masonry was exclusively employed. None of these old houses appears to have reached more than one story in height.

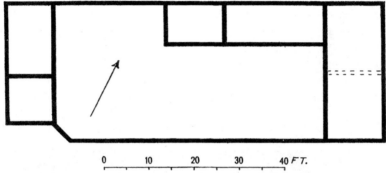

FIG. 16.—Plan of ruin, east slope of Saddle Mountain

Storage cists and single-room dwellings in shallow caves or under low, protruding ledges were occasionally observed in the rocky canyons that bar access to the slopes of Saddle Mountain. Quite typical examples of these lesser structures are shown in Plate 9, *a* and *b*.

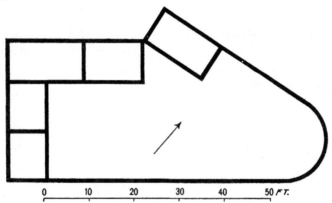

FIG. 17.—Ruin high on east slope of Saddle Mountain

The largest known cliff-dwelling east of Walhalla Plateau lies deep down under the north rim of Saddle Canyon and within 2 miles of the Rio Colorado (pl. 10, *b;* fig. 18). Because the overhanging cliff afforded but scant protection, most of the individual walls have collapsed. A few others may be projected with some degree of certainty. The masonry is generally crude. It consists of irregular and mostly unworked blocks of sandstone, bound together with thick layers of sandy mud. Several inner wall faces had been roughly plastered with this same mortar.

One of the largest rooms here possesses an inner curved wall joined to and guarding the front entrance. Two loopholes pierce this curved wall, thus suggesting its defensive function. Similar protective devices have been noted also among cliff-dwellings in White Canyon, in Grand Gulch, and elsewhere north of the San Juan River. A subterranean kiva is a still more important feature of the village under consideration. Its masonry walls rise unbroken by pilasters; the ventilator shaft, if any, is not apparent.

Along the smooth face of the cliff between and above these houses geometric and animal figures had been painted with white and red pigments or plain clay mud. In a careless moment one of the prehistoric artists had dropped his red paint, spilling it upon the rocks. Outline drawings of the human hand, made by spraying white paint

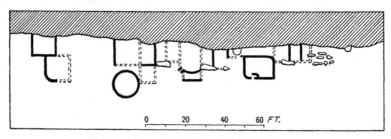

FIG. 18.—Plan of cliff village in Saddle Canyon

over outstretched fingers held close against the stone, occur frequently; spirals, pottery designs, and other symbols likewise appear, either painted or pecked upon the cliff.

Strangely enough, potsherds are not numerous at this particular site. Fragments of plain-ware vessels seem to predominate. Among these were a few superficially ornamented with red—the same fugitive decorations seen at Paragonah. A few shards only of corrugated and black-on-white ware were noted. This noticeable dearth of pottery is best explained by the very position of the settlement. Just in front the talus drops off abruptly, and such débris as would naturally accumulate near a dozen dwellings has long since been carried down the steep slope and over the cliff below.

RUINS ON WALHALLA PLATEAU

Walhalla Plateau, or "Greenland," as it is known by those most familiar with the region, is a narrow extension of the Kaibab proper pointing southward to the blue peaks of the distant San Francisco

a

b

STOREHOUSE AND CLIFF-DWELLING, SOUTH SLOPE OF
SADDLE MOUNTAIN

a, Grand Canyon from the east slope of Saddle Mountain

b, Largest cliff-dwelling seen east of Walhalla Plateau

Mountains. From almost any spot on its restricted summit one looks down into the incomparable gorge of the Rio Colorado (fig. 19).

Greenland is a lonesome place, and as such it had its attractions for the aborigine. Many small ruins are to be seen among its tall yellow pines; others lie concealed by the scraggy buckbrush and wild locust which find root in shallow, less fertile soil near the rim. None of these ancient dwellings holds any particular interest for the casual passer-by. They are all comparatively inconsequential structures, now represented by rambling piles of weathered limestone. Yet they furnish mute evidence that prehistoric man in his migrations tarried

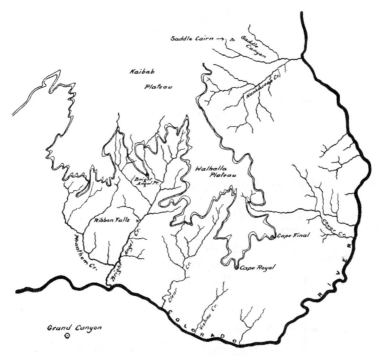

FIG. 19.—Walhalla Plateau and environs

here long enough to construct at least temporary homes while he sought out more favorable locations elsewhere. There are no inviting caves on the borders of Walhalla Plateau, and few sheltered ledges where dwellings might have been erected. Of the mesa ruins a few examples only need be cited; photographs convey no idea of their individual peculiarities.

An interesting and at the same time a large ruin (fig. 20) is to be found at the edge of the timbered area not far from Cape Royal. Its walls are of unworked limestone blocks; the lower course stands on edge, a feature noted at several other sites on the plateau. Outcroppings of limestone, extending in straight lines like walls, are to be noted in the immediate vicinity. The amount of building stone about these standing blocks is so meager one is led to believe that here, as in House Rock Valley, masonry was used only in part for construction purposes. The upper walls may have been of rubble;

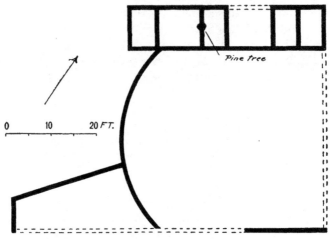

FIG. 20.—Plan of ruin near Cape Royal, Walhalla Plateau

more likely of adobe. A few potsherds, of types already mentioned, were noticed about this particular ruin.

On one of the house walls a yellow pine, 18 inches (45.7 cm.) in diameter, has taken root. This tree is probably less than 150 years old, and thus would afford no real index to the age of the dwelling.

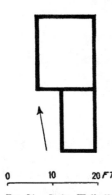

FIG. 21.—Ruin, Walhalla Plateau

South of the main house group is an area which appears to have been inclosed by a single wall of masonry. The west side of this court is curved, and adjoining its southern end there remain the foundations of a large angular space of unknown use. All together, the ruin forms one of those curious oddities of construction so frequently met with on Walhalla Plateau.

Near the wire fence which divides the lower half of Greenland is a two-room house (fig. 21). In both size and arrangement it does not differ materially from several other ruins passed hereabouts. One exception is to be noted, however. Its walls were built not of limestone but of large sandstone blocks, most of which were roughly shaped. It is rather remarkable that throughout the entire region traversed by the reconnaissance of 1918 masses of sandstone were invariably dressed to some degree of regularity before being placed in the walls of an ancient house. Limestone, on the other hand, although employed far more frequently, rarely exhibits any trace of the shaping process.

Many problems arise in connection with the prehistoric remains of Walhalla Plateau. Some of these problems seem explicable after an examination of other ruins where similar features obtain; others defy explanation. One such enigma arises in connection with our next ruin.

The dwelling itself is a simple structure of three adjacent rooms (fig. 22). In orientation, in the size of its individual apartments,

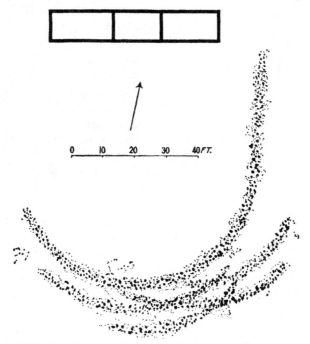

FIG. 22.—Ridges of chert spalls fronting a small ruin on Walhalla Plateau

and in the character of its stonework it does not differ in any marked degree from a dozen other ancient dwellings observed on Kaibab Plateau. If anything the ruin is less complex, less irregular than many of its neighbors. But just in front of the three connecting rooms is a semicircular court formed by low ridges of flint and chert spalls. Chunks of flint, weathered from innumerable outcroppings, are of common occurrence in the vicinity. In front of the houses, however, these fragments appear to have been raked together, forming the ridges or " windrows " indicated on the ground plan. The space between them and the ruin is totally free from chips—as free as a carefully prepared garden. The purpose of all this is not clear.

The ridges may represent the position of former rubble walls, or, what seems far more likely, the court was freed of stone in preparation for clan ceremonials. If this latter be regarded as a plausible explanation, it is almost unbelievable that this dooryard should have remained as clean and smooth as when first leveled, hundreds of years ago.

Similar ridges appear on the opposite side of the ruin, but in this instance they form rectangles of various sizes. The component stones certainly originated in the flinty ledges repeatedly seen in this section of the plateau, but how and when they were gathered into the little rows visible to-day are questions that still puzzle.

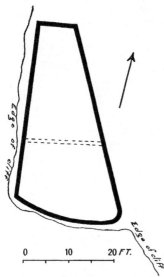

FIG. 23.—Plan of ruin overlooking the Nankoweap

This latter ruin lies among the pines between the wire fence previously mentioned and the head of Clear Creek. The house walls had been constructed with larger masses of the same flinty stone appearing in the low ridges, and much mud was undoubtedly employed in laying them. In addition, some sort of superstructure completed the stonework. Potsherds of the customary types are to be seen within and about the walls.

On the upper south rim of Saddle Canyon and at the extreme point of the mesa overlooking the Nankoweap is a rugged and somewhat isolated promontory. On top of this ledge stood the remains of a large two-room structure most easily but perhaps incorrectly described as a fortification (pl. 11, a; fig 23). Its compartments are too large to have been spanned by beams; it may well have been unroofed, for there is nothing to suggest the former presence of additional chambers. The walls are of laminate but unworked blocks of limestone. No potsherds were observed within the ruin or on the talus below.

Three storage cists occupy as many niches under ledges of the plateau neighboring this isolated butte. All are low, of small dimensions, and carry no trace of smoke stains.

The foregoing paragraphs will convey at least a general impression of those prehistoric remains visited during the hurried reconnaissance of 1918. Exposed ruins throughout House Rock Valley, on the slopes of Saddle Mountain, and on the lofty summit of Walhalla Plateau exhibit curious features not observed elsewhere

a, Promontory, with ruin overlooking Nankoweap Valley

b, Typical ruin and environs, south slope of Saddle Mountain

a, Bright Angel Creek from Walhalla Plateau

b, On the trail across Kaibab Plateau

a

b

RUINS ON WALHALLA PLATEAU

a, Room 1, Cave 1, Cottonwood Canyon

b, Slab bins, Cave 5, Cottonwood Canyon

north of the Rio Colorado. They are noteworthy because of their asymmetry. In general, limestone was the most available material for building purposes. Sandstone was utilized in some restricted areas; in others, limestone and sandstone were employed indiscriminately in the same building; elsewhere chert seems to have been most accessible. Chert and limestone were employed irrespective of their irregularities. When sandstone was utilized, on the other hand, it invariably exhibited some attempt to shape the individual blocks.

In spite of these strange features of house construction, no outstanding differences in pottery were observed between the region traversed in 1918 and those visited during the two previous years. The black-on-white ware seemed less slate-colored than at Paragonah, for example; black-on-red was perhaps a trifle more common. With these varieties there were the well-known corrugated and plain ware cooking vessels. Some few fragments of the latter even bore unfixed designs in red—the fugitive decorations of Beaver and Parowan Valleys.

V. FIELD WORK, SEASON OF 1919

Preliminary plans for the field work of 1919 contemplated a fairly thorough examination of the Uinkaret and Kanab Plateaus, in northwestern Arizona. Drovers of cattle and sheep reported the occurrence of small cliff ruins on the western border of Kanab Canyon; scattered potsherds and supposed dwelling sites had been noticed eastward from Mount Trumbull. Archeologically this wide-reaching section was entirely unknown. It invited close inspection, since the prehistoric peoples who settled along the northern margin of Antelope Valley must surely have ventured southward toward the Rio Colorado. Traces at least of their temporary habitations were almost certain to be discovered, and it seemed desirable to note the difference, if any, between these and ancient dwellings previously visited.

Upon arrival at Kanab late in May it was learned, however, that the proposed reconnaissance would prove extremely unwise. Scant winter snows, coupled with a dearth of spring rains, had left the region entirely unwatered. Forage, even for a small train of pack animals, was uncertain. The tanks or water pockets always relied upon by cattlemen were reported dry. No dependable springs were known in the area indicated. In consequence the proposed observations north of the Rio Colorado and west of Kanab Canyon, in Arizona, were once more postponed.

The initial expedition of 1915 had permitted but one day's investigation in Cottonwood Canyon, just long enough to identify it as a most promising locality for future archeological research. It was only natural, therefore, when the season's plans went awry in 1919 that Cottonwood Canyon should come speedily to mind. Those of its ruins previously visited merited reexamination; others of equal interest doubtless awaited discovery. Besides, the quiet canyon with its cool springs, its sandstone cliffs, its inclosing screen of cedar and piñon, furnished a pleasant antidote for thoughts of exploration, on foot and horseback, among the hot, barren, lava-strewn mesas toward the southwest. As in previous years, the appropriation available for the reconnaissance was very limited; Cottonwood Canyon offered a definite reward for the short time at hand.

OBSERVATIONS IN COTTONWOOD CANYON

Two laborers were engaged, and arrangements made with Mr. B. A. Riggs for transportation to his ranch. Using this as a base

90

of operations, 15 caves were visited during the two weeks which followed. The relative positions of these, one to the other, is indicated by the rough field map, Figure 24.

Cottonwood Canyon was intimately associated with the settlement of southwestern Utah. Through its winding course ox teams

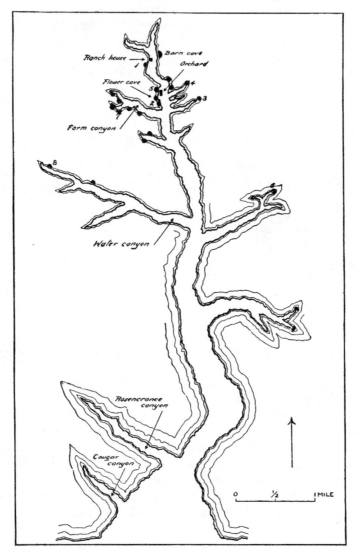

FIG. 24.—Sketch map of Cottonwood Canyon, showing location of the caves visited

hauled much of the lumber used in construction of the Mormon temple at St. George. Colonists passed through Cottonwood about 1870, bound from an old location on Muddy Creek, a western tributary of the Rio Virgin, to new homes in Long Valley. Traffic between this young colony and the older settlements to the west continued over the canyon road—it is still visible in many places—for some years after the founding of Kanab.[1] Quite naturally the more accessible caves of the canyon were utilized by these pioneers for camping purposes. But it is the archeology of the region and not its later history with which we are concerned.

CAVE 1 (Riggs Cave) is approximately 150 feet (45.73 m.) long and 40 feet (12.2 m.) deep. It lies about 200 yards (183.4 m.) below the Riggs ranch house, in the upper, well-watered, and perennially green portion of the canyon. Since our hurried inspection of 1915 a certain amount of pot hunting had occurred here. Both the dry refuse overturned by the curious ones and the several artifacts claimed from them by Mr. Riggs suggested the desirability of immediate examination of such archeologic evidence as remained.

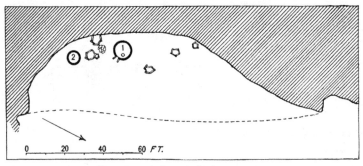

FIG. 25.—Plan of Cave 1, Cottonwood Canyon

Characteristic Basket Maker paintings had been noted during our earlier visit; stone slabs observed at that time protruding through the sand accumulations—cists subsequently exposed—were also recognized as typical of pre-Cliff-dweller occupancy. But the most prominent structure in the cave was a circular room whose adobe walls stood 10 feet (3.05 m.) in diameter and 5 feet 10 inches (1.4 m.) in height. In its relationship to the neighboring cists and in its own peculiar interest this room merits brief description.

Room 1 was a composite and apparently reconditioned structure (pl. 14, *a*). The base of its inner wall was formed by upright sandstone slabs, whose interstices were filled and plastered over with adobe mud. Several of these slabs stood more than 2 feet in height; in one place a break in the wall showed two additional contiguous stones as an outer support or backing for that one facing the room.

[1] The foregoing information was volunteered by Mr. B. A. Riggs, who participated, as a young man, in the establishment of Kanab and the conquest of its surroundings. Mr. Riggs's unfailing hospitality and helpfulness contributed greatly to the success of the bureau's reconnaissance, and enabled the writer to accomplish vastly more than would otherwise have been possible.

Above this slab base was a superstructure consisting of successive layers of individual adobe masses, usually reinforced with small twigs of sage (*artemisia*) or rabbit brush (*chrysothamnus*). In general appearance these masses were not unlike the " Vienna rolls " described from Inscription House, Navaho National Monument.[2] Those from Riggs Cave, however, were sharply rounded on top, and the uppermost or final layer disclosed no evidence of seats for roofing poles. The concave lower sides of these " bricks " resulted quite naturally when each bundle of twigs and its thick wrapping of plastic adobe was forced down upon the convex surfaces of those already in place. An additional reinforcement was provided at intervals during erection of the wall by single courses of tabular sandstone blocks. These were mostly concealed by the mud plaster with which all constructional irregularities had been smoothed; their presence and intended function, nevertheless, were quite evident upon close inspection.

The eastern wall of this circular room had been pierced by a doorway whose sill, at the level of cave occupancy, lay 27 inches (68.5 cm.) above the floor of the dwelling. Egress was facilitated by an upright stone slab set close against the wall and forming a 2-inch step within and below the door. Another slab, 19 inches (48.3 cm.) long by 12 inches (30.5 cm.) high, stood against the outer, north side of the opening; a similar jamb of reinforced adobe rested opposite. In both instances these guards were joined to the building by adobe mud. Although the inner surface of the room was plastered to or even below the tops of its foundation slabs, the plaster on the outer wall did not extend beneath the cave floor. Both sides of the door had been mutilated, but its original width was ascertained as 26 inches (66 cm.). Its lintels, if such ever existed, rested at or near the ceiling level.

The probable use of this room as a dwelling is suggested by the presence of a circular fireplace. No other depression marred its smooth clay floor. Former smoke stains on the wall had mostly been scoured away by blown sand. Fragments of customary ceiling material scattered through the débris proved, in spite of the absence of visible resting places for ceiling poles, the one-time presence of a roof. In the rear wall, 4 feet 10 inches (1.47 m.) above the floor, was a hole from which a small wooden peg formerly protruded.

The writer can not avoid the feeling that this curious structure was originally a Basket Maker storage cist, remodeled to suit the whim of a later people. Other slab cists in Riggs Cave, and especially certain objects from the surrounding débris, have every ap-

---

[2] Fewkes, 1911, p. 5; also Cummings, 1910, p. 27.

pearance of Basket Maker workmanship. Still other objects do not belong to this ancient horizon. Hence our opinion that after elapse of a seemingly short period of time only a second group of aborigines came in to reoccupy this and neighboring caves, bringing with it a more advanced culture whose outstanding contributions to the archeology of the region were pottery and fairly permanent dwellings. In these two features alone students of southwestern prehistory will detect certain affinities between the early inhabitants of Cottonwood Canyon and the builders of such ruined villages as those already described from the vicinity of Paragonah, St. George, or House Rock Valley.

It was from the narrow space behind room 1 that the digging sticks presented by Mr. Riggs (pl. 55, a–g) were taken by looters in 1917. While examining the undisturbed débris in this same section we came upon the corn illustrated in Plate 59 and several of the artifacts described on pages 145–150. From deeper refuse in the front middle portion of the cave we recovered the bag of mountain goat hair pictured in Plate 58, a. This latter specimen lay above 4 feet of cedar bark and cornstalks so thoroughly intertwined as almost to resist removal. Like material had covered the unquestioned Basket Maker cists explored by Nusbaum in the neighboring Cave Lakes Canyon.[3]

Room 2, 5 feet (1.5 m.) in diameter, stands at the south end of the cave. Here also the inside wall was supported by a base of upright slabs; above them, instead of adobe "bricks," lay the remnant of a rude masonry wall 5 inches thick. Only the inner surface of this wall had been plastered. No fireplace was present, and there remained no trace of a doorway.

Between these two circular rooms six stone slabs formed a cist 3 feet 6 inches (1.06 m.) in diameter. Adjoining it on the north was a similar, though smaller, bin, and near the latter a number of flagstones marked the former position of a third cist whose slab sides had been removed in ancient times.

Between this pavement and the cliff appears still another cist with a slightly dished stone floor 4 feet 6 inches (1.4 m.) in diameter. One's interest is attracted to this bin because its rear wall and ceiling were originally formed by the downward-sloping cave roof. Adobe adhering to the latter evidences a one-time superstructure, which inclined rearward and upward 16 inches (0.41 m.) from the perpendicular in joining the slab circle with the cliff. Although none of the connecting elements was found in the rubbish, the appearance of the completed bin must have been very similar to those

---

[3] Nusbaum, 1922.

described by Guernsey and Kidder [4] from cave 14, Sagiotsosi Canyon, northeastern Arizona.

Other bins had been exposed in the northern portion of the cavern. None of these retained any trace of superimposed walls. They undoubtedly answered for storage purposes, and originally were probably covered directly with poles and cedar bark. Shreds of bark were mixed with the blown sand thrown out from these cists.

These several slab-lined receptacles are all strongly suggestive of Basket Maker workmanship. Except for their smaller size, they are quite the counterpart of those excavated by Nusbaum in 1920. And the writer believes the slab foundations of rooms 1 and 2 of like antiquity—they stood on the same level as the cists—despite the later date tentatively accredited their individual superstructures. Shards of plain ware and corrugated jars, and still fewer fragments of black-on-white bowls were found in the cave. No shards of any description were recovered from the previously undisturbed refuse below the last general level of occupancy. Hammerstones and mullers, but no metates, were found. Use of the cavern by Basket Makers is further emphasized by the presence of their characteristic polychrome drawings (pl. 60) painted on the cave wall.

Our incomplete evidence, therefore, points to two separated periods of inhabitance for cave 1. The slab cists may have been, and probably were, completely emptied of their contents by the very individuals who constructed them. Shortly thereafter a second group of people—near-Cliff-dwellers—happened by, temporarily occupied the cave, and while so doing plundered the remains of their predecessors. As a result of these ancient depredations at least one human burial was disturbed, for several widely scattered ribs and skull fragments were recovered during our excavations.

Riggs Cave, as already mentioned, had been despoiled in 1917 by casual visitors, who obtained seven digging sticks and several other artifacts. Fortunately, Mr. Riggs commandeered these specimens as soon as he learned of the vandalism; subsequently he presented them to the United States National Museum.

His gift includes both Basket Maker and Cliff-dweller implements, and thus confirms the stratigraphic evidence as to the dual occupancy of the cave. It is indeed unfortunate that trained observers were not privileged to note here, before the site was pillaged, the relationship of these two distinct yet nearly contemporaneous human cultures. The explorations of Kidder and Guernsey [5] have established the prior existence of the Basket Makers, and have suggested that somewhere along the trail followed by these ancient folk

---

[4] 1921, p. 39; pl. 9, *e, f.*   [5] 1919; 1921.

their characteristic culture will be found to merge with that of the Cliff-dwellers. Future painstaking investigations may yet identify Cottonwood Canyon and vicinity as one section in which such contact was established.

Cave 2.—Approximately one-half mile down canyon from cave 1 and at the lower end of " the meadows " is a small orchard of apple and pear trees. Some 400 yards farther is the cavern we soon came to know as "the cave below the orchard" (fig. 24).

A considerable quantity of sand had washed in from the over-hanging cliff and formed a fanlike blanket for the entire southeast quarter of the cave. No tests were made beneath this recent accumulation. At its western and northern borders, however, stone slabs pierced the sandy cave floor just enough to mark the position of several cists similar to those examined in Riggs Cave. A number

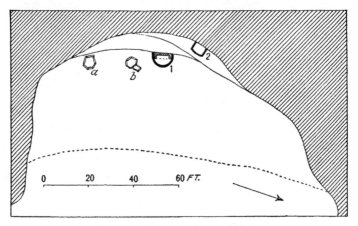

Fig. 26.—Plan of Cave 2, Cottonwood Canyon

of ruined dwellings with walls of rude masonry rested upon this same level, but in every instance their foundations lay above the floors of the slab bins. Only two of these cists were opened. The larger, measuring 4 feet 6 inches (1.37 m.) in diameter and 3 feet (0.91 m.) in depth, was filled with blown sand and a small quantity of vegetable matter; the smaller, possessing certain unusual features, is described in the next paragraph. No attempt has been made in the ground plan of this cave (fig. 26) to illustrate the relative positions either of the unexcavated bins or the destroyed cliff houses.

The second of the two cists examined measured 4 feet (1.22 m.) in diameter and 3 feet 8 inches (1.1 m.) in depth. It was lined with upright slabs, and mud had been pressed into the interstices. Above these slabs were the shattered remains of a superimposed wall consisting both of rude masonry and bundles of twigs rolled in adobe—a combination of the types noted in the two circular rooms in Riggs Cave. This wall also inclosed an adjoining bin, obviously of secondary construction, which opened into the larger cist from the north. The lesser structure tends toward the triangular in outline; its lower walls were of slabs and its adobe floor lay 20 inches (50.8 cm.) above that of the principal cist. The original purpose of this curious affair is not evident. Both cist and recess had been filled with stone spalls and adobe fragments—rubbish from razed dwellings. Covering this débris, but within the upright slabs, was a layer of cornstalks and cedar bark; this in turn was overlain by 3 inches of sandy earth conforming with the level of the cave occupancy.

In the wreckage of this irregular structure there appears to be evidence of the superposition of distinct cultures. It seems not unlikely that a Basket Maker storage cist had been reconditioned and utilized by the later Cliff-dwellers, finally to be abandoned by them also. During their occupancy of the cave these latter had built a fireplace above the western side of the pit. The heat of successive fires had charred the mass of husks and bark which covered the other rubbish of the fill.

The largest and certainly the most interesting room in this particular cave is one quite beyond satisfactory explanation. I can not recall that its like has been noted elsewhere. The structure is semicircular in plan; its lower walls are formed of sandstone slabs set on end, with all joints filled and neatly smoothed with adobe. Traces of a former masonry superstructure rest upon these slabs.

In its north-south diameter this unusual chamber measures 8 feet 4 inches (2.5 m.), but its rear floor is interrupted by a recessed depression 5 feet 8 inches (1.72 m.) long, 26 inches (66.1 cm.) wide at the top, and 20 inches (50.8 cm.) wide at the bottom. The floor of this recess lies 22 inches (55.9 cm.) below that of the main floor. Further, its sides and rear wall have been built up of masonry to meet the upward and outward sloping roof of the cave; its front wall, on the other hand, consisted of slabs of uniform size carefully joined with adobe. Just what purpose this basinlike affair originally served is not clear. No object of human workmanship was found either in it or in the room of which it formed a part.

The completely shattered walls of other masonry dwellings lie 20 feet to the north of this semicircular room, and beneath their common floor level are the outlines of several typical slab cists.

On a narrow ledge above and behind these latter ruins is a small room of rude masonry. Its walls once stood 4 feet high, to meet the slanting cliff. The 2-foot space between this structure and the edge of the shelf on which it rests bears the unmistakable marks left by the sharpening of bone awls and stone axes, the latter at least being a characteristic instrument of the Cliff-dwellers. Although ample space remained, no trace of additional structures was observed on this overhanging ledge. Access to the upper level was had by a series of notches pecked into the cliff just south of the semicircular room.

From a test trench cut through the vegetable matter, the ash, and sandy earth that formed the cave floor below and in front of this large room we recovered a cylinder of red ocher, wrapped in strips of rabbit skin (pl. 58, *b*) ; sandals, basketry fragments, corn kernels, and beans. These may all have belonged to the later period of occupancy. Here also were found the major portion of a plain-ware jar

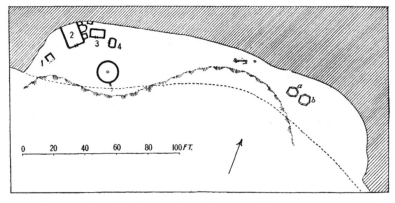

Fig. 27.—Plan of Cave 3, Cottonwood Canyon

and part of a black-on-white bowl. A small series of shards from similar vessels was gathered on the surface.

Cave 3 (Kiva Cave) received its popular name quite naturally, for it shelters the first semisubterranean ceremonial chamber we recognized and excavated in southwestern Utah. Associated with it were four wholly detached rooms (pl. 15; fig. 27). Two of these were among the best preserved cliff dwellings examined during the course of our archeological observations north of the Rio Colorado. Taken together, the five buildings were the only ruins with which residents of Kanab seemed generally familiar. Our journey to Cottonwood Canyon in 1915 had been undertaken for the sole purpose of visiting this single group. Other neighboring ruins and formerly inhabited caves had not roused an equal interest. Indeed, the writer was quite unaware of the extent to which Cottonwood Canyon had been occupied in prehistoric times until his reconnaissance of 1919 was well under way.

a, Rooms in Cave 3, Cottonwood Canyon

b, Repairing broken walls in Cave 3, Cottonwood Canyon

a, Roof and hatchway of Room 2, Cave 3, Cottonwood Canyon

b, Rooms 2 and 3, Cave 3, Cottonwood Canyon, showing doors and windows

Room 1, the westernmost of the four quadrangular rooms in Kiva Cave, was a composite structure 4 feet square. Three upright slabs formed its western wall; coursed adobe comprised its northern and rude masonry its eastern sides. The fourth wall is entirely wanting. At the time of our 1915 visit some 6 or 8 inches of masonry rested upon the three slabs; by 1919 this whole side had collapsed.

Room 2, the largest of the four, is the only one offering reasonable evidence of former use as a dwelling. Its inside dimensions average 10 by 13 feet (3.05 by 3.96 m.); its front ceiling beam is only 4 feet (1.22 m.) above the floor. Plaster still adheres to the entire inner and the lower half of the outer front wall, but it is doubtful if the others had been similarly treated. Although no fireplace is present, the interior walls and ceiling are heavily smoked. Calcareous matter, deposited by seepage throughout the greater width of the cave, is particularly abundant in the rear of this dwelling and at its floor level.

Access to the room was provided by a door in the middle front wall. The greater size of this opening—it is 28 inches (71 cm.) wide at the top, 22 inches (55.9 cm.) wide at the bottom, and 3 feet 8 inches (1.1 m.) high—as compared with those in the neighboring buildings; its unplastered and somewhat irregular sides; its adobe sill resting a mere 4 inches above the floor, all combine to indicate that this particular entrance was an afterthought, constructed sometime subsequent to completion of the dwelling. Although the upper portion of the door has fallen, impressions in both jambs show where a former slab lintel, supported by three sticks, had lain flush with the lower side of the near-by ceiling beam. Smoke stains on the fractured masonry at this point suggest that at least some of the fires so evident within the room were lighted during recent years.

A second and perhaps original entrance is a hatchway close to the south wall and directly above the lateral opening described in the preceding paragraph. This ceiling door measures 17 by 24 inches (43.2 by 61.1 cm.) and is rimmed with adobe mud. A broken sandstone slab with chipped edges, found on the floor beneath the hatchway, may formerly have covered it.

Two "windows," each approximately 6 inches (15.2 cm.) square and 2 feet 10 inches (88.4 cm.) above the floor, pierce the south wall, one on either side of the door. The inner faces of both openings are plastered. A third and similar opening, one side of which is formed by a small slab set on edge and extending 4 inches outside the room, is present in the rear half of the east wall.

Three wooden pegs or hangers protrude from both the east and west walls of the room at a height, respectively, of 3 feet (0.91 m.) and 2 feet 10 inches (88.4 cm.). Two additional pegs in the east wall support a ceiling pole at a level slightly above that of the principal beams. Other projecting sticks occupy a comparable position in the opposite wall, but in this instance they lie below the tops of the larger beams.

These two upper series of pegs are really nonessential features of room 2; they are considered thus at length only to illustrate the fact that the prehistoric artisans of Cottonwood Canyon, as elsewhere in the Southwest, sometimes altered their plans during the process of building. For living rooms a flat roof was most desired, but the beams which formed the main ceiling supports were not always of uniform diameter. It is quite obvious that the two upper pegs in the east wall of room 2 were intended to equalize this lack of uniformity, and it is equally certain that those in the west wall were placed for a like purpose, although in the completed dwelling the secondary timbers they were planned to carry rested directly upon the principal beams, several inches above the pegs.

Southwestern cliff-dwellings were invariably roofed with earth or adobe overlying a layer of willows, and sometimes grass or cedar bark. This willow layer rested upon poles of from 2 to 4 inches in diameter, and these in turn were supported by larger beams. Four major timbers were utilized in construction of room 2. One of these lay close against the inner front wall; two, placed parallel, crossed the middle room, and a fourth beam rested against the cliff. This latter timber had been braced in the middle and at the west end by posts. The roof remained in surprisingly good condition in 1919 (pl. 16, a).

Room 3 likewise boasts of a roof that shows but slight damage from time. Eighteen poles cross its shorter dimension at a point 5 feet (1.52 m.) above the floor. Upon these poles is a layer of willows, and above them a covering of adobe mud. Because of its relatively small size major beams were not required in this room; nevertheless four of its roof timbers protrude beyond the south wall in such a manner as to simulate beams (pl. 16, b). All of the ceiling poles are bound close together by three lacings of willows; the overlying willows are tied to the poles with strips of yucca leaves.

The south wall is pierced by a door 17 inches (43.3 cm.) wide and 24 inches (61.1 cm.) high; its stone sill lies 26 inches (66.1 cm.) above the floor. Both in size and height this opening is more typical of cliff-dwelling entrances than is that in room 2. Three sticks support the stone lintel; both jambs are well plastered, and on either side of the door are small holes where willow loops formerly protruded. Wedges inserted in such loops were employed as a means of holding the door slabs in position. An excellent example of this primitive locking device is figured by Cummings[6] from White Canyon, southeastern Utah.

A single hanger, protruding from the north wall, is present in room 3. The absence of smoke stains, together with the recessed door and its loop fasteners, indicate that this building served for storage rather than living purposes.

Between rooms 2 and 3 are three storage bins or mealing boxes, each built of sandstone slabs. That nearest the southeast corner of room 2 is paved with flags. No evidence remains of superimposed masonry. While these bins resemble Basket Maker cists, they were plainly utilized and most likely constructed by Cliff-dweller inhabitants of Kiva Cave.

Room 4, now partially demolished, originally served as a storage chamber. Its interior shows no trace of smoke, the unmistakable sign of living quarters. Upright slabs averaging 12 inches (30.5 cm.) in height form a base for its east, west, and south sides. Each of the four wall surfaces had been plastered, but without concealing the roughness of the underlying masonry. The only opening still visible, a door 24 inches (61.1 cm.) high, pierces the west wall 18 inches (45 cm.) above the floor. In smoothing the jambs of this entrance the ancient builders had carried their adobe plaster to either side, roughly surfacing the outer wall.

One special feature of room 4, a shelf or bench against the inner south wall, is deserving of our attention in passing. The platform itself has completely disappeared, but its former position is plainly indicated by the broken ends or the empty holes of six small logs embedded in the masonry 30 inches (76.3 cm.) above the floor at the time of construction. Owing to the presence of the door already mentioned, the western limit of this bench had been purposely restricted to a width of 16 inches (40.7 cm.), just half that of its opposite end.

Platforms such as this are not unknown to students of southwestern archeology, and yet they occur so rarely as to attract notice whenever found. Only one other was observed by the present writer in western Utah, and that in an adobe-walled dwelling exposed at Paragonah in 1917.[7] The layman's natural inference would be that such a bench originally served for sleeping purposes, but it is well known that the ancient Pueblos, like their modern descendants, preferred to spread their blankets on the bare floor. A more logical explanation, therefore, is that the shelf under consideration (it was only 4 feet long) was designed for the reception of maize or other possessions stored for future use.

---

[6] 1910, p. 23.   [7] Judd, 1919, p. 8.

The kiva, after which we named the cave, is archeologically the most important structure in this particular ruin group. Although it lacks several features of normal kiva architecture, as described by students of the San Juan field especially, there can be no question as to its original ceremonial function. It is one of two such rooms thus far observed in Cottonwood Canyon.

In diameter the kiva measures 13 feet 6 inches (4.1 m.). Its adobe floor lies 5 feet (1.52 m.) below the foundation stones of room 4. That the chamber was only partially subterranean is evidenced by the fact that its highest standing wall, now broken and incomplete, rises 1 foot above the level upon which the four rectangular rooms were erected. Excepting for the eastern one-third, upright slabs mark the base of its circular wall; above these is plastered masonry (pl. 17, a). Absence of both bench and pilasters, so frequently mentioned in kivas east and southeast of the Rio Colorado, is sufficient indication that the roof timbers of this chamber rested directly upon its inclosing stonework. Postholes for ceiling props were not disclosed.

In the middle floor is a fireplace whose sides are formed by five small slabs so placed that their upper edges come flush with the hard-packed pavement. The fireplace is unrimmed, and no screen had been used in connection with it. Three protruding points of native rock just south of the fireplace had been battered down to the general floor level. Wall recesses are not in evidence; neither is there any trace of a sipapu, the symbolic opening through which Pueblo peoples emerged into this world from an earlier, more primitive existence.

Besides its form and semisubterranean position, the chamber possesses one other characteristic feature of circular Cliff-dweller and early Pueblo kivas elsewhere, namely, the ventilator.[8] In the room now under consideration the ventilator is a simple tunnel averaging 14 inches (35.6 cm.) wide by 18 inches (45.5 cm.) high, walled and paved with slabs. This tunnel opens into the kiva at a point slightly east of south; its outer end has been demolished by cattle trailing across the loose débris in front of the cave. Cross sticks covered with cedar bark and sand roofed the passage. That a shaft once rose from its broken outer end seems extremely doubtful.

This ventilator passage connects with the kiva through a most inconspicuous opening. Its movable sandstone cover first attracted our attention. Although in line with the wall stones on either side

[8] For detailed description of, and current theories regarding, kiva ventilators the reader is referred to Cummings, Fewkes, Jeancon, Kidder, Morris, Prudden, and other students of the northern Pueblo area.

(pl. 18, *a*), this slab door, measuring 15 inches (38 cm.) wide and 14 inches (35.6 cm.) high, was somewhat smaller than its neighbors; its edges had been more carefully shaped by chipping and its upper corners were rounded.[9] The mouth of the tunnel, 11 inches (27.9 cm.) wide and 14 inches (35.6 cm.) high, was provided with thick jambs of adobe mud that, gradually thinning, reached back within the passage a distance of 10 inches. The dimensions given in the preceding paragraph (14 by 18 inches) begin at a point 28 inches (71.2 cm.) from the tunnel mouth, where the flagstones of the passage lie 9 inches (22.8 cm.) below the kiva floor. From this same point the two floors are joined by a sloping surface of adobe overlying the flags.

The sand accumulations in cave 3 were surprisingly shallow and free from household débris. Potsherds, ashes, and other refuse from the small community were thrown down the talus at the west front of the cave and are now overgrown by a tangled mass of scrub oak. In the narrower eastern portion of the cavern a small spring of clear, cool water issues from a crack in the seepage plane. Although the little sandstone basin into which the water first flows seems of fairly recent origin, roughly piled blocks in the mucky talus below it suggest that the prehistoric occupants gave some thought and effort to development of this source of supply.

A short distance south of the spring two slab-lined cists were accidentally exposed. The smaller of these measured 5 feet 8 inches (1.7 m.) in diameter; the larger 6 feet (1.82 m.) in diameter and 22 inches (55.8 cm.) in depth. Rude masonry, roughly plastered, once formed a superstructure for each cist. Both pits were filled with this wall débris and such blown sand as had lodged about it.

On the cave wall back of rooms 3 and 4 are several ancient drawings of men in white, red, and yellow clay. None of these possess the earmarks of true Basket Maker workmanship.

CAVE 4.—Hidden behind a screen of oak and box elder in a little cove opposite the orchard we found a relatively shallow cave whose level floor was literally covered with the wreckage of a Cliff-dweller settlement. A few sections only of rude masonry showed through this débris (pl. 20, *a*). There was absolutely nothing about the pile to encourage one; a ground plan of the ancient village was utterly impossible without excavation. But burned posts, standing in rows, appeared here and there to remind one of the jacal structures noted at Paragonah.[10] To test this apparent similarity a brief examination was undertaken.

---

[9] Guernsey and Kidder (1921, p. 24) describe a similar covered ventilator, 2 feet above the floor, in a kiva in White Dog Cave, northeastern Arizona. Base slabs were employed in construction of a south recess.

[10] Judd, 1919, p. 11.

With almost the first moment's work the slab base of a large circular room was disclosed. Masonry walls overlay this base. Other structures were met, and then others. Before our exploratory trench was half completed interest in the prehistoric dwellings of cave 4 had been so roused that further examination proved irresistible. Among the rooms exposed during the four days which followed were many of curious construction. Architecturally they seemed to represent two distinct periods of occupancy, but the cultural objects recovered in the course of excavation offered contrary evidence. Figure 28 illustrates the general relationship of those buildings described in the following paragraphs.

Room 1, at the east end of the cave, was traceable only in part. Its north wall and the adjoining portion of the west wall had completely disappeared. The south side of the room was built up of rudely coursed stone; the west side was indicated for a distance of 12 feet (3.6 m.) by eight posts which had been burned to the level of the accumulated sand and stone; that is, to within 12 inches (30.5 cm.) of the floor. Willows placed horizontally bound these posts together and helped support the masses of thick mud which had been pressed between them. A small amount of masonry incorporated in the south end of the west wall suggests that the existing south side of the room was constructed later than its neighbor. From the large quantity of droppings present in the débris, room 1 served as a turkey pen prior to its final abandonment.

Immediately west of this building and at the same level was a partially razed circular structure whose periphery was marked by a single row of upright slabs. The northeast quarter of this structure had been sacrificed when the west wall of room 1 was erected; its southern half had been wholly demolished, perhaps at the same time.

The unrimmed fireplace which served this round room measured 30 inches (76.3 cm.) in diameter by 8 inches (20.3 cm.) in depth. At the broken south end of the slab-stone wall and 8 inches (20.3 cm.) above its base lay a second clay-lined fireplace 14 inches (35.6 cm.) in diameter. The latter was surrounded for a short distance only by a pavement of ashy earth closely packed and smoothed by the feet of prehistoric cooks. Ten inches above this pavement and to the west of it a second similar floored area encircled a third fireplace. This latter ash-filled basin overlay a row of six partially burned posts, 3 to 6 inches in diameter, that once formed such a wall as that noted on the west side of room 1. Dried mud still stood between the uprights, but the horizontal willows, if any, which supported this filling had vanished.

Two subsequent levels of occupancy are thus represented in the 18 inches (45.5 cm.) of rubbish and blown sand which overlay the

b, Stairway, Cave 8

a, Kiva, Cave 3

ARCHITECTURAL DETAILS, RUINS IN COTTONWOOD CANYON

a, The small slab in the middle wall covers the ventilator passage in the Cave 3 kiva, Cottonwood Canyon

b, Rooms in Cave 6, Cottonwood Canyon

a, View in Cottonwood Canyon

b, Cave 3 from across canyon

a

b

RUINS IN CAVE 4, COTTONWOOD CANYON

a, North wall of Circle A, Cave 4, Cottonwood Canyon

b, Wall posts of Room 15, Cave 4, Cottonwood Canyon

a, Circle C bench with wall of Room 15 at left, Cottonwood Canyon

b, Circle C, Cave 4, Cottonwood Canyon

adobe floor of the partially razed circular room with the slab wall. And yet only a relatively short period of time elapsed during the accumulation of this débris, for potsherds recovered from the suc-

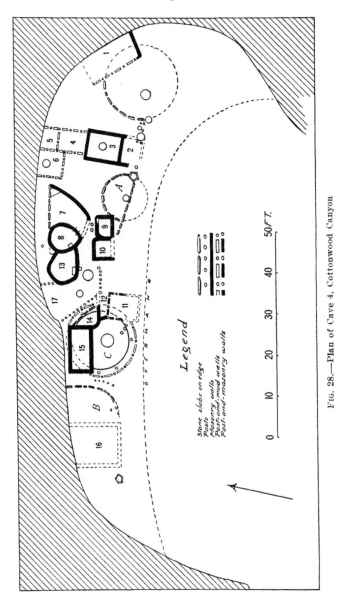

Fig. 28.—Plan of Cave 4, Cottonwood Canyon

cessive fills exhibited no differences either in vessel form or body decoration. It would appear that the round room had been first constructed; that it was abandoned and most of its wall slabs salvaged before the west side of room 1 was built; that the charred posts under the third fireplace above mentioned marked the southern limit—the sole remaining evidence—of a post-and-mud house erected after the round room had been wholly concealed and generally forgotten by its builders. Similar posts were subsequently found between circles B and C, but those now under consideration extended east and west, thus removing from the realm of reasonable conjecture any possible relationship between them and the partially razed circular room to the east. This problem of superposition and replacement will be further dwelt upon after additional dwellings in cave 4 have been described.

Rooms 2 and 3 were obviously constructed at the same time, although the floor of the former lay 10 inches (25.4 cm.) below that of the latter. Crude masonry, unplastered and smoother outside than inside, comprised the building material for both houses. Stone slabs on edge stood at the base of all except the south wall of room 3; similar stones were more sparingly used in room 2. A central stone-lined fireplace marked room 3 as a former dwelling.

Room 4 was of somewhat later construction. Excepting its south side, where the masonry of room 3 had been utilized, the walls consisted of posts, bound with willows and packed between with adobe mud. A second floor level 8 inches (20.3 cm.) below that of the room points to the probability of an open court or passageway behind room 3 prior to erection of rooms 4–6.

Rooms 5 and 6, also marked by post-and-mud walls, were undoubtedly built contemporaneously with room 4. Both because of its small dimensions and its indefinite floor, room 5 may be regarded as a storage chamber. Five inches below its probable floor level and extending beneath its west wall were the remains of a flagstone pavement that may represent either the location of an earlier cist or continuation of the surface disclosed below room 4. These flagstones, however, rested upon a layer of vegetable matter, including cornstalks and husks, not found under the adjoining room. Above room 5 the cliff had been plastered with mud.

The wall posts of room 6 averaged 4 inches (10.2 cm.) in diameter and 18 inches (45.5 cm.) from each other; horizontal willows bound them together at intervals of 6 to 10 inches (15.2 to 25.4 cm.). In the rear middle of the floor stood a slab-lined fireplace. The floor itself lay 14 inches (35.5 cm.) below the court level immediately in front of the dwelling and was covered to that depth with smoke-stained adobe and sandstone blocks from razed habitations.

Room 7, although it had been abandoned, partially destroyed, and filled with its own débris, is deserving of notice. The north and east walls only were exposed, but these carried the sooty deposits from a long-used central fireplace. Upright slabs in a hard-packed adobe floor formed a base for these two walls. On the east side rough masonry rested upon the slabs, and it may be inferred that similar stonework was originally present on the north, although the ancients left nothing but the slabs when razing this portion of the room. The floor of room 7 lay 10 inches (25.4 cm.) below that in room 6, or 24 inches (61 cm.) below the court level which reached from room 4 to room 8 and concealed the ruins of room 7.

In the northeast corner stood a triangular shelf or bench, a rather unusual feature in the prehistoric dwellings of Cottonwood Canyon. This bench, 17 inches (43.2 cm.) high, measured 24 inches (61 cm.) against both the north and east walls of the room; its western limit was marked by a large slab that joined the north wall and extended 8 inches (20.3 cm.) above the flagstone surface of the shelf.

The former position of a slab-sided bin near the southern margin of the chamber was indicated by an upright stone set in the floor and held to the wall of the room by adobe mud.

Room 8 possessed an outward resemblance to the larger circular structure in Riggs Cave, but its heavily plastered walls were composed of rude masonry rather than reinforced adobe " bricks." The room rested upon the rubbish which filled all that was left of room 7, and even utilized, in its north and southwest sections, such base-stones [11] as protruded through the débris from the abandoned dwelling.

Elsewhere in room 8 the lower interior walls were faced with slabs that rose the usual height above the floor; that is, approximately 15 inches. Above and between these slabs four separate coats of plaster appeared on the west side only. The one seemingly logical reason for this restricted wall surfacing—the eastern side of the room had not been similarly treated—was the presence against the west wall of a slab-lined fireplace.

Through the southeast wall a 14-inch (35.6 cm.) doorway opened at the level of the court extending eastward to rooms 3-6. The flat stone forming the sill of this door lay 9 inches (22.8 cm.) above the room floor.

Room 11 combined both methods of construction observed in those prehistoric dwellings already described. Its three traceable walls were formed by posts bound at varying intervals with horizontal willows; the spaces between these posts were filled, not with adobe mud alone, but with rude masonry in which adobe predominated. Upright slabs were not employed at the base of these walls, nor, indeed, do they occur in any of the post-and-mud structures.

---

[11] The writer is here coining a word to describe the large slabs of sandstone that stand against the inner wall surfaces of these ancient dwellings, occupying the same relative position, but of course not serving a like function, as do the baseboards in modern habitations.

Ceiling-pole fragments and bits of clay bearing the imprint of willows and grass gave sufficient evidence that the house had been roofed in the manner characteristic of most ancient Pueblo habitations (see p. 100).

Room 17: Certainly the most presumptuous living room in cave 4 is that represented by the remains of a post-and-mud wall immediately west of room 13. Fire had completely destroyed the structure in ancient times, but the resulting wreckage had been cleared away by the former inhabitants in order that they might continue to use the broad floor space and the two open hearths it surrounded. Only the charred butts or the empty holes of the former wall posts remained to mark the outline of this large, misshapen living room.

Posts 7 inches (17.7 cm.) in diameter stood at each end of the south wall; between them were a dozen or more smaller uprights. From the western end of this row a second series angled off a distance of 12 feet 6 inches (3.8 m.) to meet the cliff near the northeast corner of room 15. On the east the convex wall of room 13 and four posts between it and the cliff completed the inclosure. Although our hasty search may have been insufficient, no additional postholes were observed either in the hard-packed middle floor of the room or against the cave wall that formed its northern limit.

It is difficult to believe that a structure so large as this and possessed of such flimsy walls could have been successfully roofed without the aid of several central supports. The 3-inch posts in the west wall were certainly not strong enough, even with their adobe filler, to uphold the weight of a flat ceiling of poles, brush, and earth that reached more than 10 feet (3.04 m.) to the plastered masonry in room 13. And yet no evidence of central supports was disclosed.

Within the room were two fireplaces. One of these, that in the southeast corner, measured 30 inches (76.1 cm.) in diameter by 5 inches (12.7 cm.) in depth; the second, 3 feet to the west, measured 20 by 6 inches (50.8 by 15.2 cm.). Both were lined by stone slabs set edgewise, with their tops slightly above the floor level; adobe mud rounded off the outside, forming a low rim for each. But few objects of human origin were recovered from the shallow accumulation overlying the pavement surrounding these fireplaces.

East of the hearth first mentioned, at what may well have been the entrance to this extraordinary habitation, there was exposed a neat storage cist lined with four slab stones on end. The cist measured 16 inches (40.6 cm.) deep, 10 inches (25.4 cm.) square at the top, and 13 inches (33 cm.) square at the bottom. Its adobe floor was covered by a layer of grass; its upper edges rounded off to meet the surrounding pavement. The north slabstone extended 12 inches higher than its neighbors. Sand, with bits of broken stone, filled the cist.

Circle A was formed at the middle front of the cave, between rooms 2 and 9; only the northern half of its floor remained intact. Here the periphery was marked by base slabs set edgewise in the adobe pavement and supported behind by quantities of dry refuse and sand. The standing slabs were all neatly joined with mud plaster, and this rounded off in several places to indicate the former presence of a bench such as that later disclosed in circle C.

Excepting this arc of slabstone, the inclosing walls had been wholly demolished. No single trace was found in the débris to indicate the character of the superstructure that once completed circle A and made it habitable. The fragmentary north wall was overlain and entirely concealed by the pavement of the open court extending southward past room 6 and between rooms 3 and 8. Beneath this court floor were quantities of reeds, grass, and piñon boughs tightly matted in dry sand.

An unrimmed fireplace, roughly oval, occupied the middle of circle A. Single stone slabs, embedded with their upper edges at the floor level, formed the north and west sides of this ash-filled basin; its opposite sides consisted of smoothed adobe. No other depression and no holes or cists appeared in that half of the hard-packed floor which remained.

Two additional fire pits observed in this section of the cave mark successive layers of occupancy. One of the two, adobe-rimmed and 16 inches (40.6 cm.) in diameter, lay 4 inches (10.2 cm.) above and directly over the south edge of the basin noted in the preceding paragraph. The second, built at the south end of the broken east wall of circle A and with six slabs apparently reclaimed from it, rested on the same 4-inch level, but the pit obviously was not in use before the open court above mentioned had become a recognized feature of the settlement. The second fireplace was 14 inches (35.6 cm.) deep, nearly three times that of the other hearths examined.

The row of slabstones bisecting circle A probably had some connection with the first of the two fireplaces just described. The stones were set in loose sand without the customary adobe between them.

Circle C, largely overbuilt by later dwellings, was found in that degree of preservation which enabled us to form a fairly definite idea as to its original appearance and, in consequence, the nature of those parts missing in the three similar structures disclosed through excavation of cave 4.

Among the essential features of circle C these were identified: An outer inclosing wall of post-and-mud construction; a bench encircling the room within this wall; a central fireplace; and a flat roof supported by posts. The type and position of the original doorway could not be ascertained; no wall niches and no floor depressions other than the fireplace were discovered.

In constructing this room the ancient builders first prepared the site by making a shallow excavation in the rear of the cave, where wind-blown accumulations were deepest. Next they formed a ring, 14 feet 6 inches (4.4 m.) in diameter, using sandstone slabs of rather uniform dimensions set endwise with their tops in the same horizontal plane. Sand and occasional spalls were heaped against the outside of this circle; frequent stakes, driven close behind the stones, furnished additional support for them. Within the inclosure a floor of adobe, spread upon the cave sand, formed a footing for the slab-stones and securely bound them in their required position. Adobe mud filled and smoothed all interstices between the slabs.

From the character of the building, but more especially from evidence disclosed through its excavation, it would appear that after the prehistoric builders of circle C had completed both the earthen floor and the ring of slabstones at its margin they began erection of the outer wall. This consisted of posts 1 to 4 inches in diameter and set about 2 feet outside the slab circle, and adobe mud held in position between the posts by willows tied horizontally to them at intervals varying from 6 to 10 inches. Only in a few instances, and then in the case of the larger members, were these posts so deeply planted that their lower ends approached the floor level of the room. Adobe mud, neatly spread over the sandy débris separating the inner ring of stones from the outer one of posts, formed an encircling banquette 20 inches (50.8 cm.) wide by 13 inches (33 cm.) high. For the most part this bench was slightly dished; its surface rounded off to meet its facing of slabs and rose slightly in joining the outer post-and-mud wall.

Circle C had been roofed with a flat ceiling of poles, covered in turn by layers of coarse grass and adobe. The whole was probably supported by several main beams that rested directly upon studiously placed pillars. Four of these latter pierced the broad bench in the eastern half of the room; two were observed on the western side, and still others no doubt existed in that unexcavated northern portion underlying room 15. Two additional uprights in the southeast quarter were evidently introduced after completion of the ceiling as braces for one of its weaker members. One of these posts stood close to the face of the bench and was joined to it with adobe mud; the second stood near by but entirely free. No one of these several pillars exceeded 6 inches (15.2 cm.) in diameter, but, properly distributed, they doubtless withstood the tremendous weight of so large a ceiling. The lesser posts in the outer wall may have upheld protruding ends of the lighter ceiling poles, but their total contribution toward support of the massive roof must have been relatively inconsequential.

No one may say how long circle C was inhabited, nor may the purposes for which it was designed be wholly identified. The structure was destroyed by fire during its period of occupancy. No blown sand had accumulated within the room previous to this conflagration; no objects other than scattered potsherds were found in the débris. Existing portions of the outer wall; the surface and slabstone face of the encircling bench; charred timbers and fragments of roof adobe, all show the effects of consuming flames. And the fatal spark may well have come from the unrimmed fireplace near the middle of the room.

Rectangular dwellings rose upon the smoke-stained wreckage of this circular structure. Room 11, of post-and-mud construction, has already been mentioned. Room 15, with its rude masonry, was erected on a level space 16 inches (40.6 cm.) above the floor of circle C, and the latter's low encircling bench was utilized as a foundation for stones in the north wall of the former.

Room 14 is an odd affair that apparently includes the more substantial portions of a former partially razed dwelling. Its western wall was the outer east end of room 15; its southern side, of equally poor stonework, joined the former in a short curve. Neither of these two walls was traceable beyond the points indicated in Figure 28. But whatever may have been the original shape and dimensions of this reconditioned building, as last utilized it was triangular, with its third wall formed by slabs set endwise directly upon the bench of circle C. Superimposed masonry was not in evidence here as it was in the walls of room 15.

Within the row of slabs an adobe floor had been spread 3 inches (7.6 cm.) above the surface of circle C bench; on the outside, rubbish from razed dwellings filled and covered the burned and broken walls of the earlier circular structure.

The foregoing more or less detailed descriptions of typical rooms should have conveyed some understanding of the much-ruined habitations in cave 4. For the most part they illustrate types of construction quite comparable with those made known through the explorations of Morris and of Kidder and Guernsey in various sections of the San Juan drainage. But these several distinct types are all closely associated in cave 4; the too-limited collections of cultural artifacts recovered during our excavations point unmistakably to continuous, though relatively brief, occupancy of the site by the same family groups.

The rubbish of cave 4 included an unusually large proportion of desiccated human excrement. Among this many stools were noticed containing unmasticated pieces of wild gourd rind, corn husks, and even grass. Wads of yucca fiber and corn husk, matted from much chewing, were also found in quantity. Ordinarily such finds attract no particular attention, but in this instance it would appear that the ancient inhabitants for a given period had been reduced to the border line of starvation; that they resorted in this emergency to vegetable substances which from their very nature held but little of nutritive value.

FLOWER CAVE lies on the west side of Cottonwood Canyon, at the lower end of the orchard. Blown sand has swirled into a huge dune at the mouth of the cavern, now occupies the greater part of its floor, and rises well toward its roof. Such remains of prehistoric habitations as may exist here are entirely concealed by this intruder. Although no effort was made to establish the fact, occupancy of the cave in ancient times is rendered more than probable by the presence of both Basket Maker and Cliff-dweller pictographs. Many of these have been wholly or partially covered by drifted sand. A few of the more accessible, typical drawings are reproduced in Plate 60.

Behind the dune clear, cold water trickles musically from a splintered crevice, to gather momentarily into a gemlike pool, whence it is slowly absorbed by the fine yellow sand. Throughout the seepage zone columbine has spread a green carpet; the white, waxy blooms of the matted plants have given the cave its popular name, and formed a garden spot occasionally utilized by picnic parties from Kanab. As might be expected, thoughtless visitors have been tempted to carve their names on smooth sections of the cave wall, and these recent autographs too frequently encroach upon the vastly more precious records left by prehistoric sojourners.

CAVE 5, even when viewed from a short distance away, appears so shallow as to prompt the thought that ancient man could have found in it but little if any shelter. It overlooks the orchard from a point about 200 yards (183.4 m.) north of Flower Cave; and, like most of the others in Cottonwood Canyon, is fairly well screened by a tangled growth of scrub oak.

Torrents of rain water pouring off the cliff at the north end of the cave had gradually built up a mass of sticks and detritus that eventually turned the floods southward through the length of the cavern. In passing, these casual streams had accomplished two things: They had deposited many tons of sand and gravel upon the northern half of the cave floor, and in the middle portion of it they had exposed a number of regularly spaced but partially burned posts. These latter invited examination.

Room 1: Certain wooden members which had first roused our interest proved to be a circular structure (fig. 29) not unlike the round rooms in cave 4. Its outer wall was of post-and-mud construction; within this wall a slab-faced bench 30 inches (76.1 cm.) wide by 12 inches (30.5 cm.) high encircled the room. A low-rimmed fireplace occupied the middle floor. These are features already familiar to us. Several structural differences, however, are to be noted between the room under consideration and those previously described.

In the cave 4 circles, it will be recalled, adobe mud separated the wall posts, and was bound to them by horizontal willows. Osiers were less frequently utilized, apparently, in erection of room 1, cave 5; at least none was found in those fragmentary wall sections which remained in position. Cedar bark was held in place against

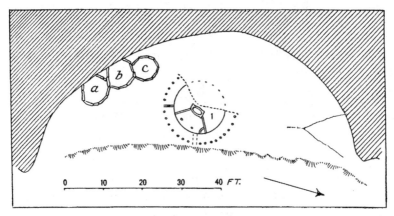

FIG. 29.—Plan of Cave 5, Cottonwood Canyon

the outside of the posts by loose sand, and for obvious reasons this sort of material could not have risen more than a foot or two in the completed structure. In the upper wall, therefore, willows may well have been employed. The inner surface of this wall had been so frequently replastered as wholly to conceal the uprights. No less than nine distinct coats of mud were counted here.

The oval fireplace in room 1 measured 34 inches (86.4 cm.) long, 26 inches (66.1 cm.) wide, and 14 inches (35.6 cm.) deep. At its northeast, northwest, and southwest corners shallow unrimmed depressions of unknown import were observed. From the first of these a buried pole reached northeastward to the peripheral bench; a second log occupied a like position at the southeast quarter. In both instances these timbers were covered by the adobe mud with which the room had been paved, but they formed, nevertheless, clearly defined ridges approximately 3 inches (7.6 cm.) in height. The writer can offer no suggestion as to the original function of these two members, but it is to be noted that the floor between them had been more thinly spread than elsewhere in the room, and in consequence was much broken when found. No evidence of sub-floor cists or burials appeared in this rimmed area; but two posts, doubtless former ceiling supports, stood near its eastern margin. A third post rose from the middle of an adobe ridge that crossed the bench at the south side of the room.

Where the first of these two buried logs joins the banquette a small earth-walled bin was constructed. At the south end of this box one of the bench slabs had been removed, as though to mark an opening. The latter could not have exceeded 10 inches (25.4 cm.) in width. It was provided with a stone sill, but its sides and the adjoining bench surface were so badly damaged as to preclude the possibility of final interpretation. On the floor in front of this conjectural opening lay three fragments of a sandstone slab whose chipped edges suggested its former use as a door cover, perhaps for a hatchway in the ceiling.

The northwestern third of room 1 was not excavated.

Rooms a–c are slab-lined cists built against the cliff in the lower section of the cave, south of room 1. Rude masonry rested upon the basestones of each pit, but this was interspersed, in the case of room b, with masses of adobe reinforced with grass and twigs. Although the original height of these broken walls could not be gauged, as exposed they measured 2 feet 4 inches (0.71 m.), 3 feet (0.91 m.), and 3 feet, respectively. Rooms a and b averaged 6 feet (1.8 m.) in diameter, and room c, 5 feet 6 inches (1.67 m.).

A fragment of a cedar-bark pot rest was the only cultural object found in cave 5. No tests were made in the sand-filled section north of room 1.

CAVE 6 lies at the head of an eastern tributary to Cottonwood and shelters the largest Cliff-dweller settlement visited by the writer during his archeological observations north of the Rio Colorado. Altogether 19 rooms and 1 possible kiva are in evidence. Plates 18, b; 23, a, b, illustrate the general appearance of these dwellings; Figure 30 shows their relationship one to the other. No excavations were made during our hurried visit to this site. Those few shards gleaned from the surface offered no variations from the fragments collected in caves 3 and 4.

In the northernmost section of the cave a small spring issues from the sandstone. Traces of ancient habitations do not appear in its immediate vicinity, nor indeed in that equally suitable section adjoining on the southeast. But there is a bare possibility that one-

a

b

DWELLINGS IN CAVE 6, COTTONWOOD CANYON

a, Storerooms, Cave 8, Cottonwood Canyon

b, Stones where axes were sharpened, Cave 8, Cottonwood Canyon

time evidence of such structures has been wholly obliterated by range cattle that frequent the spring and lounge in the shelter of its overhanging cliff. The cave is said to have been utilized for a fortnight by Mormon settlers during pioneer days, although no material evidence of such occupancy is visible to-day. Access from the old road in the main canyon is not easy; close approach can be made only on foot or horseback.

Considering the inherent crudeness of their masonry, the pre-historic buildings in cave 6 are surprisingly well preserved. Blocks of sandstone, gathered from neighboring talus slopes and oftentimes reshaped by chipping, were laid in a superabundance of adobe mud. As this primitive mortar oozed out between the individual blocks it was pressed back upon them by the workmen, who thus gave to their house walls a plastered appearance. Each dwelling bears a fingerprint record of its ancient builders. In three instances the

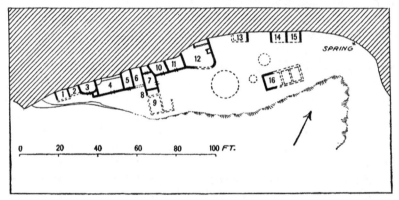

FIG. 30.—Plan of Cave 6, Cottonwood Canyon

wall plaster had obviously been rubbed down with smoothing stones. The outer walls were constructed with greater regularity than their inner faces; basestones were observed only in one room, No. 13.

At the western end of the cave, on a narrow, unevenly floored ledge, several granaries were erected. Their respective openings were grooved at each side for the reception of door slabs, which had been held in place by sticks run through willow loops. These loops have long since disappeared, but the holes they once occupied are still evident. Few only of the cave 6 dwellings merit individual consideration as a result of our incomplete observations.

Room 4 is 8 feet square. Its single doorway, through the front wall, measured 18 inches (45.5 cm.) wide by 26 inches (66.1 cm.) high; its stone sill rested a foot or more above the floor level. In the northwestern corner a triangular seat of masonry 8 inches (20.3 cm.) high had been built; later it was continued as a narrow bench across the entire width of the dwelling. Against the outer southwest corner and in the angle formed by the convex front of the adjoining room 3 stands the broken masonry of a small cist.

Room 7 resulted from a chance thought of one of the villagers. Inspired, perhaps, by the close proximity of rooms 6, 8, and 10, this primitive conserver of labor merely joined the latter two houses with 6 feet of stonework and proceeded with a roof of the customary type. The inner walls were plastered, but without apparent effort to eliminate the unevenness of their coarse masonry.

Under the overhanging cliff at the north end is a storage chamber 36 inches (0.91 m.) in width and 32 inches (0.81 m.) in maximum depth. Its front wall is only 3 feet 8 inches (1.1 m.) high. Access to the foodstuffs piled away in this little cupboard was had through a door 13 inches (33 cm.) wide and 15 inches (38.1 cm.) high. As is usual in storerooms, this opening was provided with willow loops and grooves for a close-fitting door slab.

Rooms 8 and 9 originally formed a single dwelling. The dividing partition was built in after a period of occupancy, and owing, perhaps, to settling of the talus upon which the outer walls were erected. The outline of room 9 is now barely traceable. In contrast, the north wall of room 8 stands to a height of 6 feet 3 inches (1.9 m.). Adjoining room 9 on the east are suggestions of a third habitation.

Room 10 was utilized for living purposes. Its inner walls are plastered and smoke-stained. Several sticks protrude as hangers. On the south the exposed portions of two unusually wide slabs were utilized as shelves for the reception of lesser objects. One of these lies 6 inches (15.2 cm.) above the door lintels; the second, 5 inches (12.7 cm.) wide by 7 inches (17.7 cm.) long, is seen slightly to the west of the first. The room was entered through a door 19 inches (48.3 cm.) wide and 25 inches (63.6 cm.) high; its stone sill is now missing. And, curiously enough, although the building plainly served as a dwelling, and although its door jambs were not grooved, the holes once occupied by willow loops are visible on each side of the entrance. Ordinarily such features characterize granaries, whose contents were protected from rodents by a slab firmly wedged in place.

Room 11 has much in common with its neighbor on the west. Loopholes appear at the sides of its doorway; its inner walls are surfaced. A protruding slab 3 inches (7.6 cm.) above the entrance forms a 5 by 11 inch (12.7 by 27.9 cm.) shelf; a similar repository to the east has been broken since abandonment of the dwelling.

Rooms 7, 10, and 11 probably belonged to one family. A uniformity of construction obtains in all three, as though the masonry were the work of a single individual. Each of the three boasts plastered walls, wall pegs, and stone shelves. In no other room of the village was adobe added, as it was here, solely to reduce the roughness of the inner wall surfaces.

Room 12 is at once the largest, the most unusual, and the most interesting structure in cave 6. It was built subsequent to room 11. Its south and east walls, slightly thinner than those in the adjacent buildings, were each strengthened by a single post. Excepting that on the west, which contains the superior masonry of room 11, its interior walls are rough and unplastered. The shelter afforded jointly by these walls and the overhanging cliff has provided a welcome winter refuge for cattle frequenting the cave. To them must be charged most of the destruction now evident.

When occupied, the front half of this room was covered with poles, willows, and mud; at the rear the sloping cave roof was utilized as a ceiling. This latter portion had been plastered no less than seven times with thin washes of adobe. Access to the chamber was gained through a south doorway. Just west of this entrance a fragment of broken metate appears as one of the building stones. Slightly beyond, or 3 feet (0.91 m.) from the southwest corner, a 5 by 9 inch (12.7 by 22.8 cm.) window looks out across the canyon. Against the inner east wall slabstones form a bin 16 inches (40.6 cm.) wide, 20 inches (50.8 cm.) long, and 14 inches (35.6 cm.) deep. A similar receptacle in the northeast corner measures 24 inches (61 cm.) wide and 7 feet (2.13 m.) long.

The presence of ancient smoke stains on its walls and ceiling furnish sufficient proof that room 12 was built and utilized for dwelling purposes. The fireplace is a characteristic feature of living quarters; it is rarely, if ever, present in other structures.

CAVE 7.—Of the principal tributaries to Cottonwood from the west, that nearest the Riggs ranch house is Farm Canyon (see fig. 24). Wild hay, and at times grain, have been grown here as winter feed for cattle. The larger of the areas cultivated lies at the junction of the canyon's two branches. Close by, and long used as a haymow, is cave 7.

Such ancient habitations as the cave may formerly have sheltered have been sacrificed to the requirements of modern man. No trace remains to-day of masonry walls or other structures. The blown sand that slowly accumulated during past centuries has been scraped away; a rail fence now bars the wide mouth of the cavern.

But cave 7 was known to the prehistoric inhabitants of the region. They made of its brown walls a picture gallery. With natural colors gathered on neighboring hills they traced curious red and white symbols that excite our interest but convey no meaning to us. The real significance of these ancient pictographs was lost with the passing of their creators. There is about them that which suggests Basket Maker handiwork, and they almost certainly belong to that early cultural horizon, even though the most characteristic of Basket Maker drawings, the "square-shouldered men," are wanting in the present series. A number of painted figures from cave 7 are reproduced in Plate 60.

Several other caves, mostly small and fairly inconspicuous, may be observed in the cliffs of Farm Canyon as one passes along its meandering trail. The writer visited none of these.

CAVE 8 occupies an elevated position near the head of the right-hand fork in Water Canyon. It is among the larger of all the Cottonwood caves, and quite naturally was appropriated by the ancients for residential purposes. The size of their settlement, however, and the period throughout which it was inhabited are difficult to gauge without extensive excavation.

Superficial indications point to a considerable accumulation of camp refuse, ashes, sweepings, etc. Eight buildings, mostly storerooms, are now visible on the upper terrace in the eastern half of the cavern; the jumbled remains of other houses appear along the cliff walls, and still others will be found on the lower bench. At the western end an undetermined number of dwellings and a second kiva are indicated by shattered masonry. Cattle have sought shelter in the cave, and here as elsewhere their activities have gradually and almost completely obliterated those prehistoric habitations which interposed no serious obstacle in the way of bovine progress. Large blocks of sandstone, fallen from the roof, crowd the central portion of the cave. Some of these fell before the advent of the cliff people, and were utilized by them either as a foundation for granaries or as stationary grinding stones whereon axes, bone awls, and other primitive implements were sharpened. A majority of these blocks, however, represent more recent fractures, since they overlie household débris thrown out from the ancient dwellings. Hasty examination of the most prominent of these structures (fig. 31) and one test pit on the lower terrace represent the extent of our observations in cave 8.

Rooms 1–4, of varied shape and size, were closely grouped on the edge of two massive sandstone blocks. Each of the four had been constructed for storage purposes; holes for door fasteners appear at the sides of their respective entrances. Their walls were all rough and unplastered. More than half of the floor of room 1 consisted of the bare sloping surface of the rock mass on which the structure was built. Slabs of sandstone, set in adobe mud and supported by a single piece of split cedar, form the roof of room 3. The door to the larger storeroom above opens directly upon this unusual ceiling. Basestones are incorporated in the walls of rooms

1, 3, and 4 only. At the west end of the rock on which room 1 stands is a mortar, 9½ inches (24.2 cm.) in diameter by 5½ inches (13 cm.) in depth, pecked into the stone.

Rooms 5–7 are in utter ruin. Their rude masonry has fallen to the level of the cave débris. But smoke stains on the cliff mark the width of each room and identify all three as one-time habitations. It is not improbable that shallow excavations had been made in preparation for the erection of these particular dwellings.

Other buildings, the dimensions of which may be ascertained only through more or less digging, once stood to the east of room 7. Indeed, scattered fragments of masonry and bits of mud mortar adhering to the cliff indicate that a row of one-storied structures formerly extended along the rear wall of the cave from near its eastern margin to the seepage area at the west.

Kiva: Between rooms 2 and 5 is a semisubterranean kiva very

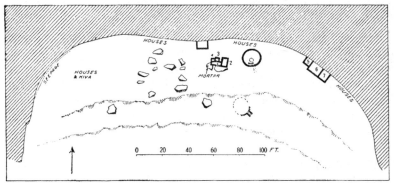

Fig. 31.—Plan of Cave 8, Cottonwood Canyon

similar to that in cave 3. Its sandy contents had already been partially removed; to complete this work and explore the meager furnishings of the room was therefore a simple task.

In diameter this kiva averages 14 feet 3 inches (4.3 m.). The periphery of its floor is marked by basestones with masonry rising above them to a height of 5 feet 6 inches (1.7 m.). Perhaps an additional foot of stonework has been dislodged since destruction of the flat roof that covered the chamber. Its ceiling beams rested directly upon the encircling wall, or more likely upon posts built into the wall at fairly regular intervals. Neither bench nor pilasters are present. The cylindricity of the room is unbroken except for a single southerly opening, 8½ by 12 inches, the inlet of an adobe-lined ventilator tunnel. The jambs of this opening are smooth and well plastered; its sill lies 4 inches (10.2 cm.) above the kiva floor. Beginning 8 inches (20.3 cm.) within the tunnel, the passage slopes sharply upward and outward. Search for its exterior orifice was not made.

The ever-present circular hearth lay 36 inches (0.91 m.) from the south wall of the ceremonial chamber. Fires that once burned in this unrimmed basin were shielded from inrushing air by a wattled screen of close-lying sticks bound to two upright stakes. There remains no evidence that this flimsy deflector had been protected in any manner; its position, midway between hearth and ventilator opening, seemingly afforded ample safeguard from flying sparks.

This is the only instance, so far as the writer is aware, in which a fire screen has been observed in a kiva north of the Rio Colorado. It differs somewhat from the typical kiva deflector of the San Juan drainage both as to its location relative to the fireplace and as to the method of its construction. Whether these slight differences have any real significance is a question which can not be answered fully from the single known western example. But its occurrence certainly adds one more mark of family resemblance between ceremonial rooms in the region under consideration and in that more familiar field east of the Colorado.

Post-and-mud room: The structures already described stand 10 feet (3.04 m.) above a lower bench. The face of the intervening terrace is covered by what appears to be a considerable accumulation of household refuse. Potsherds and other relics of ancient domestic activity strew the lower level, but no trace of house walls is evident. A momentary desire to know the character of the cave débris in this section prompted a casual test hole directly south of the kiva. The results were most unexpected.

Without any warning whatsoever a flight of steps was encountered just below the surface, leading downward from the southeast. The steps were six in number; each was formed by a log, filled in behind with sand and stone spalls and originally capped with adobe mud. Very coarse masonry walled the narrow stairway and held its individual logs in place (pl. 17, b). The uppermost step consisted of a sandstone slab; the lowermost lay 16 inches (40.6 cm.) above the indistinct floor of a circular room.

Lengthening shadows and the necessity for returning to our camp in Cottonwood Canyon prevented thorough examination of this unusual structure. But the sector exposed showed an encircling wall of close-standing posts, filled in between and plastered from the inside with adobe. These posts tend to slope toward the middle of the room, but whether this slant represents a natural feature of construction or pressure from the loose, sandy material outside was not determined. A probable posthole, 5 inches in diameter by 10 inches in depth, lies near the south wall. The fireplace, almost certainly present in the middle floor, was not uncovered. No bench occurs. Worked sticks, potsherds, corncobs, beans, squash stems, and fragments of rind were found in the blown sand and the rubbish from razed dwellings which filled this round structure. Similar objects appeared on the face of the upper terrace, but the total seemed surprisingly small when compared with the amount of visible household débris.

Most of this refuse indicates that Cliff-dwellers inhabited cave 8 for several years at least. Unprotected fireplaces and storage cists erected by them are seen here and there. But whether these house-builders were the first to utilize the site is not known. The cave could scarcely have escaped the notice of wandering Basket Makers, and yet the slab-lined bins and polychrome drawings so character-istic of their primitive culture were not observed during our cursory examination.

ADDITIONAL CAVES IN COTTONWOOD.—Besides the one last described, four lesser caverns in Water Canyon were visited in 1919. One of these, about half a mile above the lower forks, contains a much-ruined cliff-dwelling but lacks those accumulations of débris indica-tive of continued occupancy. The other three have collected such quantitites of blown sand that their prehistoric remains, if any, are deeply buried. The relative infrequency of pictographs is especially noticeable throughout this secondary canyon. No caves occur in its lower left-hand fork.

On the east side of Cottonwood and nearly a mile below the mouth of Water Canyon is a short tributary that represents the union of three small branches, two of which originate in caverns. The north-ernmost of these lies under a high sandstone cliff and shelters a one-room cliff house and two slab cists. Other and perhaps older struc-tures may well be concealed by the sandy refuse. Seepage at the south end of this cave freshens a ribbon of columbine.

Between Water Canyon and Farm Canyon is a relatively incon-spicuous ravine at the head of which three shallow caves will be seen. Two of these contain the fallen walls of masonry dwellings and numerous pictographs whose colors have grown dim before the storms of successive centuries. Beneath the sand and the ruins ex-cavation should reveal such traces of Basket Maker occupancy as escaped the destructive tendencies of later Cliff-dwellers.

Opposite the orchard is a low cave whose wide mouth is choked with massive sandstone blocks fallen from the roof. Flood waters running in from the north have added layer after layer of sand, reducing the original headway by a full third. Cattle have wintered here for many years. What archeological evidence lies buried under these more recent accumulations may not be said. But among the ancient pictures on the cave wall is an incomplete Basket Maker drawing, one of the finest and brightest of all those seen in this vicinity (fig. 32).

The writer will not venture to suggest the total number of caves in Cottonwood Canyon and its tributaries. He probably saw less than half. Most of them are at least partially screened by dense growths of scrub oak; some are no more than protected nooks or shelters. Three lesser caverns lie on the east side of the valley, between the orchard and Riggs' ranch house. Besides those already described, additional caves surely await detection between the orchard and Water Canyon; yet others will be discovered in that lower portion of Cottonwood not traversed by our reconnaissance.

Riding or walking along the canyon bottom one gains only fleeting views of what is hidden by the trees on either side. To find the caves in which prehistoric man sought refuge one must force a path through tangled brush and brambles. To retrieve the story such caves hold for the student of ancient cultures one must be prepared for slow, tedious work and many disappointments. And the resulting evidence will not always be clear-cut and positive.

FIG. 32.—Basket Maker drawing, Cottonwood Canyon

The largest cave, undoubtedly, in the whole Cottonwood drainage lies within a stone's throw from the Riggs house and now answers in lieu of a barn. I have no record of its dimensions, but during our visit it sheltered several tons of hay, two long mangers for horses, a corral with room enough for half a dozen milk cows, a calf pen, two wagons and a hay rake, a coop unused by a flock of restless chickens, and several hundred square feet of floor space not especially utilized at the time. Our bedroom was the haymow.

That this spacious cave may have been among the first occupied by prehistoric immigrants to Cottonwood Canyon is more than likely. It would seem to embody all that could be desired by primitive folk not too persistently harassed by enemy peoples. Game roamed the near-by mesas; firewood was close at hand; unfailing springs bubbled from green meadows just out in front; arable land bordered those meadows. Under the vaulted roof a dry, level floor offered ample space whereon to build such dwellings as appeared necessary in a cave that of itself furnished sufficient protection from the elements.

But any habitations that may have been erected here in ancient times are no longer traceable. Every vestige has been erased since the coming of the white man. In pioneer days, when colonists traveled back and forth through Cottonwood, the big cave offered the most desirable camping place between Long Valley and Pipe Spring, or even St. George. Eradication of the prehistoric remains probably began in that period, although no information can be gained to-day as to the number or general appearance of those remains. Since 1870 the cave has been utilized by successive owners of the surrounding range, and each in turn has made such alterations as best served his individual needs.

Cottonwood, like the neighboring Cave Lakes Canyon, harbored migratory family groups in very early times. How long that time may be in actual years no one can say even approximately. The Basket Makers were the first to arrive, as far as we know, but they were soon followed by Cliff-dwellers possessing a culture quite typical of their kind, yet less definitely specialized than that of their relatives throughout the San Juan drainage.

Both Basket Makers and Cliff-dwellers were agriculturists, the latter more so than the former. They inhabited the same caves, and the late-comers frequently rifled or destroyed the storage cists and other visible remains of their predecessors. The Basket Makers left no permanent habitations; the Cliff-dwellers were house builders who employed rude masonry at times, and again adobe mud supported by posts. At some sites, notably caves 1 and 4, there appears to be a fusion of the slab-lined Basket Maker cist with the post-and-mud wall of Cliff-dweller houses. This may prove to be only the writer's fancy, for it must be admitted that our hurried observations in this section are inconclusive. Additional and more painstaking study must be made before the two prehistoric cultures represented can be thoroughly and individually understood.

This second visit to Cottonwood Canyon was quite unanticipated; it should be regarded merely as a slightly more detailed phase of the bureau's archeologic reconnaissance north of the Rio Colorado. If it appear that too great a portion of the brief period available was devoted to a few sites, it was because these invited special consideration. Cave 1 had already been disturbed, it will be remembered; cave 3 required but little work other than excavation of the kiva; cave 4 held a mass of shattered masonry through which fragments of post-and-mud walls plainly showed. Something more than superficial examination of these two latter sites seemed desirable, in order that their house remains might be the more directly compared with ruins previously visited in other sections of the State. The writer feels that these studies, though incomplete, were entirely justified. They illustrate in a general way what might be expected at the other sites noted or an equal number yet to be sought out. After two weeks—all too short a time—the writer and his two laborers returned to Kanab, thus concluding the explorations for 1919.

VI. FIELD WORK, SEASON OF 1920

In May, 1920, the writer returned to Kanab for the purpose of bringing these archeological observations to a close. For the final season's work two main objectives were in view: (1) To gain some passing understanding of prehistoric remains west of Kanab Creek, a region we had twice been unable to enter on account of its spring-time aridity, and (2) examination of the ancient ruins on Paria Plateau, north and east of House Rock Valley (fig. 33).

For the third successive time, however, reports of cattlemen recently returned from the April round-up indicated that a horseback trip into that barren section south and west of Antelope Valley would be extremely unwise. In early fall, we were told, when the new grass has started and water pockets still contain vestiges of mid-summer rains, or during the winter months when snow may be melted, such explorations as we had in mind could safely be pursued. At other seasons the handicap imposed by nature seemed too great. The guide with whom tentative arrangements had been made refused to risk his saddle animals under existing conditions. But even though our contemplated reconnaissance was again abandoned through necessity, it did prove possible to make a brief, much-restricted survey by automobile.

With only three days at our disposal we reached the lower Toroweap Valley, examining two caves near Mount Trumbull en route, and the day following our return to Kanab left with pack outfit for Paria Plateau. From the Paria we rode down through House Rock Valley to newly reported ruins in Bed Rock Canyon, and thence across the lower end of Kaibab Plateau to Bright Angel Creek, the sole means of access to ruins near Ribbon Falls and on upper Phantom Creek. This addition to the second phase of our season's program was possible only through unforeseen curtailment of the first.

OBSERVATIONS WEST OF KANAB CREEK

Leaving Kanab early one morning in a light automobile of well-known manufacture—the only machine that could be hired for the purpose—and fortified with a barrel of water, we set out for Heaton's ranch. That far the road was known to be passable; beyond, it was uncertain.

The ranch buildings of Mr. Franklin A. Heaton are utilized chiefly during the winter months, when flocks of sheep range the

124

brown volcanic hills. Drinking water for the establishment is
provided by melting snow and by showers that drain off the metal
roofs of the shearing sheds into covered tanks. The place was absolutely deserted at the time of our visit. Near the corrals a lone

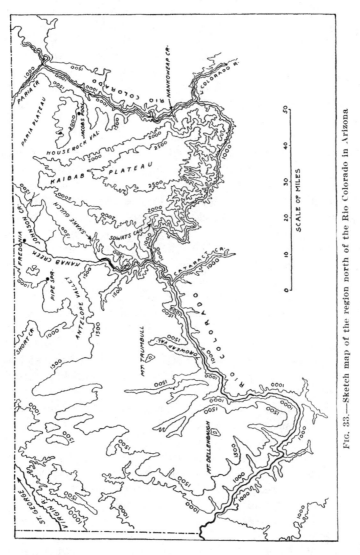

FIG. 33.—Sketch map of the region north of the Rio Colorado in Arizona

sheep wagon offered agreeable camping facilities and a place in
which to dry our clothes, soaked by a late afternoon storm.

While in Kanab we had seen a number of archeological specimens
found the previous winter by herders in the employ of Mr. Heaton.
The lot included an earthen jar, two curved clubs, a bow, and a pair

of sandals.[1] Eleven other pairs of sandals and certain unnamed objects were distributed by the herders and are now lost to science. All were said to have come from a cave near the Heaton ranch, and this cave immediately became of interest in connection with our studies.

CAVE AT HEATON'S RANCH.—The cave from which these specimens were taken lies about one-fourth mile south of the corrals and just at the edge of an ancient lava flow. The opening (pl. 25, b) is so inconspicuous that it will not be noticed until one is close by.

Within the cave a flattish ceiling leaves headway decreasing from 10 to 3 feet (3.04 to 0.91 m.). Large blocks of lava occupy much of the floor area; only where blown earth had accumulated between and over these blocks was habitable space available.* At the rear three small openings give access to half a dozen narrow passageways that wind, serpentlike, round and about, each with a gradual downward trend. These channels are dark and treacherous. They were not utilized, and perhaps not even explored, by the primitive folk who dwelt within the cave. But their yawning mouths furnished convenient receptacles for camp litter, and it was in this rubbish that the specimens above mentioned had been found. Many of them were deposited, no doubt, as mortuary offerings, since scattered human bones gave evidence of disturbed burials.

The tortuous inner passages hold nothing of archeological interest. One enters them bellywise, feeling for solid footing; within, one crawls and clambers about over the jagged rocks. Sometimes prone and sometimes kneeling, we scratched over the ancient débris with sticks and bare fingers for relics that would help identify the original occupants of the cave. Flickering candles furnished our only light. The easily disturbed dust was stifling. But potsherds, found with sandals and wooden implements, show that both Cliff-dwellers and Basket Makers had sojourned here. The evidence of the débris heaps was not exhausted, and we made no search of that portion of the cavern formerly utilized as living quarters. In this latter section there is a semicircular space that seems to have been intentionally cleared, leaving blocks of lava standing at the periphery. No trace of masonry walls is to be seen.

About 300 yards (275.2 m.) west of this cave a 4-foot hole leads vertically into a small chamber worn from the limestone. Entrance is gained by means of a dangling rope. Inspected from an uncertain point of vantage, the cavity contained nothing except three live rattlesnakes.

---

[1] These objects were very generously donated to the national collections by Mr. and Mrs. Heaton, and are now exhibited as numbers 315484–91. They are illustrated in Plates 43, a, 51, 53 of this report.

Toroweap Valley.—From Heaton's ranch an ill-defined road leads down into Toroweap Valley. The trail was made by camp wagons following sheep and cattle to and from their winter range; obviously it was never intended for automobile travel. But with the help of it we advanced to within easy walking distance of the mouth of Toroweap, gazed from the rim into the depths of the Grand Canyon (pl. 26, *b*), and returned to our camp of the night before.

Toroweap Valley is hot in May; it must be insufferable by mid-summer. The lower portion is bordered by treeless hills and paved with brown granular lava. One wonders that ancient man, no less than the herds of to-day, could find sustenance there. But occasional potsherds along the rocky ledges of the canyon give evidence that pre-Pueblo peoples had passed this way and suggest that careful search would discover the crumbling walls of their former dwellings.

The only prehistoric village we observed in this section lies in a broad, open flat about a mile north of Smoot's round-up cabin, or perhaps 8 miles (12.88 kilos) above the mouth of Toroweap Valley. Unworked blocks of limestone and lava comprised the building material; the connected rooms followed the brow of the low, unprotected knoll on which they were erected. Most of the walls are too indistinct for accurate mapping, but Figure 34 illustrates their general arrangement. Potsherds and flint chips lie scattered about, but the old ash heap, if any, is no longer visible.

This single rudely constructed village is no doubt fairly typical of the prehistoric habitations to be found west of Kanab Creek and immediately north of the Grand Canyon. Future explorations, pursued in the proper season and with less restricted means of transportation, should discover similar remains, widely distributed and not too numerous. Mesa ruins and small cliff houses (perhaps mere caches) are reported on the western border of Kanab Creek; pictographs have been seen in deeper recesses of the same canyon; caves in its limestone formation remain unexamined.

Powell makes frequent reference to ruins noted during his exploration of the Rio Colorado; some few of these pertain especially to the region now under consideration. For example, in his diary of September 18, 1870, after having traveled south from Pipe Spring past Mount Trumbull to the bottom of Grand Canyon, the major makes this entry: [2]

On a broad shelf we find the ruins of an old stone house the walls of which are broken down, and we can see where the ancient people who lived there— a race more highly civilized than the present—had made a garden and used a great spring that comes out of the rock for irrigation. On some rocks near

---

[2] Powell, 1875, p. 125.

by we discover some curious etchings. Still searching about, we find an obscure trail up the canyon wall, marked here and there by steps which have been built in the loose rock, elsewhere hewn stairways, and we find a much easier way to go up than that by which we came down in the darkness last night.

Southwest of Mount Trumbull, Dellenbaugh[3] observed on the summit of the peak which bears his name " a circular ruin about 20 feet (6.09 m.) in diameter, with walls remaining 2 feet (0.61 m.) high."

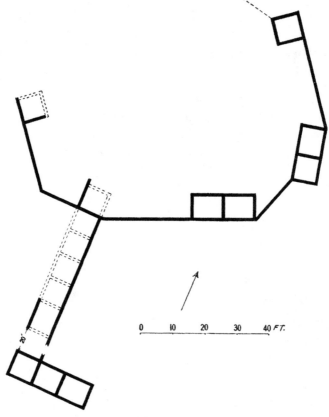

Fig. 34.—Plan of ruin, lower Toroweap Valley

These two quotations help to confirm the impression gained on our hurried trip through Toroweap Valley. Prehistoric sedentary peoples had wandered over these waste lands and left there the indubitable relics of their distinctive culture. Fragments of their broken vessels identify the makers as belonging to the same primitive Pueblo stock as that represented by the ruins near St. George, Pipe Spring, Kanab, and elsewhere. While the small shard series

[3] 1902, p. 310.

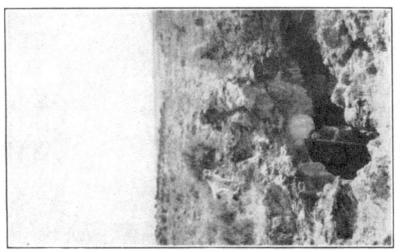

a, Mortar, House Rock Valley

b, Entrance to Heaton Cave

b, From the mouth of Toroweap Valley

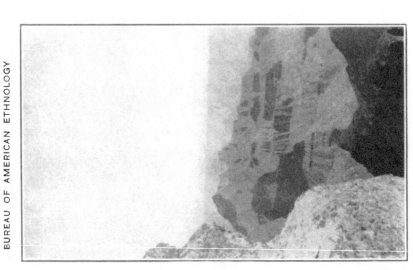

a, From Bright Angel Point

THE GRAND CANYON

a, The Painted Desert from Paria Plateau

b, Ruin near the east rim of Paria Plateau

a, View on Parla Plateau

b, Ruin-covered butte, Paria Plateau

a

b

RUIN ON WHITE BUTTE, PARIA PLATEAU

b. Buckskin Gulch, Paria Plateau

a, The White Pockets, Paria Plateau

from Toroweap Valley is less complete than those obtained at the localities just mentioned, it shows, nevertheless, the characteristic family features of the latter.

PREHISTORIC RUINS ON PARIA PLATEAU

Returning to Kanab, horses and pack mules were saddled and the second phase of the season's reconnaissance was soon under way. The route followed lay generally eastward, across Johnson Run and the upper end of House Rock Valley, with Joseph Hamblin's cow camp " somewhere up on the sand hills " [4] as our immediate destination.

Such ruins as we observed on Paria Plateau may be briefly described. Eight of them were passed one morning between Joe Hamblin's camp and a point on the east rim above the head of Badger Creek. Of these eight, one consisted of but a single room; three were made up of two rooms each; the others were larger. One of the latter, shown in Plate 27, *b*, is fairly representative of all. Its ancient walls are much fallen, and there is about them a noticeable lack of earthy accumulations. It includes two large rooms, each of which probably had been divided (fig. 35). Red sandstone was utilized in construction of these rooms, but the clay which bound the individual blocks together has long since disintegrated.

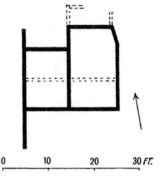

FIG. 35.—Ruin, Paria Plateau

A second ruin (fig. 36), approximately 100 yards (91.7 m.) beyond the east gate of Hamblin's horse pasture, stands on a low sage-covered knoll among the cedars. Its walls, also of red sandstone, are in no place more than three courses high. Thirty feet to the northeast is a small ash heap whose surface was strewn with potsherds. Among these were fragments of black-on-

---

[4] Paria Plateau is better known to residents of Kanab as " the sand hills." Its southern margin, fringed with cedar and piñon, reaches an elevation of 6,500 feet, rising a full thousand feet above the floor of lower House Rock Valley. Journeying northward from the south rim one descends 1,500 feet in less than 20 miles, crossing a region in which the soft, shifting sand increases in direct proportion to the decrease of vegetation. There are no living springs on the Paria. Joseph Hamblin waters his cattle from a reservoir that catches such rains as fall on 15 acres of bare white sandstone. Toward the north, near Buckskin Gulch, a sunken box of logs collects seepage partially to supply the herds of Walter Hamblin. Midway between the two camps the " lower reservoir " gathers the drainage from neighboring slopes. It was here we found the Hamblin brothers, sons of Jacob Hamblin, famed Mormon scout and Indian missionary. Joseph, the elder of the two, with his father, had been in the employ of Maj. J. W. Powell during the latter's exploration of the Rio Colorado in 1869–1872.

white, plain, and corrugated vessels. The latter ware was most frequently represented; plain shards were in a decided minority.

The largest ruin visited on the plateau occupies the flat top of a
white sandstone butte (pl. 28, *b*) 2 miles or more northeast of Hamblin's upper reservoir. Figure 37 illustrates the arrangement of rooms
and defensive walls; Plate 29, *a*, *b*, shows the present demolished
condition of the ancient village. Its walls were constructed directly
upon the bare summit of the hill, blocks of unworked sandstone from
the talus below furnishing the building material. Three upright
slabs at the south end of the house group mark the position of a
small storage cist. There is no evidence of a circular kiva. Potsherds of the usual types occur sparingly in the open court; they are
vastly more numerous on the surrounding slopes.

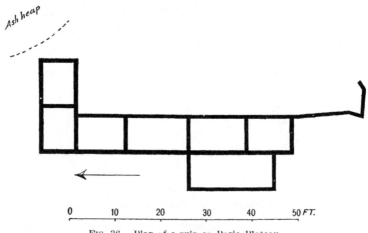

FIG. 36.—Plan of a ruin on Paria Plateau

Toward the north end of the plateau Buckskin Gulch has cut a
deep, narrow path into Paria Canyon (pl. 30, *b*). We had heard
much of an ancient dam in this section—a dam, with spillway,
constructed for irrigation purposes before raging floods bisected
it and carved out the present impassable gorge. It takes time even
for nature to dig through 300 feet of solid sandstone. But after
some search the "dam" was found—an elongate pile of waterworn bowlders and other detritus washed down from higher ground.
It has no connection whatsoever with the prehistoric occupancy
of Paria Plateau.

Buckskin Gulch proved an effective barrier in ancient times and
forced primitive man to make his way around it. As he passed
its less formidable head he pecked a series of pictographs on a
red cliff; below its mouth he pounded out holes for toes and fingers
as he marked several pathways across Paria Canyon. About 5

miles above Lee's Ferry another series of rock carvings is reported; below the latter several small cliff houses or caches are known.

Walter Hamblin's watering trough is sheltered by a dozen cottonwoods a mile south of Buckskin Gulch. Ruins we could not locate were described along the red ledges northwest of the corrals. In a short canyon behind the camp house numerous fragments of chipped flint and earthenware vessels, mostly plain ware,

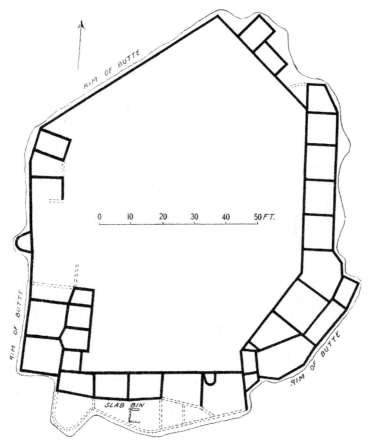

Fig. 37.—Plan of a ruin on white butte, Paria Plateau

were observed. Only one shard of black-on-white pottery was seen here. No prehistoric dwelling sites were detected during the course of our hasty inspection, but it is quite possible that several such have been covered by shifting sand or completely effaced during the centuries since their abandonment.

In the gap just north of the White Pockets (pl. 30, a), a striking landmark from almost any section of Paria Plateau, is a small cave containing the fallen masonry of several houses. Around the cliff to the southeast a somewhat larger cave likewise had sheltered prehistoric peoples. Its ceiling is still black from ancient fires, but any dwellings that may formerly have stood here have been reduced to a few scattered stones. It was in this cave, according to cowboys, that two reed arrows and a yucca sandal were found some years ago. A third cliff-dwelling was reported on the edge of a high butte in this same vicinity, but we were unable to locate it.

High up among the sand-scoured cones of the White Pockets are several small natural reservoirs that hold water throughout the greater part of the dry season. No stranger would suspect their presence, but upon more than one occasion they have proved a boon to horses and men well-nigh famished from thirst on the blistering white sands of Paria Plateau. Pecked steps lead to at least two of these tanks, showing that the ancient inhabitants drew at times upon the limited water supply.

As one rides the length of the plateau potsherds are frequently to be observed. They occur most often on those knolls and more elevated ridges that afforded some slight relief from the prevailing sand. Along the higher east and south margins of the plateau cedars and an occasional rock pine indicate a somewhat heavier rainfall than is experienced on the borders of Buckskin Gulch. These more favored sections naturally attracted the prehistoric housebuilders; it is here that we find their ruined dwellings. Many of them are situated toward the east, overlooking the desolation of the Painted Desert; still more are located along the southern rim. It was Joseph Hamblin who assured us that between the head of Soap Creek and Two-Mile Spring ruins are to be found on nearly every knoll among the cedars.

The availability of tabular sandstone was unquestionably an important factor in the aboriginal settlement of Paria Plateau. And yet it seems to have added but little to the permanence of such dwellings as were erected there. One notices especially the absence of basestones, an almost constant feature of Cottonwood Canyon ruins. They occur again at Two-Mile Spring. It is generally agreed that upright slabs were intended to hold back the sand or loose earth on which many ancient houses were built in this section of the Southwest. But basestones are often found where such precautions seem entirely unwarranted. Perhaps their use, at first a constructional necessity, ebbed with a change of environment. One might reasonably expect to find them employed in ruins at the north end of the plateau, in the vicinity of Buckskin Gulch; more rarely in those less sandy districts to the east and south.

But whatever their architectural problems, the prehistoric inhabitants of the Paria may be identified—and this, after all, is the important thing—from the pottery they made and used. The shards to be gathered at every dwelling site stamp the ancient housebuilders as relatives of those same Puebloan groups whose moldering habitations have already been described in this report. Plain and corrugated cooking pots, black-on-white bowls and jars, are represented. Vessels made from red clays and ornamented with black geometric designs occur less commonly. From superficial examination one type of pottery will appear to predominate at a given ruin; half a mile away another ware will be most in evidence. Taken as a whole, however, these fragments establish a close relationship between the occupants of Paria Plateau and those families that dwelt in House Rock Valley and the broad drainage of Kanab Creek.

The same people undoubtedly built the houses whose ruined walls, in the very gorge of the Rio Colorado, Powell, Dellenbaugh, and the Kolb brothers each in turn describe. Their respective observations pertain especially to that section of the river between the junction of the Grand and Green and the mouth of Paria Canyon, but ruins, trails, and rock carvings were seen farther down. If such occurrences are less frequent below the Paria it is only because the deeper recesses of the Grand Canyon offer fewer sites that would have tempted prehistoric Indians to the construction of permanent habitations. Such dwellings, however, were erected on the higher ledges.

Cattlemen of southern Utah report small cliff ruins in Sentinel Rock Creek, which joins the Colorado just north of the Paria. Both cliff-dwellings and pictographs have been observed at the Kitchen Corrals, near Molly's Nipple, on the headwaters of Paria Creek.

The Ruins of Bed Rock Canyon

From Paria Plateau we rode southward past Two-Mile Spring and Cane Spring, more intimately associated with the explorations of 1918, to Bed Rock Canyon, at the south end of House Rock Valley. Bed Rock Canyon is a shallow, waterless, rock-walled gorge just north of Saddle Canyon. Mr. Eric Cram, of Kanab, had reported ruins in this vicinity not seen during our earlier reconnaissance, and it was desired to make cursory examination of them.

The prehistoric habitations here are more numerous than one would suspect. They are to be found on each side of the canyon, situated, in most instances, on bare projecting points. Their ancient walls were built up of undressed limestone blocks gathered from near-by ledges. These walls are now rarely more than two or three courses high; the highest wall we saw in a dozen ruins stood less than 4 feet. The amount of fallen stone outlining the individual rooms is insufficient to have formed a wall of more than half the required height. It would seem, therefore, that at least the upper walls in the Bed Rock Canyon ruins had been constructed of adobe or other disintegrable material.

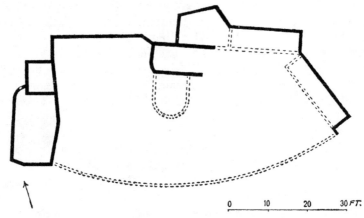

FIG. 38.—Plan of a ruin, Bed Rock Canyon

Three of these prehistoric villages are represented by the accompanying ground plans. Figure 38 shows an irregular group of houses, more or less complete and conforming to the outline of the bluff on which it stands. On the east side of the canyon is a second ruin (fig.

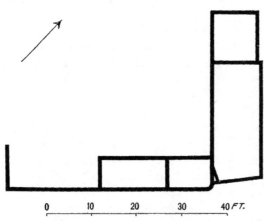

FIG. 39.—Plan of a ruin, Bed Rock Canyon

39), likewise made of undressed blocks of l i m e s t o n e. It is L-shaped and includes four rooms, with a projecting wall at the south end suggestive of unfinished dwellings. Inasmuch as no stones were f o u n d across the open side of this long room, wattled work or adobe may have completed the structure.

The third ruin (fig. 40) to which more than passing attention was given stands on the canyon edge in a less easily defended position than that occupied by most of its neighbors. Two large rooms of exceptional shape adjoin a series of three rectangular structures. Near by, but at the base of a 4-foot ledge, is a room 15 feet (4.57 m.)

square. The walls of these six houses are in no place more than 2 feet (0.61 m.) high. Since surprisingly few fallen stones are present, one is almost convinced that some additional, less permanent material had been utilized in completion of these dwellings. Pottery scattered over the surface indicates that here, as at all the other groups visited, occupancy had continued throughout a given period.

Many additional ruins of from one to four rooms each lie along the borders of Bed Rock Canyon. Most of these appear on the upper ledge, which varies in thickness from 2 to 4 feet (0.61–1.22 m.); a few, however, were constructed at the top of the low talus just beneath the limestone cap. Some distance back from the rim are several one-room buildings. Two of these were also noted in the bottom of the canyon, a rather precarious location.

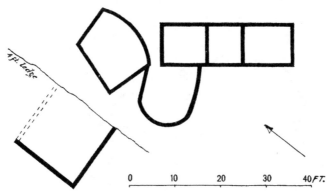

Fig. 40.—Plan of a ruin, Bed Rock Canyon

Potsherds are extremely plentiful at all these sites, and decorated ware apparently predominates. Fragments of bowls and jars showing black-on-white decoration are especially numerous. The surface slip is well polished; the designs seem to be more intricate and varied than those represented at other ruin sites throughout northwestern Arizona. Black-on-red shards likewise seem more numerous here than elsewhere. Among them are several fragments of what Kidder would probably call proto-Kayenta ware; that is, red decorations outlined in black over a cream-colored slip.[5] A number of bowl shards possess the outflaring Kayenta rim. Boldly hachured designs are also present on both red and white pottery. The ruins along Bed Rock Canyon were seemingly built and occupied by more progressive groups than those who dwelt in upper House Rock Valley. A certain time element may be involved, but our brief examination tends to indicate that the prehistoric peoples of this locality were somewhat more advanced culturally than those

---

[5] Kidder, 1924, p. 72.

represented by the slab-walled houses near Two-Mile Spring, for example, or the rude valley dwellings above New House Rock corrals.

Future exploration should disclose numerous village sites along the south and east margins of House Rock Valley. Its tilted west wall, and especially those little twisted canyons that break into it, are known to shelter small ruins.

Saddle Canyon is a northern tributary of the Nankoweap, and storage cists or caches are reported at frequent intervals throughout the length of both. Such structures should indicate the proximity of cliff-dwellings or mesa ruins. Some few of them were examined in 1918; others, two years later. In general their size was governed by the space available. They are uniformly built of crude masonry, in weathered holes and under overhanging ledges. Plate 32, *b*, gives

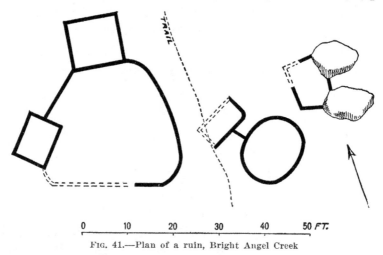

FIG. 41.—Plan of a ruin, Bright Angel Creek

a fair impression as to the character and location of these isolated storehouses. Rarely are they grouped.

One such series, however, we did find—half a dozen or more small, unprotected rooms whose walls, at the base of a limestone cliff, were barely traceable. The group was divided by a cave, perhaps 7 feet (2.13 m.) wide and 10 feet (3.04 m.) deep, utilized as living quarters by the prehistoric farmers. Pack rats had preempted the cavern, crowding it to the very roof with sticks, cacti, and other rubbish. A masonry wall with doorway barred the entrance; smoke stains showed plainly on the rounded ceiling. It seems quite plausible that hidden granaries such as these, occasionally accompanied by houses, were owned by more or less independent families who erected their principal habitations back upon the mesa tops. Those ruins we saw in 1918 on the south slope of Saddle Mountain are quite typical of such dwellings. They are mostly one-, two-, and three-room structures, built of rough, undressed limestone blocks.

Our 1920 trail followed that of 1918 through upper Saddle Canyon and out upon the summit of Kaibab Plateau. Fallen timber, treacherous rocks, and snow banks added spice to the ride. Southward lay the head of Bright Angel Creek, in whose deep gorge two groups of ancient ruins invited inspection. One of these was reported at Ribbon Falls, the other on Phantom Creek. Neither could be reached, except from the north, through Bright Angel.[6]

OBSERVATIONS IN BRIGHT ANGEL CREEK

As one journeys down toward the Grand Canyon, Beaver Creek[7] is the first large tributary entering Bright Angel from the east (fig. 19). About a mile and a quarter above the mouth of Beaver

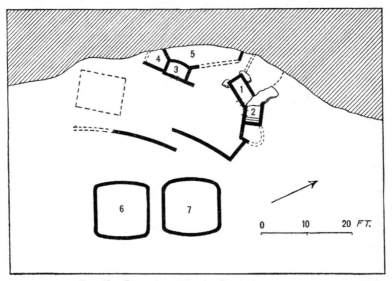

FIG. 42.—Plan of a cliff ruin, Bright Angel Creek

Creek the trail bisects a small ruin (fig. 41) whose irregular walls were constructed of unshaped limestone and sandstone blocks. These have mostly collapsed; all traces of mortar have disappeared, and at first sight the house group seems no more than a mere temporary camp where loose stones had been piled up for protection. In and about the old walls, however, many fragments of pottery are to be found, including black-on-red. Two views of these ruins are reproduced in Plate 33, a, b.

---

[6] The suspension bridge that now connects the north and south rims of the Grand Canyon was not completed until May 15, 1921.

[7] A National Park Service sign on the trail at the mouth of this stream in 1920 bore the name "Wall Creek," although it has been known for the past 30 years as Beaver Creek. Beavers still inhabit the canyon. During the summer of 1923 representatives of the Milwaukee Public Museum visited and described a number of ruins in Bright Angel Canyon. See West, 1925.

On the opposite side of the canyon, directly under but far below Bright Angel Point, is a small cliff house (pl. 34, *a, b;* fig. 42) partially sheltered by a high, perpendicular cliff. Rooms 1–4 were obviously granaries, although their doorways were neither grooved nor provided with loopholes for the retention of door slabs. The fairly level though rock-strewn platform on which these storerooms stand is fronted by a two-section retaining wall with passageway between. Eighteen feet below is a second terrace, on which the fallen masonry of two large houses may be seen. The indistinct walls of other habitations are present on both the upper and lower platforms. All were built of sandstone blocks roughly put together. Room 2 is of particular interest, owing to the fact that against its inner southeast wall a split cottonwood log 10 inches (25.4 cm.) wide had been embedded in the masonry 16 inches (40.6 cm.) above the floor. This bench or shelf is visible through the open door of the right-hand room in Plate 34, *b.*

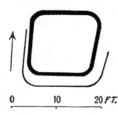

0   10   20 *FT.*

Fig. 43.—Terraced ruin, Bright Angel Creek

Corncobs, squash stems, and fragments of pottery were noted on the face of the débris heap northeast of room 2. Only one shard of black-on-red was observed at this particular site. Three metates or milling stones lay exposed on the upper terrace.

Perhaps half a mile north of Beaver Creek an elevation of some prominence looks out upon the canyon floor. Surmounting it is a single room of prehistoric construction. From opposite ends of this room masonry walls protrude as though to form two sides of a square. Close on the east piles of stone mark the sites once occupied by other dwellings now in total ruin. Below this hill and west of the trail is a very large "yant pit,"[8] a relic of those days when Kaibab Indians wintered on Bright Angel Creek.

A quarter mile farther down canyon, 75 feet (22.8 m.) west of the trail and about 200 feet (60.9 m.) from the stream, one notices a lone room resting upon a man-made terrace averaging 16 inches (40.6 cm.) in height. Plate 32, *a,* shows the irregular limestone blocks with which this dwelling was constructed, but does not illustrate its retaining wall. The latter lies down slope; by aid of it level space for the old house was provided. The greater area of the terrace left a platform on three sides of the building (fig. 43). Puebloan pottery with its characteristic types of decora-

---

[8] "Yant" or "yamp" is also known as "Indian potato" by the Mormons of southwestern Utah. It is the yampa (*Carum gairdneri*) of the Paiute. Formerly the Indians roasted large quantities of the root in shallow pits of greater or less diameter. After a large fire had been reduced to glowing coals green grass was thrown on, then the yampa, then more grass, and finally earth, leaving the mass to steam for several hours.

a

b

RUINS ON BED ROCK CANYON, HOUSE ROCK VALLEY

b, Small storeroom in Saddle Canyon

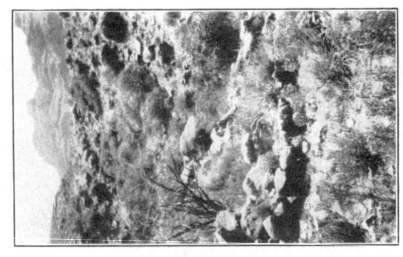

a, Ruin, Bright Angel Creek

a

b

RUIN, BRIGHT ANGEL CREEK

a

b

CLIFF-DWELLING, BRIGHT ANGEL CREEK

a

b

RUINS NEAR UPPER RIBBON FALLS

a

b

IN BRIGHT ANGEL CREEK

tion may be gathered near by. High in the opposite wall of Bright Angel Canyon stand the remnants of an isolated granary.

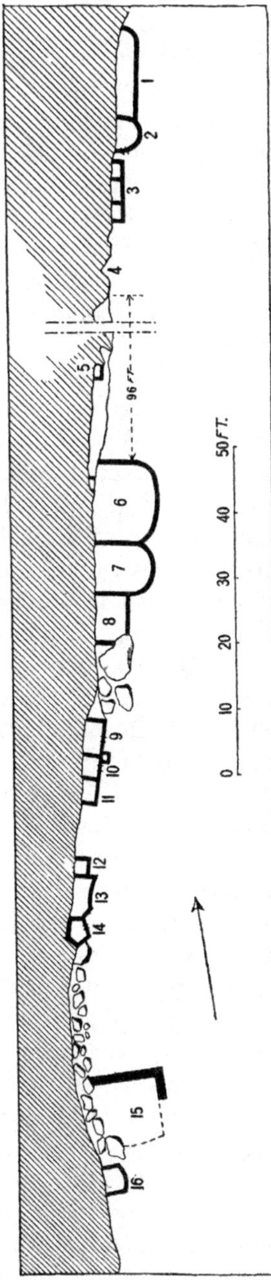

Two hundred yards below the terraced house the trail passes a second yampa pit 20 feet (6.1 m.) in diameter. Additional ovens of the same character probably exist throughout the upper half of the canyon, wherever the Paiutes found suitable sites for their brush shelters.

RUINS NEAR RIBBON FALLS.—Lower Ribbon Falls may be seen from Bright Angel Trail. It wins exclamations from all who pass this way. But if one climbs the bowlder-covered dome to the north and advances a half mile or so one enters a huge amphitheater whose rock walls, towering a full thousand feet, echo the rushing waters of the upper falls. Few people have looked upon the beauty of this secluded valley.

Under the most prominent cliff and close by the cataract is a long series of storerooms (pl. 35, *a*, *b;* fig. 44). They occupy every weathered hole that promised protection from such storms as beat against the cliff. Toward the south end of this group several larger rooms served as dwellings; basestones were present in three of them. About 100 feet (30.5 m.) southeast of these houses a large bowlder furnished a buttress against which two additional habitations had been constructed. Like the granaries, these houses were built of unworked sandstone; their masonry is rough and unplastered. Other similar structures would doubtless be disclosed were one to make careful search of the grassy valley.

It should be noted that almost no pottery was observed near the upper Ribbon Falls ruins. Less than a double handful of shards were found, and this small lot contained but one fragment each of black-on-white and black-on-red.

FIG. 44.—Plan of cliff ruins and storerooms near upper Ribbon Falls

Our original plan had been to continue down Bright Angel to ruins reported on upper Phantom Creek. Melting snows and late spring rains conspired, however, to prevent materialization of this plan. Bright Angel Creek was abnormally high, and after fording it six times, not without danger, it seemed advisable to leave our horses at Beaver Creek and proceed on foot to Ribbon Falls. Below this point Bright Angel enters a narrow gorge and its single trail is forced into the very stream bed. With raging torrents running, the lower canyon was obviously impassable. Occasional ruins probably rest on the ledges below Ribbon Falls, although the writer is inclined to believe that the prehistoric peoples erected most of their dwellings in that more habitable middle portion of Bright Angel Canyon through which we passed. Here was space for isolated houses; tillable land lay near by; and the rock ledges on either side offered sheltered nooks for storage chambers. But such ruins as we saw bear no evidence of long-continued occupancy.

Of the ruins on Phantom Creek little is known other than that they exist. Descriptions vary somewhat. They have been pictured as sizable cliff villages, and again like the granaries at upper Ribbon Falls. A map of Kaibab National Forest published in 1917 represents " ancient ruins " not only at Ribbon Falls and on upper Phantom Creek, but below Cape Royal and at many other localities on the reservation. The larger number of these ruins, as described by rangers and trappers familiar with the whole plateau, are storage rooms built under sheltering ledges. But with these present there is every reason to believe that ancient dwellings, now mere piles of stone, no doubt, are to be found not far away.

Major Powell discovered a small group of ruins at the mouth of Bright Angel Creek in 1869. On the afternoon of August 15 he and his men camped on a sand bar; the next day the major explored a little gulch just above camp, and in it found the fallen walls of two or three masonry houses.[9] Here he observed an old mealing stone and a large quantity of broken pottery. The published notes of this indefatigable explorer show that traces of prehistoric habitations were seen at intervals throughout much of the distance he traveled. Quotations from his reports have been made in the preceding pages without exhausting the list.

Powell gave to the prehistoric Indians who once dwelt in this plateau country the name of Shinumo, and " Shinumo Creek," some 20 miles (32.2 kilos) below the mouth of Bright Angel, suggests that he observed ancient dwellings here also. A short distance farther down canyon the Powell party camped on August 20, 1869, and here, " on a terrace of trap," writes the major, " we discovered

---

[9] Powell, 1875, p. 87.

another group of ruins. There was evidently quite a village on this rock. Again we find mealing stones and much broken pottery, and up on a little natural shelf in the rock back of the ruins we find a globular basket that would hold perhaps one-third of a bushel. It is badly broken, and as I attempt to take it up it falls to pieces. There are many beautiful chips, as if this had been the home of an old arrow maker."[10]

Still other ruins, to cite but one more example, were noted in Tapeats Creek, about 12 miles (19.3 kilos) east of Kanab Canyon.[11]

References such as these confirm the statements of " Uncle Jim " Owens and other trappers that small caches are to be found under the canyon rim almost any place east of Powell's Plateau. Very few of these structures, however, are large enough to have been utilized as dwellings.

Archeological Remains West of Kaibab Plateau

From Bright Angel Creek we turned toward Kanab, following the main road through Big Park (De Motte), without making particular search for ruins, and on to the ranger station at the north end of Pleasant Valley. From this point our trail bore northwest to the head of Moquitch Canyon,[12] a southern tributary of upper Snake Gulch.[13] This deviation from the easier route was prompted by the thought that Moquitch Canyon must have received its name on account of some evidence within its borders of prehistoric ruins.

Although careful watch was kept throughout the entire length of this short canyon, only three small ruins were observed. These occupied restricted shelters underneath overhanging ledges; in each instance their masonry walls had almost completely collapsed. Very few caves suitable for human occupancy exist in the main canyon; its many branches are even less promising. Ruins may, indeed, be found on the sage-covered terraces, although none was observed by us. Fragments of pottery or other artifacts of like antiquity were rarely to be seen along the trail.

Like Moquitch Canyon, Shinumo Canyon (or Snake Gulch, as it is now called) possesses a name that savors of prehistoric remains. Previous inquiry had elicited the information that extensive series of pictographs are to be found in lower Snake Gulch, and Mr. J. C. Roak, former supervisor of Kaibab National Forest, recalled that

---

[10] Powell, 1875, p. 90.

[11] Dellenbaugh, 1908, p. 240.

[12] Moquitch is the Paiute corruption of Moqui (dead people), a name expressing the contempt in which the Hopi have long been held by their tribal enemies.

[13] On the U. S. Geological Survey topographic sheet, edition of 1886, reprinted in 1915, Snake Gulch is marked " Shinumo Canyon."

he had seen in the general neighborhood of these drawings small caves with smoked ceilings and traces of masonry walls. Our intention had been to examine such sites as might be found there, but the trip was necessarily abandoned, both on account of the exhausted condition of our saddle animals and the reported lack of forage and water. Because Snake Gulch has been cut through the limestone and down into sandstone formations, it is not at all improbable that prehistoric remains exist there—ruins more extensive than those observed in Moquitch Canyon.

Supervisor Roak also mentioned several round rooms seen by him on a ridge overlooking Sowats Canyon, a branch of the southernmost tributary of Kanab Creek from the east. His observations had been most casual, but the circles were remembered as being of stone, the tops of which just showed above ground. Pottery was not observed in their vicinity.

Leaving the cool forested summit of Kaibab Plateau, our trail led rather abruptly down into the broad sandy valley of Johnson Creek, blistering hot under the noonday sun, to Fredonia and then to Kanab. The season's reconnaissance was thus brought to an end, and with it the bureau's archeological observations north of the Rio Colorado. It goes without saying that these six successive years of reconnaissance were not exhaustive; indeed, they were not intended to be. Many sections of northwestern Arizona and southwestern Utah, in addition to those enumerated herein, unquestionably contain evidence of prehistoric sedentary peoples. Such remains, however, should agree very closely with those described in the foregoing pages. This is especially true as regards the degree of culture they represent. It is to be hoped, nevertheless, that intensive excavation may be undertaken at several of the sites we visited or at other equally desirable locations in order that the prehistoric culture of these western canyons may be better understood and more accurately compared with the culture of those related peoples who dwelt east of the Colorado.

There now remain for brief consideration the lesser antiquities gathered during the course of these observations.

VII. CULTURAL MATERIAL

Inasmuch as the explorations reviewed in the foregoing pages were planned and pursued as a reconnaissance only, it would be presumptuous to attempt at this time more than a general description of the cultural material collected during these explorations. Detailed consideration must await thorough investigation at individual sites, yet a preliminary understanding of the problems involved is not only desirable but quite possible from the specimens now in hand. Some mention has already been made of the objects recovered at Paragonah in 1917 by the joint Smithsonian Institution-University of Utah expedition.[1] These represent but a single locality; it remains now to compare them with like objects collected at other sites north of the Rio Colorado. In this preliminary presentation brief attention will be directed to the pottery, the bone implements, stone implements, wooden artifacts. textiles, vegetal food, and the skeletal remains.

POTTERY

No bowls are represented among the shards collected at Willard. All the pottery fragments are from plain-ware jars;[2] a few rim pieces have handles attached (pl. 37, c, d, h). The paste from which these vessels were made was fairly even, though friable; in general it was not overtempered. Minute particles of mica appear in some fragments, sand in others. The larger proportion of the shards are dark gray in color and blackened by use over fires. Most of them are well smoothed, though less highly polished than is characteristic of vessels at more southerly sites. No surface slip was employed.

The only evidence of decoration on the Willard fragments occurs on three which show thumb-nail impressions at the base of the neck— impressions like those on a specimen found at Salt Lake City by Hayden in 1870 (pl. 37, e). One shard (pl. 37, h) bears pinched-up nodes; another carries a narrow band of red ocher, perhaps accidentally applied after the vessel had been fired. Maguire notes the finding of three or four black-on-white fragments during his excavations here and his statement is confirmed by local residents. No

---

[1] Judd, 1919a.

[2] The statement made by Judd, 1917a, p. 120, that corrugated ware was found at Willard is obviously an error. A review of the series shows nothing but plain jar fragments.

decorated fragments other than those mentioned were disclosed during the bureau's investigations in 1915.

At Beaver and Paragonah plain-ware jars apparently represented about 50 per cent of the pottery in use. But unlike those from Willard, the Beaver and Paragonah jars are characterized by a fine gray clay and are exceptionally well polished. This light gray paste and superior finish together form the earmark of such vessels when found at the two sites last indicated. Corrugated jars also evidence a high skill in the potter's art; most of them are well polished inside. The coils range from exceptionally fine to coarse; some few specimens are especially ornamented by alternating indented and short plain coils, as in Plate 37, *n*. Rubbed-over coils with grooves that tend to be vertical are not uncommon at these more northern sites. Holmes [3] figures a cooking pot with wide flat neckbands and plain globular body—a typical pre-Pueblo specimen—from Palmer's St. George collection. Like vessels are rarely represented in our shard series,

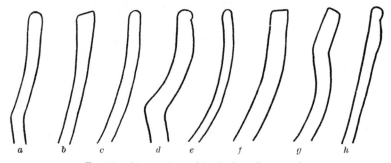

FIG. 45.—Rim sections of bowls from Paragonah

and then only from ruins south of the Utah-Arizona border. Painted jars were rare at Paragonah and apparently unknown at Beaver; they were present but not common on Paria Plateau and in House Rock Valley.

Although bowl fragments from Beaver and Paragonah are sometimes plain, most of them carry a black-on-white ornamentation. Decorated bowls with exterior coiling were used sparingly from Paragonah southward. Where a surface slip appears on vessels from these northerly ruins it is a slaty gray rather than the clear white found throughout the San Juan drainage, for example. This dull color is especially characteristic of decorated pottery at Beaver and Paragonah; it forms a distinguishing base color unlike that found elsewhere in the Southwest, so far as we are aware. In addition, bowl rims are often dished, as shown in Figure 45. *a*, *d*, *g*, and in Plate 39, *c*, a specimen from Beaver. Interlineal and external ornamentation with "fugitive" red paint, applied after firing and

FRAGMENTS OF JARS AND COOKING POTS

FRAGMENTS OF DECORATED POTTERY

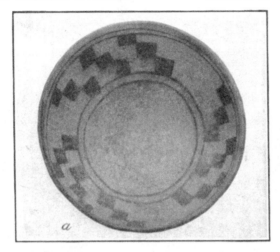

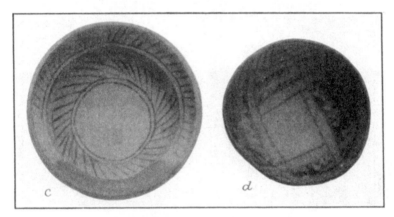

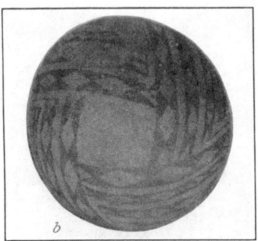

FOOD BOWLS

SMALL JARS AND PITCHERS

PLAIN AND COILED WARE COOKING POTS

a

b

COILED COOKING POTS FROM BEAVER

COOKING POT FROM HEATON CAVE

WATER JAR FROM KANAB

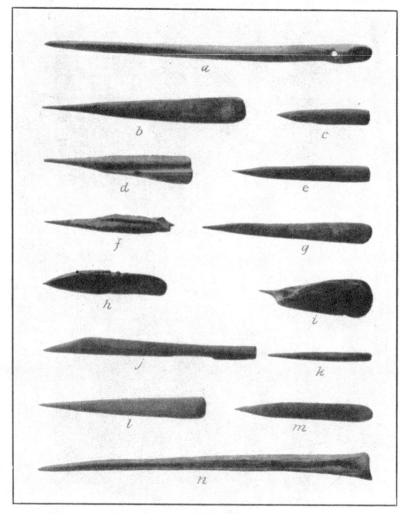

BONE AWLS

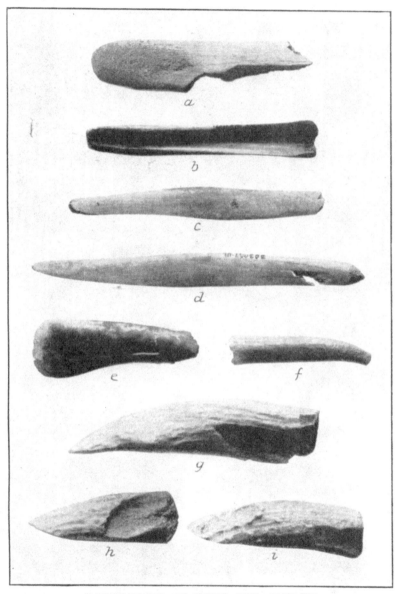

IMPLEMENTS OF BONE AND ANTLER

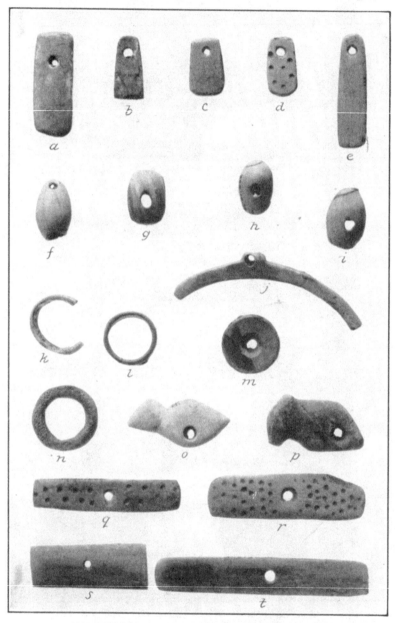

ORNAMENTS OF BONE, STONE, AND SHELL

PIPES OF CLAY AND STONE

METATES OR MILLING STONES

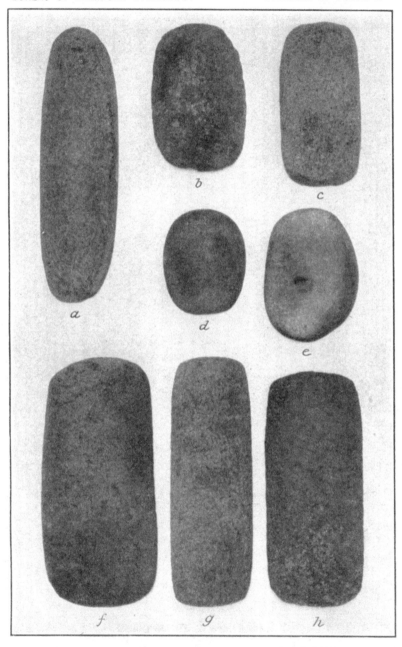

STONES FOR GRINDING AND SMOOTHING

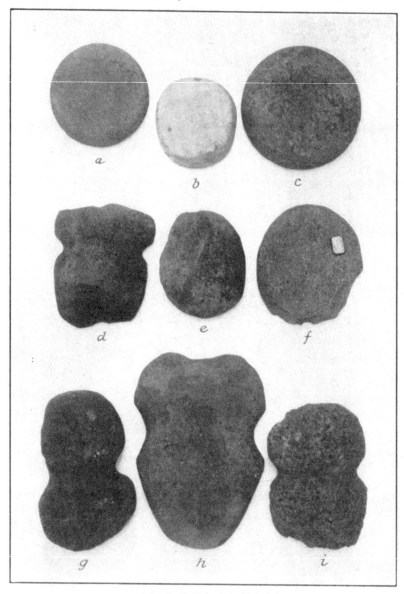

IMPLEMENTS OF STONE

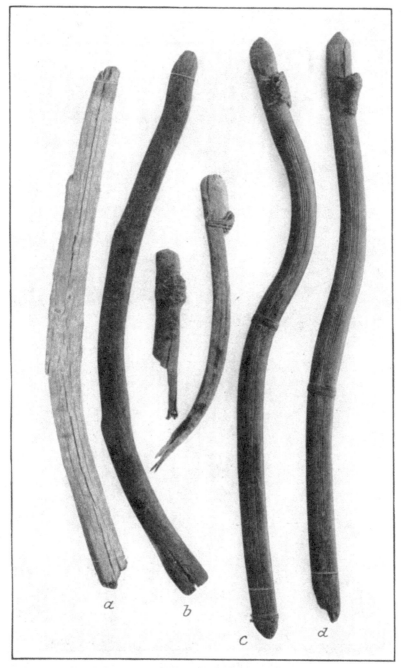

CURVED CLUBS FROM HEATON CAVE

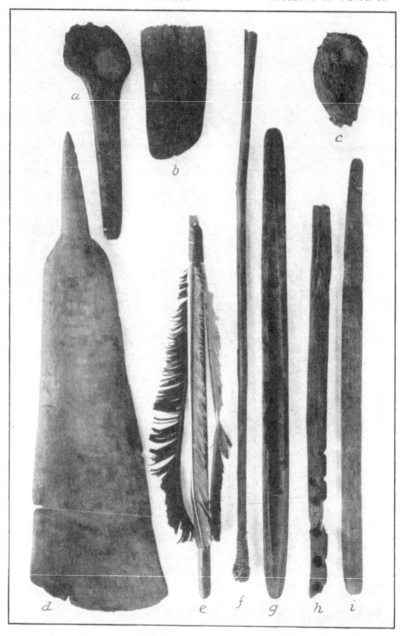

VARIOUS OBJECTS FROM UTAH CAVES

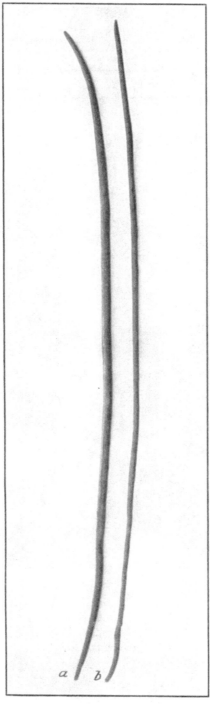

a, BOW. *b*, POINTED STICK.
HEATON CAVE

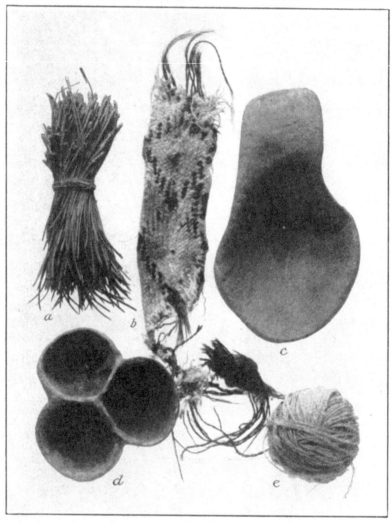

OBJECTS FROM UTAH CAVES

a, Hairbrush of pine needles; *b*, fragment of carrying band; *c*, dipper of mountain sheep horn; *d*, pottery paint cup; *e*, ball of cord

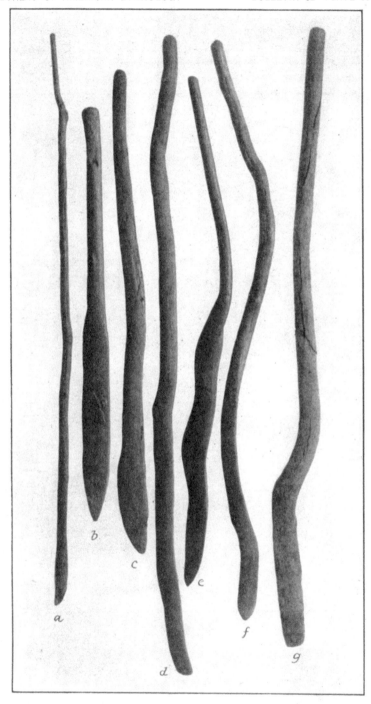

AGRICULTURAL IMPLEMENTS OF WOOD

BASKETRY

SANDALS

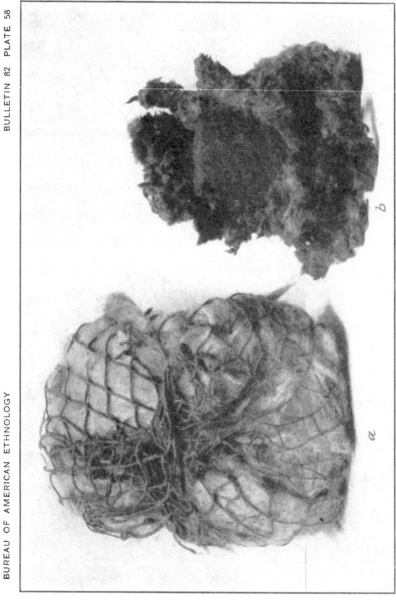

a, Netting containing mountain goat hair

b, Red ocher wrapped in rabbit fur

CORN FROM CAVE 1, COTTONWOOD CANYON

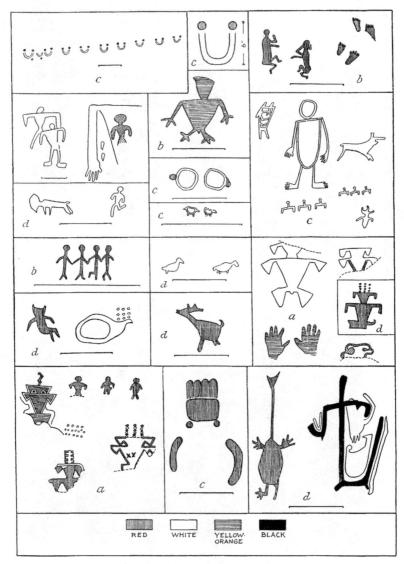

COTTONWOOD CANYON PICTOGRAPHS

a, Cave 1; *b,* Cave 5; *c,* Cave 7; *d,* Flower Cave.   The bar scale represents 12 inches

DESIGNS ON FOOD BOWLS

a–e, From Paragonah, cat. no. 303209; *f–n,* from Beaver

hence easily removed, is frequently encountered in Beaver and Parowan Valleys; less often, apparently, farther south.

In contrast to such sites as those represented by the mounds at Beaver and Paragonah, the stone-walled ruins in Cottonwood Canyon, in House Rock Valley, in Bright Angel Creek, and on the Paria Plateau are accompanied by bowl fragments with a slip much whiter in color. There is less of the slaty gray so characteristic of more northerly ruins. The white is whiter and the black of the decoration is blacker. Also there is a greater variety of design. Black-on-red ware occurs more frequently, and especially in lower House Rock Valley shards of Kidder's proto-Kayenta ware [4] are occasionally seen. Only in these rather limited areas closely bordering the Rio Colorado south of Paria Creek and east of Kaibab Plateau were shards found bearing the polychrome decoration, the peculiar design, or the outflaring rim of proto-Kayenta pottery.

BONE IMPLEMENTS

Implements and ornaments made from mammal bones, chiefly deer, form a noticeably large proportion of the artifacts recovered during explorations at Paragonah. It seems that almost every kind of object capable of being carved from bone with flint knives was manufactured here by the prehistoric inhabitants. Numerically, awls rank first. These range from the small, slightly worked metapodial of the deer to longer, heavier instruments fashioned from the cannon bone. In general these awls were shaped from broken bones and splinters; those which have been carefully worked and smoothed are in a decided minority. The proportion of crude to finished awls is even more marked at other sites represented in this report, yet it must be borne in mind that our only intensive excavations were undertaken at Paragonah. Awls found in Cottonwood Canyon and in Heaton's Cave are rather short and stubby.

Wedges and punches made from antler are rather common at Paragonah; also scrapers or knives fashioned from deer ribs. Other characteristic bone objects from Parowan Valley are "game counters" (pl. 46, q–t) and pendants. These range from plain to highly specialized forms and vary widely in size and workmanship. Many of them were painted red on the chipped side. "Game counters" do not appear in our collections from ruins south of the Great Basin.

STONE IMPLEMENTS

Metates, or mills, were the largest stone utensils employed by the prehistoric peoples of western Utah. A striking yet fairly characteristic feature of these mills is the small depressed area at the upper end of the grinding surface (pl. 48, a–c). At Willard fully

---

[4] Kidder, 1924, p. 72.

75 per cent of the metates piled along field fences possess this lesser depression. Milling stones of the same type occur less frequently farther south, but even there they were not wholly displaced by those of simpler form. Kidder photographed a like metate near Moab, in southwestern Utah, where adobe-walled houses are known; Hough[5] described examples of the same apparent type from pit dwellings at Luna, New Mexico. The present writer recalls no other localities where this specialized milling stone has been found. A tentative explanation of this secondary basin is that it served to hold grain or meal during the grinding operation.

Manos for use on these metates, smoothing and rubbing stones, hammers, and pottery polishers from ruins north of the Rio Colorado are not especially different from those found in other Pueblo areas. Perhaps the only exception that need be made to this general statement is that the manos of western Utah were rarely used on more than one side. Thin manos and those triangular in cross section are absent. Any rubbing or grinding stone within reach served for pulverizing the red paint so habitually employed in Parowan Valley. Carefully rounded stone balls, doubtless used in some kicking game, were astonishingly numerous at Paragonah; they occur far less frequently in southern ruins. Two similar balls of adobe came from the 1917 excavations; to one of these a portion of its original clay covering was still attached.[6]

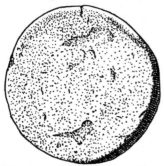

FIG. 46.—Stone door cover from Paragonah

Only two stone axes were obtained during the six seasons of observation, and these, from Cottonwood Canyon, are illustrated in Plate 50, *d*, *h*. Five grooved mauls, all of basalt, are in the collections.

Chipped arrow points were gathered in considerable numbers at Paragonah and Beaver. The fact that they seem less common farther south is perhaps due only to the more restricted excavations in that section. But wherever found, they average somewhat larger than those from ruins on the opposite side of the Colorado.

Two arrow-shaft smoothers (pl. 50, *e*, *f*) and fragments of three others came from the mounds at Willard. Similar stone implements are not represented in our collections from other districts, although a fragment of drilled mountain sheep horn, supposedly a shaft smoother, was obtained in Cottonwood Canyon.

---

[5] 1919, p. 416, figs. 15–16.   [6] Judd, 1919a, fn. p. 17.

Wooden Artifacts

Certainly the most interesting wooden objects collected during the bureau's entire investigation are those which came from Heaton's Cave, near Mount Trumbull. Reference is made especially to two curved clubs (pl. 51, c, d) presented to the United States National Museum by Mr. and Mrs. Franklin A. Heaton. Although the original purpose of these clubs remains, for the present at least, entirely unknown, they are representatives of a definite type of prehistoric implement widely distributed and apparently of Basket Maker handiwork.

It will be noticed that each is fitted with a pitch-covered yucca "bumper" at one end; that each is incised longitudinally on both sides with four parallel lines; that these lines are interrupted in the same relative place on both specimens, and that the sinew wrapping is identical on each. Guernsey and Kidder [7] figure two similar specimens from White Dog Cave, northeastern Arizona; Hough [8] illustrates one of slightly different type from a guano cave 9 miles east of Lava, N. Mex.; Doctor Parsons [9] notes the finding of a sixth example, almost the duplicate of Hough's, in a shrine cave near Laguna pueblo; one other specimen, from Grand Gulch, Utah, is displayed in the Museum of the American Indian, Heye Foundation, New York City. None of these latter, however, exhibits the pronounced S shape of the Heaton Cave clubs.

As has been said, the intended function of these remarkable implements is at present unknown. Guernsey and Kidder found theirs associated with unquestioned Basket Maker remains; Basket Maker sandals were present in Heaton's Cave; Grand Gulch is the locality in which the Basket Maker culture was first identified. The curved clubs, therefore, probably belong to this pre-Cliff-dweller period. Granted, for the time being, this greater antiquity, it would mean that the implements in question, whether offensive or defensive in nature, must have been contemporaneous with the atlatl, or "throwing stick," a well-known and distinctive Basket Maker weapon.

Atlatls were not found during the course of the bureau's explorations, but the shafted fragment of an atlatl dart (pl. 52, e) was obtained from a cave in Cottonwood Canyon. Its butt end is notched (in itself an unusual feature), thus indicating that the throwing stick used by the aborigine who fashioned this particular dart had been fitted with a string instead of the typical atlatl spur. [10] The only

---

[7] 1921, p. 88.
[8] 1914, p. 19.
[9] 1918, p. 385. A fragment of another New Mexico specimen, collected near Carlsbad by Dr. Willis T. Lee in 1924, is now in the U. S. National Museum (Cat. No. 330644).
[10] Guernsey and Kidder, 1921, pp. 80–88.

specimen of this type (with forked end and string) known to the writer is in the museum of the Affiliated Colleges, San Francisco.

In addition to these incised clubs, two fragments of like instruments were found in the same cave. With them were two plain clubs (pl. 51, *a, b*) that more closely resemble the well-known Hopi rabbit sticks. Neither of these two latter specimens is grooved; neither is wrapped with sinews, but it will be observed that one of them (pl. 51, *a*) is scored at one end as though originally fitted with the "bumper" still attached to the two first mentioned.

Although it is doubtless a safe conjecture that these interesting specimens were made and used by Basket Makers, it should be noted that an exceptionally fine bow (pl. 53, *a*), also presented by Mr. and Mrs. Heaton, came from the same cave. The bow is a Cliff-dweller weapon; no specimen has yet been found in undisturbed Basket Maker sites. Besides the bow, sandals, basketry fragments, and pottery—all definitely Cliff-dweller—were found in Heaton Cave. It is certain, therefore, that these two distinct yet nearly contemporaneous peoples—Cliff-dwellers and Basket Makers—not only inhabited upper Kanab Creek but also penetrated the lava-strewn region surrounding Mount Trumbull, and may even have left their distinctive records in the very gorge of the Grand Canyon.

TEXTILES

Our best specimens of basketry (pl. 56, *a–d*) came from Cottonwood Canyon. All of these are undoubtedly of Cliff-dweller workmanship. A noticeable feature of their construction, however, is that the two larger specimens were woven over a single rod, without welt. The two smaller baskets also have a single rod, but with this is a filler through which the splints were introduced.

Both Basket Maker and Cliff-dweller sandals are represented in the collections from Heaton Cave. One of the former is figured in Plate 57, *a*. The same illustration also shows a pair of Cliff-dweller sandals woven from yucca fiber, a braided Cliff-dweller sandal, and a post-Basket Maker sandal, all from Cottonwood Canyon.

The Cliff-dwellers spun cotton and wove it into cloth. Several ragged fragments were collected in Cottonwood Canyon. No specimens of Basket Maker textiles were found, but the piece of red ocher illustrated in Plate 58, *b*, is wrapped with portions of a rabbit-skin robe, a typical Basket Maker garment. Yucca wrapped with rabbit skin and the well-known feather cord of the Cliff-dwellers were found associated in at least three of the Cottonwood caves. Spindle shafts and so-called whorls of pottery, wood, and gourd rind were obtained not only in Cottonwood Canyon but at other sites as well.

VEGETAL FOOD

The prehistoric house builders of the region covered by this report were primarily farmers. They raised squash, corn, and beans; in addition, they harvested piñon nuts, acorns, and various grass seeds.

Charred corn and a single squash seed were recovered during the excavations at Beaver. Charred corn was found at Paragonah. Wheat and related grains were naturally unknown prior to the advent of the Europeans. Those numerous metates observed at Willard were doubtless intended primarily for the grinding and crushing of maize. These characteristic utensils, together with the pottery, tend to identify the prehistoric peoples of Willard as essentially sedentary. Agriculture, and especially the cultivation of corn, has always been associated throughout the southwestern United States with fairly permanent places of abode.

Corncobs were observed in Cottonwood Canyon, upper Kanab Creek, Heaton's Cave, Bright Angel Creek, and in storage cists below the rim of Walhalla Plateau. But by far the best examples of this native American food plant collected during the bureau's reconnaissance were 11 well-preserved ears from cave 1, Cottonwood Canyon (pl. 59). They were submitted for examination to Mr. G. N. Collins, United States Department of Agriculture, who reports them as follows:

" The collection of maize ears from the pre-Pueblo ruins of Utah is of very special interest, and the ears are the most perfectly preserved of any prehistoric specimens I have ever examined.

" There is a rather wide range of characters exhibited in the different specimens. Thus corneous or flinty and amylaceous or soft endosperm are both represented. In some ears the seeds are nearly as long as broad; in others they are much flattened. In two of the ears the seeds are slightly but distinctly dented. The number of rows varies from 8 to 16. There is also a variety of aleurone colors. Notwithstanding this diversity, the ears exhibit no characters not found in existing varieties.

" Of the Indian varieties with which we are familiar, the ears of this series most nearly resemble in general appearance the small-eared varieties of the Hopi. Some of the ears, however, are not unlike specimens among the varieties grown by the Zuñi, while others find their nearest counterpart in Papago varieties.

" The collection immediately suggests a series of ears collected by Guernsey and Kidder in the Basket Maker ruins of Arizona. This resemblance is probably closer than that with any existing variety, although the resemblance may be overestimated from the fact that both are discolored in much the same way.

" In the Arizona series all the ears were of a flinty texture, while in the present series all but two must be classed as soft.

" In aleurone color the resemblance to the Arizona specimens is striking. The yellowish brown common in both of these collections is unknown in any of the existing varieties of North America. Yellowish-brown aleurone has been found in a variety from Bolivia, but I am inclined to believe that the resemblance is superficial and that the color in the prehistoric ears is due to a partial disintegration of the common blue aleurone.

" One of the most interesting specimens of the collection is the ear with split seeds. Seeds which split open or pop while still on the plant are observed frequently in present-day varieties. This behavior has been ascribed to the presence of a fungus, and if this should prove correct it is of interest that the same or a very similar fungus attacked maize in these remote times.

" On the other hand, we have during the past year succeeded in isolating a strain in which all the plants show this characteristic. If, as I believe, we can demonstrate that this behavior is due to a simple Mendelian character, it will be further evidence of the close similarity between existing varieties and those represented in the ancient remains." [11]

Piñon nuts, acorns, and various grass seeds were observed in many of the ruins examined. At Beaver and Paragonah such perishable materials had been preserved only on account of their charred condition; in Cottonwood Canyon, on the other hand, vegetal foods had escaped complete decay owing to the dryness of cave sites.

SKELETAL REMAINS

No human burials were disclosed during the excavations of 1915 at Willard.

In the Bradshaw mound, at Beaver, an adult male skeleton (288804) [12] was found, incased by adobe, in the so-called kiva (p. 33). The skull exhibits medium occipital deformation. A second male skeleton (288805), but with undeformed skull, appeared during trenching operations in the Geordge mound. An infant had been buried in the same grave.

At Paragonah five adult skeletons were found during the investigations of 1916 and 1917. Of these five, one is male and four are female. Of the female skulls, two (292010, 292014) are undeformed

---

[11] For further reference to Basket Maker corn see Kidder and Guernsey, 1919, p. 154; Guernsey and Kidder, 1921, p. 41; Collins, 1923, p. 417. In the latter Mr. Collins unwittingly ascribed the above Cottonwood Canyon specimens to southern Colorado.

[12] The numerals in parentheses are catalogue numbers of the Division of Physical Anthropology, United States National Museum, which division has given the descriptive information incorporated herein.

and two (292011, 303211) show slight deformation. The male (292012) also shows slight occipital compression.

Three additional Paragonah skulls, presented by Dr. James Green, of Parowan, should be mentioned here. One (291862) is an adult male exhibiting pronounced deformation; two are adult females. Of the latter, one (291863) shows slight occipital compression and the other (291864) pronounced compression.

The four skulls exhumed from a cave owned by Mr. Thomas Robinson, in upper Kanab Creek (p. 50), are entirely undeformed. One of these (315643) represents a young adolescent, probably female; two (315644, 315646) are adult females; one (315645), adult male. It will be recalled that Mr. Robinson had previously exposed four burials while preparing the cave for service as a haymow; that three of the craniums had been reinterred. From inconclusive evidence it is thought Basket Makers inhabited this particular cave in ancient times.

No deduction, of course, is to be ventured from so small a series of skeletal remains. Its chief interest lies in the fact that both deformed and undeformed skulls are included. Occipital compression, resulting from pressure of a rigid cradle board, is characteristic of Cliff-dweller and other recognized Puebloan peoples of antiquity. The Basket Makers used a different type of cradle; Basket Maker skulls are undeformed. But here, in the adobe ruins of west central Utah—ruins that exhibit a rather distinct prehistoric Pueblo culture—meager skeletal remains show that the rigid cradle board was not generally employed. In other words, what is regarded elsewhere as a fixed Puebloan custom or cultural result had in western Utah reached only its incipient form, or, with perhaps equal plausibility, had advanced to the point of gradual decline.

81069°—26——11

CONCLUSION

Six successive periods of brief annual exploration have been reviewed in the foregoing chapters. This intermittent reconnaissance has traced prehistoric human habitations from Great Salt Lake, in Utah, to the Grand Canyon, in Arizona—homes of ancient Indians who were agriculturists after a fashion, and in consequence chiefly sedentary in their habits. But these prehistoric dwellings and the cultural objects found in them are not always the same.

We note changes in the type of habitation as we pass from one valley to another, and changes in the character of the utensils employed daily by the occupants of those habitations. We note, too, the effect of changes in interfamily relationship—what seems to be the beginning of village life and community organization. Isolated dwellings are brought together, forming hamlets. And from the very location of those settlements we may know that fear of enemy attacks was practically nonexistent.

Before these annual surveys had been concluded the writer felt reasonably convinced that he had followed the course of tribal migrations and witnessed the result of aboriginal community development. He is less certain now. The evidence is too inconclusive. More detailed investigation is necessary. There are too many weak links in the chain; too many gaps still to be bridged. Our hurried reconnaissance does not show progressive development in the art of pottery making, for example. There is too little of the very primitive. Incipient stages are not sufficiently represented.

Future, more intensive research throughout the field of this report may show either a gradual cultural development from north to south, as we first suspected, or cultural retrogression from south to north. The archeological evidence would be much the same in either case. In ruins near the Rio Colorado and east of Kanab Canyon a relatively higher degree of culture was evidenced than appeared in ruins of Beaver and Parowan Valleys. That culture may have originated within the drainage of the Rio San Juan, or it may have come into being on the northern and western borders of the Great Interior Basin. But it is Puebloan in fact; it is definitely and directly related to those pre-Pueblo and Pueblo cultures represented by the prehistoric ruins of northern Arizona, New Mexico, and Colorado. These archeological observations north of the Rio Colorado have extended far to the north and west that area known to have been inhabited by ancient Pueblo peoples.

APPENDIX I

Figure No.	National Museum Catalogue No.	Locality	Figure No.	National Museum Catalogue No.	Locality
Pl. 37, a___	291962	Paragonah.	Pl. 40, c___	288474	Kanab.
b___	291964	Do.	d___	288469	Johnson Canyon.
c___	288756	Willard.			
d___	288756	Do.	e___	292028	Meadow.
e___	9761	Salt Lake City.	f___	291955	Paragonah.
f___	291963	Paragonah.	g___	291860	Meadow.
g___	288614	Beaver.	Pl. 41, a___	288468	Johnson Canyon.
h___	288792	Willard.			
i___	288709	Beaver.	b___	292026	Meadow.
j___	291962	Paragonah.	c___	134524	Fillmore.
k___	288614	Beaver.	Pl. 42, a___	288704	Beaver.
l___	291962	Paragonah.	b___	288705	Do.
m___	291964	Do.	Pl. 43, a___	315484	Heaton Cave.
n___	291963	Do.	b___	315474	Kanab.
Pl. 38, a___	315593	Bed Rock Canyon.	Pl. 44, a___	288488	Beaver.
			b___	288731	Do.
b___	315594	Paria Plateau.	c___	288731	Do.
c___	315593	Bed Rock Canyon.	d___	288731	Do.
			e___	288731	Do.
d___	315593	Do.	f___	288731	Do.
e___	315591	Bright Angel Creek.	g___	288731	Do.
			h___	309615	Cottonwood Canyon.
f___	315591	Do.			
g___	315591	Do.	i___	309615	Do.
h___	319705	Cottonwood Canyon.	j___	309609	Do.
			k___	303070	Paragonah.
i___	309705	Do.	l___	288565	Do.
j___	309705	Do.	m___	288565	Do.
k___	309705	Do.	n___	303060	Do.
l___	309705	Do.	Pl. 45, a___	303092	Do.
m___	309705	Do.	b___	315606	Cottonwood Canyon.
n___	309705	Do.			
o___	309705	Do.	c___	303087	Paragonah.
p___	309705	Do.	d___	303087	Do.
Fig. 45, a___	303210	Paragonah.	e___	315585	Heaton Cave.
b___	303210	Do.	f___	288564	Paragonah.
c___	303210	Do.	g___	303151	Do.
d___	303207	Do.	h___	303151	Do.
e___	303210	Do.	i___	303151	Do.
f___	303210	Do.	Fig. 46 _____	303001	Do.
g___	303210	Do.	Pl. 46, a___	303130	Do.
h___	303210	Do.	b___	303144	Do.
Pl. 39, a___	292030	Meadow.	c___	303144	Do.
b___	315477	Kanab.	d___	303146	Do.
c___	288484	Beaver.	e___	303144	Do.
d___	315479	Kanab.	f___	303117	Do.
Pl. 40, a___	288470	Johnson Canyon.	g___	303118	Do.
			h___	303118	Do.
b___	291859	Meadow.	i___	303118	Do.

LOCALITY AND CATALOGUE NUMBER OF OBJECTS ILLUSTRATED—Continued

Figure No.	National Museum Catalogue No.	Locality	Figure No.	National Museum Catalogue No.	Locality
Pl. 46, j	315622	Cottonwood Canyon.	Pl. 51, a	315577	Heaton Cave.
k	303099	Paragonah.	b	315576	Do.
l	303097	Do.	c	315578	Do.
m	315615	Cottonwood Canyon.	d	315578	Do.
n	303098	Paragonah.	e	315488	Do.
o	288483	Beaver.	f	315489	Do.
p	291871	Paragonah.	Pl. 52, a	315641	Riggs Canyon.
q	303140	Do.	b	309580	Cottonwood Canyon.
r	303140	Do.			
s	303130	Do.	c	309597	Do.
t	303130	Do.	d	288473	Kanab Creek.
Pl. 47, a	303180	Do.	e	309577	Cottonwood Canyon.
b	288554	Do.			
c	291872	Do.	f	309574	Do.
d	301976	Do.	g	309572	Do.
e	291874	Do.	h	309585	Do.
f	303177	Do.	i	309573	Do.
g	288539	Beaver.	Pl. 53, a	315487	Heaton Cave.
h	291873	Paragonah.	b	315570	Do.
i	288540	Beaver.	Pl. 54, a	309611	Cottonwood Canyon.
j	303178	Paragonah.			
k	309510	Beaver.	b	315640	Riggs Canyon.
l	303179	Paragonah.	c	309619	Cottonwood Canyon.
Pl. 48, a	288793	Willard.			
b	288499	Beaver.	d	309508	Do.
c	288496	Do.	e	309655	Do.
Pl. 49, a	288772	Willard.	Pl. 55, a	309506	Do.
b	291983	Paragonah.	b	303361	Do.
c	288684	Beaver.	c	309504	Do.
d	309696	Cottonwood Canyon.	d	309501	Do.
			e	309503	Do.
e	288691	Beaver.	f	309502	Do.
f	309700	Cottonwood Canyon.	g	309505	Do.
			Pl. 56, a	309682	Do.
g	288683	Beaver.	b	309684	Do.
h	291984	Paragonah.	c	309683	Do.
Pl. 50, a	288551	Do.	d	309681	Do.
b	309692	Cottonwood Canyon.	e	315491	Heaton Cave.
			Pl. 57, a	309671	Cottonwood Canyon.
c	288463	Willard.			
d	309694	Cottonwood Canyon.	b	315588	Heaton Cave.
			c	309673	Cottonwood Canyon.
e	288787	Willard.			
f	288788	Do.	d	315639	Do.
g	309693	Cottonwood Canyon.	e	315588	Heaton Cave.
			Pl. 58, a	309612	Cottonwood Canyon.
h	309695	Do.	b	309685	Do.
i	288471	Johnson Canyon.	Pl. 59	309641	Do.
			Pl. 61, a-e	303209	Paragonah.
			f-n	288709	Beaver.

APPENDIX II

Locality	Room	Length			Width		
		Feet	Inches	Meters	Feet	Inches	Meters
PAYSON, 1876 [1]		11	0	3. 30	9	0	2. 74
BEAVER, 1915:							
Geordge mound	1				5	6	1. 67
	2	6	2	1. 88	5	6	1. 67
	3	6	0	1. 83	4	3	1. 30
	5	10	3	3. 12	6	0	1. 83
	`6	10	0	3. 05	5	4	1. 62
	7	13	3	4. 03	5	4	1. 62
	8	10	6	3. 20	5	10	1. 77
	9						
Bradshaw mound	1	12	2	3. 70	6	1	1. 85
	2	7		2. 13	5	7	1. 70
	3	20	3	6. 17	5	3	1. 60
	4	5	6	1. 67	5	6	1. 67
	5				4	5	1. 34
	6	8	10	2. 69	5	8	1. 72
	7	10	3	3. 12	5	6	1. 67
	10	11	4	3. 45	7	3	2. 21
	11	13	10	4. 21	5	5	1. 65
	12	12	11	3. 93	5	3	1. 60
	13	10	4	3. 15	5	3	1. 60
	14	10	0	3. 05	5	2	1. 57
	15	15	4	4. 67	12	6	3. 81
	Kiva, diameter.	16	0	4. 87			
PARAGONAH:							
1915	Mound 1	20	3	6. 17	6	4	1. 93
	Mound 2	14		4. 27	7	0	2. 13
1916	1	30	3	9. 21	8	10	2. 69
	2	24	1	7. 33	7	4	2. 23
	3	8	7	2. 61	7	6	2. 28
	4	21	11	6. 68	8	4	2. 54
	5	16	9	5. 10	6	10	2. 08
	6	35	2	10. 71	6	7	2. 00
	7	12	4	3. 76	6	2	1. 88
	8	21	7	6. 58	6	9	2. 05
	9	17	3	5. 26	7	6	2. 28
	10	15	0	4. 57	5	8	1. 72
	11	9	10	2. 99	5	6	1. 67
	12	33	6	10. 21	8	0	2. 43
	13				7	4	2. 23
	14	13	10	4. 21	6	9	2. 05
1917	1	18	6	5. 64	8	8	2. 64
	2	6	8	2. 03	6	5	1. 95
	3	6	10	2. 08	6	6	1. 98
	4	11	6	3. 50	5	4	1. 62
	5	10	10	3. 30	8	11	2. 71
	6				7	2	2. 18

[1] Palmer, 1880, pp. 170–171.

AVERAGE DIMENSIONS OF ROOMS EXCAVATED—Continued

Locality	Room	Length			Width		
		Feet	Inches	Meters	Feet	Inches	Meters
PARAGONAH:							
1917	7	11	3	3. 43	7	10	2. 38
	8	13	3	4. 03	5	5	1. 65
	9				5	4	1. 62
	10	22	0	6. 70	5	5	1. 65
	11	22		6. 70	5		1. 52
	12	6	2	1. 88	5	10	1. 77
	13	12	3	3. 73	5	8	1. 72
	14	18		5. 48	6	11	2. 10
	15	7		2. 13			
	16	10	10	3. 30	5	4	1. 62
	17	9	8	2. 94	5	4	1. 62
	18	19	11	6. 06	6	5	1. 95
	19	11	5	3. 47	6	6	1. 98
	21	22	0	6. 70	6	7	2. 00
	22	29	0	8. 84	4	6	1. 37
	23	13	3	4. 03	5	8	1. 72
	24	14	9	4. 37	5	10	1. 77
	25	12	4	3. 76	6	6	1. 98
	27				6	0	1. 83
	29	7	3	2. 21	5	7	1. 70
	30	12	10	3. 91	5	9	1. 75
	32	14	6	4. 42	9		2. 74
	33	12	10	3. 91	6	4	1. 93
	34	10	5	3. 17	6	5	1. 95
	35	21	0	6. 40	6	7	2. 00
	36	18	4	5. 58	5	6	1. 67
	37	9		2. 74	4	0	1. 22
	38	6	7	2. 00	4	3	1. 30
COTTONWOOD CAN-YON:							
Cave 1—1919	1, diameter	10	0	3. 04			
	2, diameter	5	0	1. 52			
Cave 2	a, diameter	4	6	1. 37			
	b, diameter	4	0	1. 22			
	1, diameter	8	4	2. 54			
	2	5	0	1. 52	4	0	1. 22
Cave 3	1	4		1. 22	4	0	1. 22
	2	13	0	3. 96	10	0	3. 05
	3	8	6	2. 59	4	10	1. 47
	4	5	2	1. 57	4	0	1. 22
	Kiva, diameter.	13	6	4. 11			
	a, diameter	6	0	1. 83			
	b, diameter	5	8	1. 72			
Cave 4	1	12		3. 65	6	0	1. 83
	2				7	0	2. 13
	3	8	0	2. 43	7	4	2. 23
	4	6	6	1. 98	5	0	1. 52
	5	3	10	1. 16	5	0	1. 52
	6	6	0	1. 83	7	0	2. 13
	7	16		4. 87	9	4	2. 84
	8	5	8	1. 72	7	0	2. 13
	9	5	0	1. 52	3	4	1. 04
	10	4	9	1. 44	3	10	1. 16
	11				5	9	1. 75
	13	7	0	2. 13	5	4	1. 62
	15	9		2. 74	4		1. 22

AVERAGE DIMENSIONS OF ROOMS EXCAVATED—Continued

Locality	Room	Length			Width		
		Feet	Inches	Meters	Feet	Inches	Meters
COTTONWOOD CAN-YON:							
Cave 4_____	16_____	12	_____	3. 65	10	0	3. 05
	17_____	12	3	3. 73	8	9	2. 66
	A, diameter__	11	_____	3. 30	_____	_____	_____
	C, diameter__	17	10	5. 43	_____	_____	_____
Cave 5_____	1, diameter__	13	4	4. 06	_____	_____	_____
	a, diameter__	6	0	1. 83	_____	_____	_____
	b, diameter__	6	4	1. 93	_____	_____	_____
	c, diameter__	5	4	1. 62	_____	_____	_____
Cave 8_____	1_____	7	0	2. 13	2	3	. 68
	2_____	5	0	1. 52	2	10	. 86
	3_____	2	6	. 76	1	8	. 50
	4_____	1	11	. 58	1	8	. 50
	Kiva, diame-ter.	15	2	4. 62	_____	_____	_____

BIBLIOGRAPHY

BANCROFT, H. H.
  1875. Native races of the Pacific States, Vol. 4, Antiquities. New York, 1875.
  1890. History of Utah. (1540–1887.) San Francisco, 1890.
BANDELIER, A. F.
  1892. Final report of investigations among the Indians of the Southwestern United States. Part II. Papers of the Archaeological Institute of America. American Series, No. IV. Cambridge, 1892.
CARVALHO, S. N.
  1858. Incidents of travel and adventure in the far west. New York, 1858.
CHITTENDEN, H. M.
  1902. American fur trade of the far west. New York, 1902.
COLLINS, G. N.
  1923. Notes on the agricultural history of maize. Reprint from Annual Report, American Historical Association for 1919, vol. I, pp. 409–429. Washington, 1923.
CONANT, A. J.
  1879. Footprints of vanished races. St. Louis, 1879.
CUMMINGS, BYRON.
  1910. Ancient inhabitants of the San Juan valley. Bulletin of the University of Utah, vol. III, no. 3, pt. 2, Salt Lake City, 1910.
  1913. Quoted by Salt Lake Tribune, April 21, 1913, and Semiweekly Tribune, May 16, 1913. Salt Lake City, 1913.
  1915. Kivas of the San Juan drainage. American Anthropologist, n. s., vol. 17, no. 2, pp. 272–282. Lancaster, 1915.
DALE, H. C.
  1918. The Ashley-Smith explorations and the discovery of a central route to the Pacific, 1822–1829. Cleveland, 1918.
DELLENBAUGH, F. S.
  1877. The Shinumos—a prehistoric people of the Rocky Mountain region. Bulletin, Buffalo Society of Natural Sciences, vol. III, no. 4. Buffalo, N. Y., 1877.
  1902. Romance of the Colorado River. New York, 1902.
  1908. A canyon voyage. New York, 1908.
DUFFIELD, M. S.
  1904. Aboriginal remains in Nevada and Utah. American Anthropologist, n. s., vol. 6, no. 1. Lancaster, 1904.
EPLER, WILLIAM.
  1898. The Indians of the Great Basin from 1861 to 1865. American Archaeologist, vol. II, pt. 5, pp. 119–122. Columbus, Ohio, 1898.
FEWKES, J. WALTER.
  1909. Prehistoric ruins of the Gila valley. Smithsonian Miscellaneous Collections, vol. 52 (quarterly issue, vol. 5, pt. 4). Washington, 1909.
  1910. Notes on the occurrence of adobes in cliff-dwellings. American Anthropologist, n. s., vol. 12, no. 3. Lancaster, 1910.

FEWKES, J. WALTER—Continued.

1911. Preliminary report on a visit to Navaho National Monument, Arizona. Bulletin 50, Bureau of American Ethnology. Washington, 1911.

1911, a. Antiquities of the Mesa Verde National Park—Cliff Palace. Bulletin 51, Bureau of American Ethnology. Washington, 1911.

1912. Casa Grande, Arizona. Twenty-eighth Annual Report, Bureau of American Ethnology. Washington, 1912.

1920. Field work on the Mesa Verde National Park, Colorado. Smithsonian Miscellaneous Collections, vol. 72, no. 1, pp. 47–64. Washington, 1920.

GUERNSEY, S. J., and KIDDER, A. V.

1921. Basket-maker caves of northeastern Arizona. Papers of the Peabody Museum of American Archaeology and Ethnology, vol. VIII, no. 2. Cambridge, 1921.

HARRINGTON, M. R.

1925. Pueblo site near St. Thomas, Nevada. Indian Notes, Museum of the American Indian, Heye Foundation, vol. II, no. 1. New York, 1925.

1925, a. "Pueblo Grande de Nevada." Arrowhead Magazine, March-April. Los Angeles, 1925.

1925, b. Archeological researches in Nevada. Indian Notes, Museum of the American Indian, Heye Foundation, vol. 2, no. 2, New York, 1925.

1925, c. Ancient salt mine near St. Thomas, Nevada. Indian Notes, Museum of the American Indian, Heye Foundation, vol. 2, no. 3, New York, 1925.

1926. Western extension of early Pueblo culture. Indian Notes, Museum of the American Indian, Heye Foundation, vol. 3, no. 2, New York, 1926.

HOLMES, W. H.

1886. Pottery of the ancient Pueblos. Fourth Annual Report, Bureau of Ethnology. Washington, 1886.

HOUGH, WALTER.

1907. Antiquities of the upper Gila and Salt River valleys in Arizona and New Mexico. Bulletin 35, Bureau of American Ethnology. Washington, 1907.

1914. Culture of the ancient Pueblos of the upper Gila River region, New Mexico and Arizona. Bulletin 87, U. S. National Museum. Washington, 1914.

1919. Exploration of a pit house village at Luna, New Mexico. Proceedings, U. S. National Museum, vol. 55. Washington, 1919.

JEANCON, J. A.

1922. Archaeological research in the northeastern San Juan basin of Colorado during the summer of 1921. State Historical and Natural History Society of Colorado and the University of Denver. Denver, 1922.

JUDD, NEIL M.

1916. Archeological reconnaissance in western Utah. Smithsonian Miscellaneous Collections, vol. 66, no. 3, pp. 64–71. Washington, 1916.

1916, a. The use of adobe in prehistoric dwellings of the Southwest. Holmes Anniversary Volume. Washington, 1916.

1917. Archeological reconnaissance in western Utah. Smithsonian Miscellaneous Collections, vol. 66, no. 17. Washington, 1917.

JUDD, NEIL M.—Continued.

1917, a. Notes on certain prehistoric habitations in western Utah. Proceedings, 19th International Congress of Americanists, 1915. Washington, 1917.

1917, b. Evidence of circular Kivas in western Utah ruins. American Anthropologist, n. s., vol. 19, no. 1. Lancaster, 1917.

1918. Archeological work in Arizona and Utah. Smithsonian Miscellaneous Collections, vol. 68, no. 12. Washington, 1918.

1919. Archeological reconnaissance of northwestern Arizona. Smithsonian Miscellaneous Collections, vol. 70, no. 2. Washington, 1919.

1919, a. Archeological investigations at Paragonah, Utah. Smithsonian Miscellaneous Collections, vol. 70, no. 3. Washington, 1919.

1920. Archeological investigations in Utah and Arizona. Smithsonian Miscellaneous Collections, vol. 72, no. 1. Washington, 1920.

1921. Archeological investigations in Utah, Arizona and New Mexico. Smithsonian Miscellaneous Collections, vol. 72, no. 6. Washington, 1921.

1924. Two Chaco Canyon pit houses. Annual report of the Smithsonian Institution for 1922. Washington, 1924.

KIDDER, A. V.

1910. Explorations in southeastern Utah in 1908. Journal, Archaeological Institute of America, 2nd ser., vol. XIV, no. 3. Norwood, Mass., 1910.

1917. Prehistoric cultures of the San Juan drainage. Proceedings, 19th International Congress of Americanists, 1915. Washington, 1917.

1920. Ruins of the historic period in the upper San Juan valley, New Mexico. American Anthropologist, n. s., vol. 22, no. 4. Lancaster, 1920.

1924. An introduction to the study of southwestern archaeology. Department of Archaeology, Phillips Academy, Andover, Mass. New Haven, 1924.

1925. Notes on State archeological surveys during 1924. American Anthropologist, n. s., vol. 27, no. 4. Menasha, Wis., 1925.

KIDDER, A. V., and GUERNSEY, S. J.

1919. Archeological explorations in northeastern Arizona. Bulletin 65, Bureau of American Ethnology. Washington, 1919.

KOLB, ELLSWORTH and EMERY.

1914. Experiences in the Grand Canyon. National Geographic Magazine, vol. 26, no. 2. Washington, 1914.

MALLERY, GARRICK.

1886. Pictographs of the North American Indians. Fourth Annual Report, Bureau of Ethnology. Washington, 1886.

MINDELEFF, COSMOS.

1896. Casa Grande ruin. Thirteenth Annual Report, Bureau of Ethnology. Washington, 1896.

1897. The repair of Casa Grande ruin, Arizona, in 1891. Fifteenth Annual Report, Bureau of Ethnology. Washington, 1897.

MONTGOMERY, HENRY.

1894. Prehistoric man in Utah. The Archaeologist, vol. 2, nos. 8, 9, 11. Waterloo, Ind., 1894.

MORRIS, EARL H.
  1915. Excavation of a ruin near Aztec, San Juan County, New Mexico.
        American Anthropologist, n. s., vol. 17, no. 4. Lancaster, 1915.
  1919. Preliminary account of the antiquities of the region between the
        Mancos and La Plata rivers in southwestern Colorado. Thirty-
        third Annual Report, Bureau of American Ethnology. Washington,
        1919.
NELSON, N. C.
  1914. Pueblo ruins of the Galisteo Basin, New Mexico. Anthropological
        Papers of the American Museum of Natural History, vol. XV, pt.
        1. New York, 1914.
NUSBAUM, J. L.
  1922. A Basket-maker cave in Kane County, Utah; with notes by A. V.
        Kidder and S. J. Guernsey. Indian Notes and Monographs (no.
        29), Museum of the American Indian, Heye Foundation. New
        York, 1922.
PALMER, EDWARD.
  1876. Exploration of a mound in Utah. American Naturalist, vol. X, pp.
        410–414. Cambridge, 1876.
  1880. Review of published statements regarding the mounds at Payson,
        Utah, with an account of their structure and origin. Proceedings,
        Davenport Academy of Natural Sciences, vol. II, 1876–1878, pp.
        167–172. Davenport, 1880.
  1880, a. Cave dwellings in Utah. Reports of the Peabody Museum, vol.
        II, pp. 269–272. Cambridge, 1880.
PARSONS, ELSIE CLEWS.
  1918. War god shrines of Laguna and Zuñi. American Anthropologist, n. s.,
        vol. 20, no. 4. Lancaster, 1918.
POOLE, H. S.
  1874. The great American desert. Proceedings and Transactions, Nova Sco-
        tian Institute of Natural Sciences, vol. III. Halifax, N. S., 1874.
POWELL, J. W.
  1875. Exploration of the Colorado River of the West in 1869–1872. Wash-
        ington, 1875.
PRUDDEN, T. M.
  1903. Prehistoric ruins of the San Juan watershed in Utah, Arizona, Colo-
        rado and New Mexico. American Anthropologist, n. s., vol. 5, no.
        2. Lancaster, 1903.
  1918. Further study of prehistoric small-house ruins in the San Juan water-
        shed. Memoirs, American Anthropological Association, vol. 5, no. 1.
        Lancaster, 1918.
PUTNAM, J. D.
  1876. Hieroglyphics observed in Summit Canyon, Utah. Proceedings, Dav-
        enport Academy of Natural Sciences, vol. 1. Davenport, 1876.
RAE, W. F.
  1871. Westward by rail. 2nd ed., London, 1871.
REMY and BRENCHLEY.
  1861. A journey to Great Salt Lake City. vol. 2. London, 1861.
SEVERANCE, M. S., and YARROW, H. C.
  1879. Notes upon human crania and skeletons collected by the expeditions
        of 1872–1874. U. S. Geological Surveys west of the 100th Meridian,
        vol. VII, Archeology. Washington, 1879.

SHIMER, H. W., and F. H.
    1910. The lithological section of Walnut Canyon, Arizona, with relation to the cliff-dwellings of this and other regions of northwestern Arizona. American Anthropologist, n. s., vol. 12, no. 2. Lancaster, 1910.

STANSBURY, HOWARD.
    1852. An expedition to the valley of the Great Salt Lake of Utah. Philadelphia, 1852.

STEVENS, I. I.
    1855. Exploration for a route for a Pacific railroad, vol. XII, bk. 1. Washington, 1855.

WEST, GEORGE A.
    1925. Cliff-dwellings and pueblos in the Grand Canyon, Arizona. Yearbook of the Public Museum of the City of Milwaukee, 1923, vol. 3. Milwaukee, 1925.

WHEELER, G. M.
    1889. Report on United States Geological Surveys west of the 100th Meridian, vol. I, Geographical Report. Washington, 1889.

WIRT, JULIA J.
    1880. Quotations from letters regarding mounds at Payson, Utah. Proceedings, Davenport Academy of Natural Sciences, vol. II, 1876–1878, pp. 28; 82. Davenport, 1880.

INDEX

○